365
Meditations
for
Young Adults

365 Meditations for Young Adults

Sally D. Sharpe, Editor

Esther Cho - Christian Coon - Christopher Cropsey
Richard Evans - James A. Harnish - Elizabeth Hunter
Kwasi Kena - Mitch McVicker - Barbara Mittman
Ellen Mohney - Jason Moore - Julie O'Neal
Harriet P. Willimon - William H. Willimon

DIMENSIONS
FOR LIVING
NASHVILLE

Library of Congress Cataloging-in-Publication Data

365 meditations for young adults / Sally D. Sharpe, editor ; Esther Cho...[et al.].
    p. cm.
    ISBN 0-687-09576-X (pbk. : alk. paper)
    1. Young adults—Prayer-books and devotions—English. 2. Devotional calendars. 3. Meditations. I. Title: Three hundred sixty-five meditations for young adults. II. Sharpe, Sally D., 1964- III. Cho, Esther.
    BV4850 A143 2002
    242'.2—dc21

                                                                    2002005075

CONTENTS

INTRODUCTION

WHAT DO YOU WANT TO BE WHEN YOU "GROW UP"?

What do you want to be when you grow up? It's a question we heard a lot as children, and it's a question we continue to ask ourselves even as adults. Our young adult years certainly are a time of "becoming"—choosing a career, getting the education or skills we need, finding a job, discovering our place in life, making our way in the world, and perhaps getting married and starting a family. And all these experiences, many of which involve life-changing crossroads, are extremely important. The challenge is to walk with God day by day so that we may become all that God wants us to be.

This book is intended to help you do just that. As you make your way through the year (whether you start in January or June), encountering a different writer or writing team each month, you will find practical and spiritual insights, encouragement, and a sense of camaraderie for the challenge of walking with God day by day. Though the writers have diverse backgrounds and personalities, there is a common theme among them: God is with us. It may seem obvious, yet we're so prone to forget it.

In all the changes and the challenges, in both the mundane and the mysterious, in every moment of every day, God is with us. No matter where we've been, where we are, or where we may be headed, God never deserts us. Though we may try to hide from God or "go it alone," we can't escape God's love. God loves us from the cradle to the grave. And when we accept this love, we discover life abundant.

It's so easy to get caught up in striving to become something: educated, employed, financially secure, physically fit, outstanding in our field, well-liked—the list goes on and on. But, as the writer of Ecclesiastes says, all of these things "are meaningless, a chasing after the wind" (1:14 NIV).

7

There's really only one pursuit worthy of our full attention, our complete focus. A successful career woman and mother expressed it so well. She said that it has taken her a long time to decide what she wants to "be" when she "grows up," but she thinks she has finally figured it out: She wants to be completely God's. That's really what life's all about it, isn't it?

Young adulthood is a time of change and challenge, a time of seeking and searching, a time of exploration and discovery, a time of establishing deep and long-lasting roots and relationships—in other words, a time of tremendous opportunity for personal and spiritual growth. It is a time to walk with God and to "become."

The question is still a good one: What do you want to be when you "grow up"?

Sally D. Sharpe, Editor

ABOUT THE WRITERS

Esther Cho (NOVEMBER) currently is a student at the Harvard Divinity School, working on an advanced degree in biblical studies. For three years she was a minister at St. Luke's United Methodist Church in Highlands Ranch, Colorado.

Christian Coon (MARCH) is the pastor of Christ United Methodist Church in Deerfield, Illinois. Chris is a native Iowan and a graduate of Simpson College, the Medill School of Journalism at Northwestern University, and Garrett-Evangelical Theological Seminary. He has written articles for various periodicals, including *The Christian Century* and *The Christian Ministry*. He and his wife, Anne, are the proud parents of their new daughter, Caroline Ruth. He enjoys running, following the Cincinnati Reds, watching *The Simpsons*, and listening to Lyle Lovett.

Christopher Cropsey (JULY) spent most of his childhood in Mt. Juliet, Tennessee, where his parents and younger brother still reside. Currently, Chris is studying classical piano and youth ministry at Belmont University in Nashville, where he is a Presidential Scholar and Honors Program participant. Previously he has served the people of the Cumberland Mountains as a staff member for the youth service mission trip Mountain T.O.P. In his free time, Chris loves to play and listen to music, read, and watch sports. He also has been a contributor to *365 Meditations for Teens*.

Richard Evans (NOVEMBER) is a minister at St. Luke's United Methodist Church in Highlands Ranch, Colorado. He has a Ph.D. in pastoral counseling from the University of Denver and the Iliff School of Theology, and is an emeritus Supervisor of Clinical Pastoral Education.

James A. Harnish (DECEMBER) describes himself as "a Boomer who really loves Gen-Xers." His passion for ministry with young adults grows out of his relationship with two Gen-X daughters and one son-in-law as well as the growing number of young adults who share the ministry of Hyde Park

United Methodist Church in Tampa, Florida, where he is senior pastor. He is a graduate of Asbury Theological Seminary and served three previous congregations in Florida. He is the author of ten books including *Passion, Power, and Praise: A Model for Men's Spirituality* and *Journey to the Center of the Faith: An Explorer's Guide to Christian Living*. He and his wife, Marsha, have been married for thirty-two years and are avid fans of the University of Florida Gators football team.

Elizabeth Hunter (OCTOBER) is a section editor for *The Lutheran* magazine and a graduate student in education. She lives with her husband, Leslie, a youth pastor, in Oak Park, Illinois, a suburb of Chicago. They share interests in spirituality, music, poetry, philosophy, theater, martial arts, and writing stories.

Kwasi Kena (AUGUST) currently serves as the Congregational Development Coordinator for the Greater New Jersey Annual Conference of The United Methodist Church. Prior to this appointment, Kwasi and his wife, the Reverend Safiyah Fosua, served as commissioned General Board of Global Ministries missionaries to Ghana, West Africa, for four years. Kwasi enjoys teaching and writing. He has taught various courses in communication, social science, and religion at colleges and universities in Oklahoma and Iowa. He is the author of three books*: The Resurrected Jesus; In Plain View of the Cross;* and *40 Days in the Wilderness: Meditations for African American Men*. He also has been a contributor to *365 Meditations for Teens,* and *365 Meditations for Families*. Kwasi writes regularly for teens and young adults with Urban Ministries Publications, Inc.

Mitch McVicker (MAY) is a Christian music singer/songwriter who began as a supporting guitar player and vocalist for Rich Mullins. They traveled, performed concerts, wrote songs together, and were roommates for two-and-a-half years before the tragic accident that claimed Rich's life and severely injured Mitch. During his year-long recovery, Mitch wrote many of the songs on his new release, *Chasing the Horizon*. He says the songs are an expression of "where he was" during that year and of what God has done in his life and the lives of those around him. One of the songs, "Burning the Fields," is about renewal, which is the theme of his devotions. "Coming to renewal," he says, "isn't necessarily an easy or comfortable process. It's gonna hurt; it's gonna burn. But we are being remade into what God would have us become." Mitch grew up in Topeka, Kansas, and has been living in Nashville for three years. He travels much of the year, which gives him plenty of time for listening to music and "the quiet." When he's not on the road, he likes to watch movies and sports and just do "nothing."

Barbara Mittman (SEPTEMBER) is an ordained deacon in full connection, certified in Christian Education and youth ministry. Barb currently serves as one of the pastors at First United Methodist Church in Ames, Iowa. Previously she has served on conference and local church program staffs. She has written church school curriculum for youth and was the author for two volumes of *20/30 Bible Study for Young Adults.* Barb, her husband, Bob, and her daughter, Katie, live in Nevada, Iowa.

Ellen Mohney (FEBRUARY) is a graduate of the Baylor School of Chattanooga, Tennessee, where she received the Jumonville Award as Best All Around Student and the Herb Barks Award for the Most Representative of the School's Spirit. Currently a sophomore at Samford University in Birmingham, Alabama, she is preparing to be in full-time youth ministry. She has worked as a guide at The Rock at Ute Trail Ranch, a Christian camp in Colorado, taking high school youth on backpacking trips in the Rockies. Her interests include all sports, especially soccer, track, hiking, and mountain biking.

Jason Moore (JANUARY) is a Director of Christian Education at a church in Taylors, South Carolina. Previously he has been a summer camp counselor and trip leader and a high school English teacher. He has written articles for various periodicals, and his poem "Memory" is included in the National Library of Poetry. Jason says that writing is an extension of himself—not in some flighty, metaphysical way, but in how he grapples with the doubts, problems, and questions of life. It allows him to dig deep within, as one might with a scalpel, and pick, pulling back the protective folds to see what he truly believes.

Julie O'Neal (JUNE) is a student at Saint Paul School of Theology in Kansas City, Missouri. She has been involved in all levels of The United Methodist Church, from the local church to the General Boards. She is a member of the Shared Mission Focus on Young People (a general church initiative), and has contributed to *Devo'Zine,* a magazine produced by the Upper Room. Julie's home is in Scottsdale, Arizona, where her parents, two younger brothers, and younger sister live. She enjoys journaling, music, and Krispy Kreme doughnuts.

Harriet P. Willimon and William H. Willimon (APRIL) have collaborated on many projects through the years. Harriet is a young adult and a psychiatric social worker at Piedmont Medical Center in Rock Hill, South Carolina. She holds recent degrees from Wofford College and the University of South Carolina. Currently she is living in Charlotte, North Carolina. Will, her father, is Dean of the Chapel and Professor of Christian Ministry at Duke University, Durham, North Carolina. He preaches on most Sundays to students in Duke University Chapel, where he also leads the programs of campus ministry. He is the author of more than sixty books, many of them written for young adults.

January

LIVING FROM THE CENTER

Jason Moore

January 1 ~ Into the Chaos

In the beginning God created the heavens and the earth. The earth was without form, and void; and darkness was on the face of the deep. And the Spirit of God was hovering over the face of the waters.

—Genesis 1:1-2 (NKJV)

Mrs. Susie was my second-grade teacher. She taught math and science, and she had a wonderful way of simplifying complex theories, of fitting the universe in a paper sack. Maybe that's why I can still remember my first science project—a mobile of the solar system.

Looking back, there wasn't much to it: two clothes hangers taped into an "x," some string, nine foam balls colored like the pictures in our encyclopedia, and a big orange cardboard sun in the center. I used different sized balls for the planets and connected them carefully to the hangers. When I was done, I put it in a grocery bag and went to bed. The next morning, however, I reached into the bag to find a jumbled mess where my mobile had been. The string was tangled and the planets were in the wrong places. Worst of all, when I pulled the mobile out, the sun was in the bottom of the sack.

I'm twenty-three now, and though I don't worry with science projects anymore, my life often seems as tangled as that second-grade mobile.

There are days, weeks even, when nothing seems to work out right, when it seems that life is spinning out of control. This is where God comes in. For just as the sun holds the planets in place, so also a life with God at its center is one of peace and grace and order—one lived in the proper perspective.

Living from the center means living a life that is focused on God. This, however, is not an easy task. We are a busy people, easily distracted. So we must daily refocus our attention. In the days to come, as I reflect on the commonplace, I invite you to look beyond the surface, to see metaphors in the simple things, to see how you might come to live from the center.

Prayer Focus: What does it mean for me to live with God at the center?

January 2 ~ Above the Noise

The LORD is near to all who call on him . . . in truth.
—Psalm 145:18 (NRSV)

During my first two years in college, I lived on the sixteenth story of the tallest building on campus. For some reason it was quieter up there, as if everyone had talked themselves out on the long elevator ride—or worse, had endured thirty-two flights of stairs. But for whatever reason, there was a stillness up there, a kind of separateness seldom interrupted.

There was no one above us, so you never heard footsteps thudding or floorboards creaking. And I can remember so many nights up there, typing away, as my roommate slept, in almost absolute quiet save for the clicking of the keys. Even with him there, I felt completely alone. Sometimes, however, I would grow tired of the quiet, so I'd throw the window open to hear the sounds of the city below, which were so different from those of my youth.

The tracks were only a stone's throw from my dorm, and every night around 4:00 A.M., the train would let out a moan and come rumbling by, rattling the windows and calling me from my reverie. The whole room seemed to shimmy, and it amazed me that something so far below was not only heard but also felt.

But let's face it, most of us don't live above the noise. We're in it. Thus, living a life from the center means finding a way to follow God's will even

14

in the midst of all the crazy racket. And this requires a new perspective: You see, God is not like I was, tucked away in some room in the sky. Rather, God is like the train, rumbling through the center of our lives, calling us away from our selfish desires, offering us a better way to travel through life.

Prayer Focus: Where do I hear God calling me to get involved?

January 3 ~ Better Days

For lo, the winter is past,
The rain is over and gone.
The flowers appear on the earth;
The time of singing has come.

—Song of Solomon 2:11-12 (NKJV)

It was late afternoon and the beach was all but deserted. I was standing barefoot at the end of the pier, watching as the umbrellas disappeared one by one. The wind was warm and salty, and I sat for the longest time, watching the breakers tumble and roll, clawing softly at the sand below. Closing my eyes, I could feel the sun warm on my face, the pier gently swaying, the subtle stinging of skin made tight from salt and sun, as a feeling of peace washed over me.

I often think of that summer day when life seems overly gray, when the winter doldrums have gotten the best of me. And I wonder if the disciples did the same thing. In those days after the crucifixion, as reality began to sink in, I wonder if they remembered better, brighter days, when they walked with Christ and felt the warmth of his love.

I guess that's what I'm doing now. When my soul seems cold and frosted over, I think of warmer days when my walk with Christ was closer, when sunshine seemed to flood my soul. Those memories bring me hope and comfort, for I know that no season lasts forever. And that's what living from the center means: we accept that there are times in our journey when we feel lost, cold, forsaken. Nonetheless, we keep walking, knowing that eventually we can say once more, "The winter is past. . . . The time of singing has come."

Prayer Focus: How close do I feel to God today?

January 4 ~ Faith in the Dark

Now faith is the substance of things hoped for, the evidence of things not seen. . . . By faith Abraham obeyed when he was called to go out. . . . And he went out, not knowing where he was going.

—Hebrews 11:1, 8 (NKJV)

Sometimes I wake up in the night and don't know where I am. It's a strange, unsettling feeling. There in the dark, with the alarm clock staring coldly back at me, for a moment at least I am afraid. Bars of light pass dimly through the blinds, painting a dark web of shadows along the wall. The ceiling creaks and moans; the bed seems alien—not my own. And as I fumble with the lights, it takes some time to get my bearings, to remember where I am.

Usually, it only takes a minute or two to piece it all together. I flip on the lights, and the mystery's solved. Still, it's not the dark that frightens me— or sleeping in strange places. It's the unknown. Yet this is a fear that confronts us daily—not only in the dead of night, but also in the daily circumstances of our spiritual lives. How often do we look around, entangled in the trappings of our lives, and wonder, *Where am I?* or *How did I get here?* And it's this feeling of being lost, this fear of the unknown, that can paralyze us if we let it.

This, however, is where faith comes in. Only faith can bridge the chasm between the known and unknown, for faith covers distances that reason, intellect, and science simply cannot. Through faith, we vanquish our fears, and in each sunrise we behold a promise of opportunity instead of anxiety. But this is a choice. We choose to believe as surely as we choose to brush our teeth, and we choose how we will approach each day. Living from the center, therefore, does not mean that we'll always understand what God is doing in our lives; rather, it means we have faith that God will lead us through.

Prayer Focus: What doubts do I need to give to God?

16

January 5 ~ Help Wanted

Then suddenly a woman who had been suffering from hemorrhages for twelve years came up behind him and touched the fringe of his cloak, for she said to herself, "If I only touch his cloak, I will be made well."

—Matthew 9:20-21 (NRSV)

After several hours in the van, we turned off the highway onto a long dirt lane. You could see the house from the road—how it sagged in the middle, broken like a loaf of communion bread. John and I hopped out of the van to have a look around and see if someone might be home. We eased onto the porch, gave two solid knocks, and waited.

Soon, a short, stout woman appeared. We explained to her that we were with the church and that we wanted to do some work on her house. We said it wouldn't cost her a thing. I thought she'd be excited. She wasn't. I thought she'd invite us in, give us a tour of the place, tell us exactly what needed work. She didn't. Five minutes later, we were back in the van, going back the way we had come.

A week later, I'm still thinking about that lady who didn't want our help. Most people in her situation would have jumped at the opportunity she rejected. How can one with so much need turn away hands so eager to help? Even now, it bothers me—not because she didn't want our help, but because it reminded me of the many times I've rejected God's help. How often I have turned away from God, refusing to allow him to pull me from the mire of my circumstances. How many times he has reached out to me and I have been too frightened to take his hand, afraid of the changes it would require.

Living from the center requires that we accept God's help to battle the sin in our life. Like the lady in search of healing, we must seek the grace offered by our Savior; we must take his hand if we are ever to be made whole.

Prayer Focus: How have I rejected God's help in my life?

January 6 ~ Letting Go

"Submit to God and be at peace with him; in this way prosperity will come to you."

—Job 22:21 (NIV)

When I was growing up, we used to play a game called Mercy. You and your opponent would lock hands, palm to palm, and start squeezing. Very quickly your knuckles would turn white from the pressure, and tiny beads of sweat would line your brow as the efforts of your hands and fingers passed down your arms, tightening every muscle along the way. Soon your whole body would be tense. You'd squeeze and twist fingers until, finally, the other person would give up, crying, "Mercy, mercy!"

The funny thing is that the game is much easier if you don't squeeze back. You see, all the tension is created by our own bodies, by our response to the pressure being applied. When we stop squeezing, the pressure lessens, and the pain begins to disappear. It's the struggle that creates the pain and causes the tension. It's just a matter of letting go.

But we're stubborn people. We hate to throw in the towel, to cry "Mercy" and give up. We're afraid to seem weak—afraid that if we let our guard down and stop squeezing for even a moment, we'll be taken advantage of. And sometimes we do need to hang on till the bloody end. After all, some things are worth the struggle.

Yet most things aren't. Often we struggle and worry over things we have absolutely no control over. We fret and stew and wonder *What if?* as though it were simply up to us. It's like worrying about the weather. Besides, some things are inevitable—like change, or death. We end up spending so much energy trying to put off the inevitable that we can't enjoy what we have right now.

So we must learn to accept what we cannot change; to put our faith in God and trust in his will for our lives; to never neglect the joys and opportunities each day presents; to accept whatever challenges and difficulties come our way.

Prayer Focus: *What do I need to let go of today?*

January 7 ~ Mine!

Since there will never cease to be some in need on the earth, I therefore command you, "Open your hand to the poor and needy neighbor in your land."
—*Deuteronomy 15:11 (NRSV)*

My niece, Heather, is two years old. I don't get to see her very often, but when I do, we always play together. Last weekend was no different. I'd hardly made it through the door when she asked me to play. Before I knew it, I was down on all fours, playing dinosaur and chasing her around the house.

Later we got down to some serious LEGO construction. The LEGO bricks were in a bucket, which I strategically placed between us. Heather reached in, grabbed a handful, and put her creative genius to work. I started to do the same, but then something happened. As I reached in for a piece, Heather said, "Mine!" and tried to take it from me. So I gave her the piece and tried again, only to be greeted with the same response. Then she just reached out and took the bucket.

It occurred to me that maybe we aren't much different. Most of us have everything we need. We have money in our pockets, nice clothes, good homes. We have more than enough, and yet, like little Heather, we are always grasping for more. We have a hard time sharing—afraid to loosen our grasp lest all we have be taken from us. So we pull our buckets closer, squeeze a little tighter, build our walls higher and higher.

Yet when we close ourselves off and fence ourselves in, we hold on to the least important things while letting potential blessings slip through our fingers. We forget what it means to be generous; we forget that God calls us to be a compassionate people. Most important, we forget that all good things are from God—that we are called not to be owners but stewards.

Prayer Focus: *What am I clinging to other than God?*

January 8 ~ Satisfied

"I will feast the soul of the priests with abundance, and my people shall be satisfied with goodness, says the LORD."

—*Jeremiah 31:14 (RSV)*

Sometimes I look at my dog, Jake, and I can't help feeling jealous. I'll come in after a long day at work to find him sprawled out on the floor, resting peacefully. He'll get up very slowly, let out a yawn, and give me a look that says, "What're you so worked up about?" And to tell you the truth, I don't know. After all, we live in the same apartment, go to the same parks, and, most nights, share the same bed. I'm not sure why his life seems so simple and mine seems so complicated.

But, then again, maybe it doesn't have to be. I think we complicate life by trying to do too much, and by worrying that we don't do enough. Yet all our hurrying and busyness, more often than not, just lead to fatigue and frustration.

Living from the center demands not only that we place God at the center, but also that we free ourselves from the need to be busy, from the need to seem productive. Instead, God calls us from a life of movement to a life of meaning.

Prayer Focus: *How can I slow down and make myself more available to God?*

January 9 ~ The Quiet Game

"Be still, and know that I am God!"

—*Psalm 46:10 (NRSV)*

There's a game we used to play in first grade. It's been a while now, but I can still remember it. You've probably played it before: the quiet game. This is how it worked. After recess we'd come pouring into class, hot and sweaty, loud and laughing, bouncing off the walls. Then Mrs. Poe would kill the lights, and above our cries she would announce that it was "time to play the quiet game." Quickly, our voices fell silent; we put our heads down, hoping that our still bodies would prove how very quiet we were.

But that was a long time ago, and I think I was much better at it then. Sometimes it's hard for me to slow down now; it's hard to truly be *still.* Many days are scheduled away before they even begin. And often the days just seem to slip away from me: there's a meeting, an unexpected phone call, a few hours spent on a report; and before I know it, the day is almost over—with so much left undone. Perhaps this is true for many of us. We rush around; we hurry everywhere. Still, it seems we're just chasing our tails.

Maybe we could learn a lesson or two from my first-grade teacher. She found a way to quiet and calm us; she stilled our bodies so our minds could focus on the lessons ahead. With heads bent and hands folded, we were better prepared to listen. Sounds a bit like prayer, doesn't it? Prayer is like that: a calming of the soul, a quieting of the mind, so that we might truly hear God's call in our lives. It is my hope that we might learn to play the quiet game all over again; that in our daily living, we would learn to be still, and in the quiet moments that follow, begin to feel the soothing presence of the Living God.

Prayer Focus: How can I better learn to be still?

January 10 ~ Shine

"Let your light so shine before men, that they may see your good works and glorify your Father in heaven."
—Matthew 5:16 (NKJV)

Two weeks after I was notified of my acceptance to the Citadel, my first pair of uniform shoes arrived, along with a note suggesting I begin breaking them in and adding a few coats of polish. The first part was easy enough. I put on two pairs of socks and wore them practically everywhere. But the second part seemed a bit trickier, so I called in my dad, who was in the military.

Still, I couldn't quite understand why I had to do it. The black patent leather was slick and smooth, without a mark or crease. They looked fine as they were. But Dad knew better. Pulling out a small tin of polish and an old, ragged T-shirt, he went to work, explaining as he went: "The polish protects the leather from water, dirt, whatever. They won't look like much at first; but after you build up a good base, they'll really start to shine. Just keep working on them until you can see your reflection."

A few years have passed since that shoe-shining lesson, but those words still ring true—not so much in the way I care for my shoes, but in the way I walk with God. Experience has taught me that if others are to see God's face in me, if I am to reflect his love and compassion in all that I do, then I've got to build a solid base on his Word and spend some time every day in prayerful self-examination. As I seek God's face in prayer, I feel his breath upon me; the dirt and haze of life are stripped away to reveal the reflection of his face. But this takes time. It doesn't happen overnight.

In those first few weeks at the Citadel, I spent several hours every day just shining shoes. And so it is with God. We cannot expect to reflect God's love if we don't spend time with him on a daily basis.

Prayer Focus: Can others see God's love reflected in my actions?

21

January 11 ~ Unpacking

This is the day which the LORD has made;
We will rejoice and be glad in it.

—Psalm 118:24 (NKJV)

The other day I helped a friend of mine unpack. She had recently moved to a new place, and I thought she could probably use some help getting situated. After taking a stack of boxes upstairs, we came across a box, sitting off by itself, simply marked "fragile." We had no idea what was inside. Peeling away the tape, we opened the box to find a collection of carefully wadded newspapers. Soon the floor was covered with newspaper, and I listened as the story of the picture frames, coffee mugs, and lemonade glasses unfolded. Every one had a story—some precious memory tied to it.

Driving home that afternoon, with the last rays of sun bleeding through the windshield, I kept thinking about the box of treasures we had found. And I wondered how many "boxes" I've left unpacked. You see, every day is a treasure. Many days may be wrapped in doubt, depression, or loss, but they're still worth opening. The trouble is that we can't store our days. We don't have a shelf or cellar where we can stash all our unopened days for safekeeping.

I haven't been around very long, but I've lived long enough to know that life is short. I don't know how long God plans on keeping me here, but I know that every day I have one less than the day before. So I can't afford to let a single day slip by unnoticed. I've let too many days go unopened; I don't want to waste another.

God never said life would be all sunshine and roses, but that doesn't mean we can't live joy-filled lives. But to do this, we must treat every day as a gift from God. Living from the center means that we must begin to see each day, each moment, as an opportunity to live in his presence.

Prayer Focus: How can I better appreciate each day?

January 12 ~ Bad Days

I waited patiently for the LORD;
And He inclined to me,

And heard my cry.
He also brought me up out of a horrible pit,
Out of the miry clay,
And set my feet upon a rock,
And established my steps.

—Psalm 40:1-2 (NKJV)

With the first hard frost, the last leaves let go and float to the ground. The brown, fallow fields are powdered white; the windows fog up; the grass crunches beneath your feet. The sycamore trees, stripped bare by wind and cold, glisten gray as their limbs clatter in the early light. You rub your hands together as you wait for your car to warm up, longing for the warm bed you just left. It's Monday and you'd rather be in bed.

Well, so would I. In fact, there are many days like that—days when I just feel so *unnecessary*, when it's all I can do to just get out of bed. I trudge off to work wishing I were headed someplace else. When I take a long, hard look at my life, when I take the life I imagined and put it beside the life I live, when I see how far I am from the person I want to be, I feel like those sycamore trees. Stripped of pretense, naked before God, I must confront who I am. Burdened by my past, afraid of the future, I wilt beneath this heavy frost. But what cuts me to the core is the sinking feeling that I'm trapped by my circumstances, that I'm spinning like a tire in the snow.

You see, it's awfully easy to get bogged down in our circumstances. We feel so weighed down by life. And as depression begins to creep in, we lose sight of our calling; we lose all sense of purpose and direction. We end up feeling useless, of little worth. But God calls to us in the midst of the mire. He is just as present on our worst day as on our best.

Prayer Focus: *How do I handle bad days?*

January 13 ~ A Consuming Fire

Therefore, since we are receiving a kingdom that cannot be shaken, let us give thanks, by which we offer to God an acceptable worship with reverence and awe; for indeed our God is a consuming fire.

—Hebrews 12:28-29 (NRSV)

23

It was well after 7:00 when I climbed into Stella, our old white truck, and headed down to the lake. It was July, so there was plenty of light left—enough to see the row of black thunderheads closing in. I wasn't having the best of days, and, in keeping with that theme, the clouds let go. The rain was falling in buckets before I could make it to the lake.

Normally, the rain wouldn't have been a problem, but on this particular night of summer camp, the campers were supposed to sing songs and roast marshmallows around the fire. So when I pulled up to the lake, I darted from the truck to cover the wood, which, unfortunately, was already good and soaked. I climbed back inside the truck and spent the next half-hour wondering what we'd do instead.

Almost as suddenly as it had begun, the rain ended and the sun came out. There was still hope. Immediately, I took the wood we'd need and laid it out on the pier to dry. I headed up to the gym to grab some pine cones and rally the fire brigade. Two hours and about two dozen pine cones later, we melted marshmallows and sang songs around a small but adequate fire.

As I write, it's raining once again, and I wonder how many of our "fires" are burning low, almost out—for as hard as it can be to get the fire going, it is infinitely more difficult to *keep* it going. It takes work and dedication, especially when the rains of this world—the inconsiderate spouse, the unfaithful friend, the tedious job, the negative boss—keep dousing the flames. Remember, however, our God is a "consuming fire." He can consume us—wet wood and all.

Prayer Focus: *How's my fire burning?*

January 14 ~ A Lesson in Christian Physics

Therefore, if anyone is in Christ, he is a new creation; old things have passed away; behold, all things have become new.
                                                    —2 Corinthians 5:17 (NKJV)

Objects at rest tend to stay at rest—it's one of the fundamental laws of physics. And though there are numerous formulas and computations that can be used to support this statement, personal experience is more than enough to prove its validity. Case in point: If I'm asleep in bed, I

24

tend to remain that way unless an outside force (my alarm clock) compels me to move.

The same is true when it comes to change. I, myself, am not fond of it. Once I get settled in, once I find my niche, once I'm all comfortable, I don't want to change. And after I've established a routine, I find it even more difficult. You see, with the routine comes security, structure, certainty. With all my receipts clipped together, with my coupons stacked neatly in a drawer, with my calendar covered by appointments and meetings, very little seems left to chance. Life seems in order, so why go out on a limb, why rock the boat, why try something new?

It's a question for all of us. So how do we handle this inertia, this unwillingness to change? Well, there must be a force that breaks us from our comfort zone—not the external force that we learned about in physics class, but an internal one, an upheaval of the soul, that finally brings about change. But it must start within, and it must come from Christ. Therefore, whenever we find ourselves in a spiritual rut, we need to remember that we are new creations in Christ. We are not confined to our former ways but are free to see and hear and live in a new way.

Prayer Focus: *What changes do I need to make to better serve God?*

January 15 ~ A Sense of Wonder

For since the creation of the world His invisible attributes are clearly seen, being understood by the things that are made.
                                                                —*Romans 1:20 (NKJV)*

One day I was sitting by the pool at my apartment complex, reading a book and beginning to doze in the midday heat. I had been staring at the same page for a few moments, my mind drifting away on the breeze, when I heard the sound of voices. Soon a lady and her young son appeared through the gate, their voices low and excited as if they were pleasantly surprised.

It wasn't hard to see that they had just moved in. The mom was looking about, obviously pleased at what she'd found. I could hear her saying, "Isn't the pool nice? It'll be open in just a few weeks, and then you can swim here with all your little friends. Look, they have chairs, and nice, big umbrellas for when it's hot." She was still rattling off her sales pitch when the little boy piped in, "Mommy, Mommy, a caterpillar!" as he crouched to get a better look. The mom just kept walking and making plans, and I couldn't help smiling at the irony of it all.

But isn't that how it is? We're so caught up in our lives and schedules that we walk right past a million wonders without even noticing. We're too busy to hear the child within—to see if it might be God calling out to us, urging us to stop and look, urging us to breathe, urging us into a closer walk with him. It would be much better, I think, if we were like the boy, and had not lost our sense of wonder.

Prayer Focus: *How might I regain my sense of wonder?*

January 16 ~ Hunger

Oh, that men would give thanks to the LORD for His goodness,
And for His wonderful works to the children of men!
For He satisfies the longing soul,
And fills the hungry soul with goodness.

—Psalm 107:8-9 (NKJV)

It was almost midnight when they turned the lights off, and I lay down to sleep. We were barely halfway through our fast, and I could already hear my stomach rumbling—feel the hunger growing inside. As I closed my eyes, I prayed that the night might pass quickly, and that the hunger would disappear with the coming of the light.

Unfortunately, this wasn't the case. I awoke the next morning feeling hollow, tired, and stiff from a night spent on the floor. As I stretched, my stomach reminded me once again that it was time to eat. But the fast wasn't over, so I just grabbed a bottle of juice and gulped it down, hoping to fill the emptiness gnawing inside.

We all survived the fast, completing our time with Holy Communion and a sumptuous meal. Having eaten too much, I waddled out of the church feeling stuffed. But after a few days had passed, I was thinking of a different kind of hunger—a spiritual hunger; one not satisfied with food or drink or sex or money or anything of the sort; one that swallows up all we pour in; one that lingers in spite of our best efforts to "feed" ourselves.

26

We hunger for love and acceptance, for hope and forgiveness. We hunger for that which cannot be bought or sold, for that which is eternal, for that which is beyond all understanding, for that which truly satisfies—the presence of God. Only God can fill that emptiness within; only God can make us whole.

Prayer Focus: What do I hunger for?

January 17 ~ Learning to Play

Whoever has no rule over his own spirit is like a city broken down, without walls.

—Proverbs 25:28 (NKJV)

For some time now, I've been wanting to learn how to play the guitar. I'm not musically inclined, so I've always put it off. But, finally, I took the plunge; I bought a guitar from a friend and started taking lessons last week.

Now, I have several buddies who play, and to be honest, it never looked that hard. You just strum with your right hand and wiggle your left hand between the frets. Well, as you can imagine, it's not that simple. Just learning to finger the chords has been difficult. You have to wrap your left hand around the neck with your wrist poking out at a funny angle while managing to press the proper strings without pressing the other ones. "It doesn't feel natural," I complained to my teacher. "I don't think my fingers are designed to move like that." Luckily, however, my teacher is very patient. "All it takes is a little practice," he said.

Isn't life like that? Doing the right thing isn't always easy, and often it takes practice. We are sinful by nature, so, more often than not, our first impulse is not the right one. This means that we must constantly struggle against ourselves, seeking to overcome our selfish desires and do what Christ would have us do. Nonetheless, we constantly fall short; we miss our goal; we play the wrong notes. How lucky we are, then, to have such a patient and loving Teacher, one who forgives our mistakes and encourages us to keep practicing.

Prayer Focus: What areas of my spiritual life need more "practice"?

27

January 18 ~ Lost in the Crowd

We are hard pressed on every side, yet not crushed; we are perplexed, but not in despair; persecuted, but not forsaken; struck down, but not destroyed.
—2 Corinthians 4:8-9 (NKJV)

I've participated in numerous celebrations, but nothing compared to this. As soon as I jumped the railing, I was caught up in the crowd, swept closer and closer to the goalpost—my excitement growing all the while. I was lost in the moment; I didn't realize the danger until it was too late. People began to pile up around the goal, and there wasn't room for the rest of us.

Yet the crowd went forward, and I went with it. I watched as fans continued to spill over the railing, flooding the already congested field. There seemed to be no end. I could feel the crowd pressing upon me, crushing me with its weight, and I struggled to keep from going down. The crowd continued to sway and pulse, twisting upon itself, constricting like a noose. Soon it was hard to breathe. I was drowning in a sea of people with no way out.

Finally, the goalpost was brought down, and a section of the crowd broke loose to follow it. I quietly made my way back to the railing, climbed it, and stood for a long time watching the crowd. Never before had I felt so trapped, or witnessed the overwhelming force of a crowd possessed.

But isn't that, at least in some degree, our daily situation? Every day we are adrift in a sea of faulty thinking and values. We are swept away by the currents of popular culture—surrounded by a society with decaying morals. And so we swim through the wreckage, clinging to the battered remains of our faith, looking for anything to hold on to. Yet Christ offers us hope. In him, there is the strength to stand out, to be different, to be his chosen people.

Prayer Focus: *Do others know what I stand for?*

January 19 ~ Still Running

Commit your way to the LORD,
Trust also in Him,
And He shall bring it to pass.

He shall bring forth your righteousness as the light,
And your justice as the noonday.

—Psalm 37:5-6 (NKJV)

When I started running a few years ago, it was something of a chore. I was struggling with a relationship that was falling apart, and I began to run as a coping mechanism. It gave me the outlet I needed. Still, it wasn't easy. I ran with a close eye on my watch, panting and praying that I could just make it over the top of the next hill or around the next corner. I felt awkward, unsteady; and as I lumbered along, it was a constant battle just to keep from turning back.

Things are a little different now. I still have those days when I have to make myself run, when those first few miles seem more punishment than pleasure, but it comes much easier now. You see, there's a moment in every run when I stop fighting myself, when everything just seems to come together. My breathing slows, my shoulders relax, my steps fall steady and sure. I forget about my watch; I half forget myself, and all that remains is this blessed feeling of freedom, of peace, of wholeness.

Now, many people aren't physically able to run, and others just don't enjoy it. But there's a different kind of *run* that we're all capable of, for it is a movement of faith, a daily search for God's will in our lives. Like my early runs, it's hard at first. Yet when we begin to take those first awkward strides, God reaches out to us and, like a good coach, guides us through those difficult days. If we are faithful and diligent in our efforts, we soon find that what was once awkward and unnatural is now second nature. Centered in Christ, we begin to want what he wants for us, and we long to live more fully in his grace. We wake each morning eager to see God move in mighty ways; we look forward to the "daily run" of faith.

Prayer Focus: Am I running with God or away from God today?

January 20 ~ The Lonely Miles

"Fear not, for I have redeemed you;
I have called you by your name;
You are Mine.

When you pass through the waters, I will be with you. . . .
When you walk through the fire, you shall not be burned."

—Isaiah 43:1-2 (NKJV)

We were in the middle of our first marathon, and everything was going well. The miles were still clicking by quickly as we wound through cozy neighborhoods and back into downtown. But somewhere around mile twenty-two, real pain began to set in. My longest runs had never taken me this far, and I was in uncharted territory. My body was not responding well, and each step became a struggle. Finally, I stopped by the road, hoping the pain would fade, and watched my friend disappear over the next hill. By this point, the crowds that had cheered us on earlier had thinned out, as had the runners. We were stretched all along the course; and with no familiar faces around, I suddenly felt very alone. I had four miles left to run, and I could barely walk. All the adrenaline was gone; I had no idea how I would finish. Looking back, I don't think I've ever felt as tired, as helpless, as lonely as I did right then.

Doesn't it seem that the toughest times come when we're already tired, when we feel deserted and utterly alone? Ironically, these are often the times of our greatest spiritual growth; for when we feel our weakest, then, and only then, can we realize the strength of our faith and our utter dependence on God. Prayer begins to rise from the depth of our being; and though the pain may endure, we receive reassurance and comfort seldom experienced.

I have my medal hanging in my office now as a reminder of those last few painful miles and the struggle they required. Although you may never run a marathon, it is my prayer that you may, one day, look back on times of difficulty and suffering and see how God strengthened and nourished your faith during those lonely miles.

Prayer Focus: *Have I felt God's presence during difficult times?*

January 21 ~ The Simple Things

Not that I speak in regard to need, for I have learned in whatever state I am, to be content: I know how to be abased, and I know how to abound. Everywhere and in all things I have learned both to be full and to be hungry, both to abound and to suffer need.

—Philippians 4:11-12 (NKJV)

Yesterday after church, I stood in my apartment with a warm cup of coffee in hand, smiling out at the falling snow. My dog, Jake, was curled up at my feet—both of us hypnotized by the softly swirling crystals. And in the gray afternoon light, with the cars and sidewalks beginning to disappear under a blanket of shimmering white, I just stared out the window feeling blessed.

A few hours later, I took Jake for a stroll in the woods behind my apartment. The trees were heavy with snow—the limbs bending low beneath the weight, with the snow falling faster all the time. I could feel the snow cold against my face, and every few minutes Jake would shake the snow loose from his coat. But we kept walking, not wanting to leave the solemn peacefulness that enveloped us.

And I thought to myself, it's funny that it takes something like an early snowfall to remind us of our blessings. Perhaps we are so blessed that we take the simple things for granted. What a shame that it takes something big, something out of the ordinary, to grab our attention. Because we are well fed, we take food for granted. Because we have nice homes, we take warmth and shelter for granted. But I say to you, we are blessed. Every day God's blessings pour forth from heaven like snow softly falling. Yet many times we cling so tightly to what we have—our jobs, possessions, and social status—that our hands are not open to receive what God would give us. Instead, we scrape away our blessings like snow from a windshield. And as we busy ourselves looking for something bigger and better, we trample his blessings to the ground.

Prayer Focus: *What am I thankful for today?*

January 22 ~ A Place in the Son

"But from there you will seek the LORD your God, and you will find Him if you seek Him with all your heart and with all your soul."
—*Deuteronomy 4:29 (NKJV)*

A friend of mine has a beach house on the Isle of Palms. It's nothing fancy—just a small house about three blocks from the ocean. There's no ornate landscaping, no expensive car out front, nothing to make it stand out. Still, I go there every chance I get—not as an escape from everyday life, but as an escape to a deeper life. It's a good place to walk or think, without all the distractions that most beaches offer. So I find myself rising early in the morning, trying to catch the tide going out and the sun coming up. And sometimes I hit it just right: before the great yellow egg spills its yolk across the water, when the rays are still pink and pleasant. Then it seems as if the sunshine has somehow crept inside me, warming up my very soul.

So it often is in church. When I come and sit alone in the early morning sunlight, with the sun playing through the glass, the sanctuary grows in proportion to my solitude, and that strange warmth comes over me again; for then I feel most intensely the presence of the Living God. But it's a long time from Sunday to Sunday. Our batteries get low. So we need to find—or rather make—time to spend with our Creator. It's too easy to become overburdened, to fall out of step. Therefore, if we are to live from the center, we must have those sacred places and holy moments every day where we can seek God and know that he will be found.

Prayer Focus: *Where do I go to feel close to God?*

January 23 ~ A Work in Progress

Unless the LORD *builds the house,*
They labor in vain who build it;
Unless the LORD *guards the city,*
The watchman stays awake in vain.

—Psalm 127:1 (NKJV)

Right down the street there's a house going up. They cleared the lot over six months ago, not long after I moved here. I really thought it would be done by now, but it's not. It has been a slow process, and most days I see the same white van out front—the same two guys inching along, with little change in the house.

Over the last few months, I've watched it evolve: from the first bricks of the foundation, to the bare frame and rafters, to the walls and windows and shingled roof. And it seems to come in spurts. Weeks will pass with no noticeable change; then suddenly, as if by magic, a house has risen from the piles of brick and lumber.

I guess that's how we are. We go through long periods where our spiritual lives seem to be at a standstill, as if the workers are all out to lunch. Then suddenly, a radical change comes over us, and we undergo an intense period of spiritual growth, seemingly without justification. My hunch is that God is like those carpenters. Even while the outside may go relatively unchanged for months at a time, he's hard at work inside. Sometimes we're not even aware that he's working on us. We're so caught up in the daily trappings of life that we don't notice the subtle changes. But then one morning we wake up and realize that there's a new light inside—a holy light that has just been installed.

Prayer Focus: What do I need to work on in my spiritual life?

January 24 ~ Apple Trees

Blessed be the God and Father of our Lord Jesus Christ, the Father of mercies and God of all comfort, who comforts us in all our tribulation, that we may be able to comfort those who are in any trouble, with the comfort with which we ourselves are comforted by God.

—2 Corinthians 1:3-4 (NKJV)

Out the backdoor of my grandparents' house—past the shed, past the blueberry bushes—you'll find a row of apple trees. They're not much to look at—shrunken and shriveled from frost and winter wind. But Grandpa always took wonderful care of them, and I can't look at them without thinking of him; so whenever I'm over there, I make a point to pay those trees a visit.

In the summer, their branches are full, brought low from the weight of the ripening apples until they drag the ground. So a few summers back, Grandpa had braces built to keep the branches from sagging and breaking beneath the weight. How strange it was, however, when I returned one weekend to see those bony branches blowing stiffly and leafless in the wind, barely touching the braces below. The braces seemed unnecessary with the limbs so empty; and as I stood looking at them, it was hard to imagine them brimming with fruit—green and full of life.

Then I thought of something I hadn't before. Maybe God is like those braces—always present no matter the season; there to support us, to lift us when life seems too much. Perhaps this is when God is most real to us; for where there is pain, there is God: ready to comfort, ready to heal, ready to restore, ready to brace us even through the bitterest wind.

Prayer Focus: What do I need God's help with today?

January 25 ~ Born to Fly

But those who wait on the LORD
Shall renew their strength;
They shall mount up with wings like eagles,
They shall run and not be weary,
They shall walk and not faint.

—Isaiah 40:31 (NKJV)

I didn't notice him at first. He had been playing on the other side of the green, closer to the band than I. But before long he ran my way, came right at me, and veered off to the young couple sitting a few feet away. From a distance, I noticed only the incredibly blond hair—hair that seemed almost white in the late afternoon sun. But as he drew near, with his arms swept back airplane-style, I noticed part of his "wing" was missing. His right arm stopped just below the elbow, with only a nub where his forearm should be. Yet again and again, without the least bit of self-consciousness, he circled by, smiling broadly as he ran and leapt into the arms of his proud papa. Lifting him up, his father pulled him close; and they smiled and laughed when the boy put his arms about his father's neck as his father squeezed him tight.

Later that night, after the music had stopped and everyone had gone home, I thought of the boy, of his arm, of the proud father who held him high. Even now, when I close my eyes, I can still see him, running fast with his arms swept back, ready to leap. And I admire him. In spite of what some might think of as a limitation, he wasn't content to sit and watch. He wanted to run and leap and *fly*.

I wonder if we can be as brave. Though we all may not have a physical disability, we all do suffer from certain weaknesses of the spirit. We all have wounded hearts and hurting souls. Yet if we have the courage to truly live as we are called, the courage to run after God, then maybe we can have a life like the little boy—a life of joy; a life free of spiritual limits; a life where we can leap into the arms of our heavenly Father who lifts and loves us.

34

January 26 ~ Counting the Cost

"And whoever does not bear his cross and come after Me cannot be my disciple. For which of you, intending to build a tower, does not sit down first and count the cost, whether he has enough to finish it."

—Luke 14:27-28 (NKJV)

This morning didn't begin as I had planned. Halfway out the parking lot, my car, Betty, died. She didn't just cut off this time; she wouldn't go. I tried all the gears before finally putting her in neutral and letting her roll back into my parking spot. It was a cold ride to work on my bike; and once I thawed, I thought about laying Betty to rest and finding a replacement.

The thing is, I haven't had a car payment before, and I'm not that excited about having one now. My parents bought Betty; but now that I'm on my own, it'll all be up to me. I know I've got to have something other than my bike; but no matter what I choose, I'll have to consider the cost. A brand new car won't seem nearly as appealing six months down the road if I'm living on bread and water, or pitching a tent in my pastor's backyard because I can't pay my rent.

You see, everything has a price. Nothing in this life is free. Whether it's our time, our money, or the sweat of our brow, there's always a cost. But Christ calls for our unwavering commitment. Though God's love, grace, and forgiveness are offered freely to us all, there is a cost to following Christ. A deep spiritual commitment requires not only our time and energy, but our hearts as well.

Prayer Focus: What will serving Christ cost today?

January 27 ~ Getting Up

If we confess our sins, He is faithful and just to forgive us our sins and to cleanse us from all unrighteousness.

—1 John 1:9 (NKJV)

I've never been much of a roller skater, so I'm not sure why I thought ice-skating would be easier. After all, ice is as hard as cement—not to mention slicker and colder. You would think that I would have drawn upon my previous experiences and been content to watch from the safety of the bleachers. But time has a way of dulling the memory, and we tend to forget even the hardest lessons learned. So I skated and fell, and it hurt. Gradually, however, I got the hang of it and managed to spend the better part of the afternoon standing up instead of falling down.

You see, we all fall down—not just in skating, but in life. And it hurts. Sometimes our actions affect only ourselves, yet many times we take others with us when we fall. But falling is natural, and to some degree, inevitable. The trick is to keep getting up.

Every day I fall in ways big and small. Every day I sin and fall short of who God wants me to be. Then I dust myself off, I take a good look around, and I get up—not because I'm so great or good. In fact, it has little to do with me. Rather, it is God's awesome, unending love and forgiveness that lift me up and allow me to try one more time.

Living from the center doesn't mean that you won't fall anymore. What it does mean is that you understand that "getting up and staying up" has much more to do with God's grace than your desire.

Prayer Focus: How have I fallen today?

January 28 ~ Off the Leash

There is therefore now no condemnation for those who are in Christ Jesus. For the law of the Spirit of life in Christ Jesus has set you free from the law of sin and of death.

—Romans 8:1-2 (NRSV)

My dog, Jake, and I have this routine. Every day when I get home from work, I walk through the door, make for the closet, grab his leash, and fasten it; then out the door we go. Jake's always excited about it. After being inside all day, he's ready to get out and stretch his legs—to just run and run and run.

There's a nice, wooded trail that winds behind my apartment complex, so that's where we go. Because it has become such a routine, Jake knows

36

that when we pass the pool he's getting close. With freedom just seconds away, he begins to tug even harder, until I have a hard time getting him to calm down long enough to let him go. Then, as soon as he hears the leash click free, he explodes into motion and races into the woods. I usually walk slowly behind him, watching him dart here and there, watching his tail wagging happily. After being held back so long, he's free to run and play, to just do what dogs were designed to do.

I wonder why we can't be as happy, as joyful, as free—for hasn't God freed us from the penalty of sin? Hasn't death just become a doorway for all believers? I am continually amazed at the lack of joy we exhibit. How often we seem still chained to sin, still carrying the baggage of a life's worth of hurts, as if some great leash has been holding us back so long that we've grown tired of pulling against it. Somehow we've forsaken our joy. But the leash has been removed. Sin and death and all that would steal our joy have been defeated, and freedom is ours!

Prayer Focus: What's keeping me from joyful living today?

January 29 ~ Tender Feet

A new heart I will give you, and a new spirit I will put within you; and I will remove from your body the heart of stone and give you a heart of flesh.
—Ezekiel 36:26 (NRSV)

Sometimes it seems I'm just not as tough as I used to be—at least, my feet aren't. There was a time when I could go barefoot almost anywhere. When I was younger, I hardly ever wore shoes in the summer. It felt good to walk outside early in the morning, with the grass still slick with dew and the smell of wet tobacco in the air. I'd spend most of the day outside, playing in the yard or walking through the fields—my feet growing tougher all the time. Yet when I remember those summers, the best part was always those first few days when my feet were still tender—when I could still feel the tickle of the grass, the gritty sand, the sudden, painful prick of an unexpected thorn.

But things are different now. The other day I could barely cross the parking lot. I was taking out the trash, and since I was too lazy to put on shoes, I suffered all the way there and back. Still, it made me think. Life seems a little easier with calloused feet. You no longer feel all the thorns and barbs; you can walk almost anywhere without worry or feeling or pain.

The problem is that our hearts are often more calloused than our feet. Having been hurt before, the heart begins to harden so that the thorns of life don't cut as deep or hurt as bad. Yet we cannot truly experience love or joy or any good thing without risking pain as well; for it is only when we open our hearts, when we take the chance of being hurt, that we're able to love and be loved.

Prayer Focus: Do I have a heart of stone or flesh?

January 30 ~ The Comfort Zone

Not that I have already attained, or am already perfected; but I press on, that I may lay hold of that for which Christ Jesus has also laid hold of me.
—Philippians 3:12 (NKJV)

For as long as I can remember, there have always been two places that I have avoided like the plague: hospitals and nursing homes. They always seemed such unhappy places—places of sickness and disease and death, places where everyone spoke in quiet voices and the antiseptic air stifled me and made it hard to breathe. I was never comfortable there—and certainly never went there of my own accord.

But it's funny what God can do to a fellow. Not long after I started working for the church, I was out visiting shut-ins with our pastor. He offered to drop me off before he visited the hospital and the nursing home. Almost without thinking, I asked if I could go. I'm still not quite sure why.

That was a year ago, and now I find myself trucking on down to the hospitals and nursing homes about once a week. But the truly amazing thing is that I actually enjoy it. You see, I think God is constantly calling us out of our comfort zone. God knew that I needed to grow in my faith, that I had done all I could where I was.

Living from the center means that we must constantly press on, forgetting what we have already attained, to follow as God leads. We must leave the safety and security we're accustomed to and venture out in faith, trusting that God will enable us to do all he requires.

January 31 ~ Waiting for the Rain

O God, you are my God, earnestly I seek you; my soul thirsts for you, my body longs for you, in a dry and weary land where there is no water.
— Psalm 63:1 (NIV)

Not long ago, I was sitting on my grandfather's front porch, staring out at a cornfield, waiting for the rain. We were in the middle of a severe drought: the grass was brown, the flowers were faded, the corn was already beginning to die. Without rain soon, the whole crop would be lost.

It was dusk, and every time a car passed, I could see dust rising in the air, suspended in the last rays of daylight. It had been a hot day, with the thermometer dipped deep in red since morning. But as I sat, slowly rocking, I felt the air turn cool and the wind pick up. Clouds rolled in, piling up in the east, and I could almost smell the rain. A few minutes later, the first echoes of thunder rumbled long and low, and I smiled at the thought of big drops falling and the road steaming late into the night.

Funny thing, though: it didn't rain that night, and I went inside feeling more than just disappointed. You see, I was going through a drought of my own—a spiritual drought. Inside, I felt as parched as those fields, and I couldn't understand why my prayers for renewal had gone unanswered—why I felt so empty. I was ready to give up, to look somewhere else. But then I thought of the corn—how in times of drought its roots plunge deeper; how it just stood there, waiting. And many times that's exactly what we need to do. God hasn't forgotten or forsaken us. The rain will come—if we wait. And while we wait, if we'll keep our eyes open to the simplest things around us, we will see God.

Prayer Focus: What am I waiting for?

39

February

SEEING GOD

Ellen Mohney

February 1 ~ Recognizing Our Savior

At this, she turned around and saw Jesus standing there, but she did not realize that it was Jesus.

—*John 20:14 (NIV)*

God never ceases to amaze me. He is so *huge,* and we are so small; yet he cares deeply for us and longs to have a personal, intimate relationship with each of us. But in order to have this deep relationship with God, we must spend time with him daily in Scripture and prayer. We will be richly blessed if we take time to be with God, but we will be blessed even more if we recognize the ways God actively works in our lives and the lives of others.

This month we will look at the many ways God reveals himself to us. Sometimes, God speaks to us by sending special people into our lives at the times we need them most. Other times, he may reveal himself through the circumstances we are in. Still other times, he uses his beautiful creation to reach us. We must always be aware of the ways God may be trying to speak to us, because if we are not watchful, we can forgo the blessings he freely pours out on us. By recognizing some of the ways God moves and works, we may come to understand more of his character and his undying, all-encompassing love for us, his children.

41

Prayer Focus: *Do you desire to know God more personally and to be blessed through recognizing the many ways he is revealing himself to you? Pray that he will open your eyes to see him more clearly.*

February 2 ~ Seeing God on an Airplane

Trust in the LORD with all your heart and lean not on your own understanding; in all your ways acknowledge him, and he will make your paths straight.
—Proverbs 3:5-6 (NIV)

Recently I was on an airplane, and it was apparent that we were going to have to fly through a rainstorm. I made a comment to the woman next to me about the ugly weather. She responded, "The sky is never ugly; it is always beautiful." She was right. Once we flew through the storm clouds, I saw that the sky was as clear, peaceful, and beautiful as I had ever seen it. Though the clouds made the sky appear dreary, in reality, the sky above had not changed.

Flying higher than the storm clouds, in the peaceful sky above, reminded me of our shortsighted vision as Christians. So many times we cannot see past the storm clouds in our lives, whatever form they may take. We worry and get anxious because we can never be sure what is beyond the clouds. However, we must never forget that, just like the sky, God is unchanging. God is always beautiful, always faithful. Though our future may seem cloudy, we can trust that God sees it clearly, for he is above all our problems and frustrations. Then, if we trust in the Lord with all our hearts, he will make our paths straight. It is only in that knowledge that we can rest in his peace.

Prayer Focus: *Are you worried about what the future holds? Pray for God to give you a heart that fully trusts him.*

February 3 ~ Seeing God Through Pets

"But while he was still a long way off, his father saw him and was filled with compassion for him; he ran to his son, threw his arms around him and kissed him."
—Luke 15:20 (NIV)

After reading today's title, you may be thinking that I'm going a bit too far in my suggestions of ways God can reveal himself to us. But it is true! God can even use our pets to show his unconditional love for us. If you've ever had a dog, you will know what I am talking about.

When I left home for college, I could tell that my dog knew I was not coming back for a while by looking at her sad eyes. I felt sure she wouldn't love me as much when I returned, because I assumed that in my long absence she would find other people to replace me. Thankfully, that was not the case at all. The first time I came home, she saw my car from down the street, and she took off running. She made it to the car and was jumping up and down, so excited to see me; when I got out of the car, she was leaping up and licking my face.

What a joyous picture of the love of our Father. My dog, like the father of the prodigal son, and like our Heavenly Father, didn't care that I had been gone for so long. All she cared about was that I had come home. Our Father is even more loyal to us than a dog could ever be; he doesn't care where we have gone or how long we've been there. All that's important is that we've come home.

Prayer Focus: Have you or someone you love strayed from God? If so, pray that the one who has gone astray will know the loyalty and love of the Father and have courage to go home.

February 4 ~ Seeing God in "Bubbles"

Every good and perfect gift is from above, coming down from the Father of the heavenly lights, who does not change like shifting shadows. He chose to give us birth through the word of truth, that we might be a kind of firstfruits of all he created.

—James 1:17-18 (NIV)

One summer I went to Jamaica on a mission trip to take part in the children's ministry. Every day we would walk to the elementary school down the street, and there would be a classroom full of children. For arts and crafts one day, we brought bubbles, not realizing that most of the children had never seen bubbles before. They squealed with joy every time we blew the bubbles at them; as soon as the bubbles popped, they would

43

scream, "More, more!" I have never in my life seen children get so excited about something. When we had to leave, they were very sad, and many started to whine and complain.

Isn't that how we act with God? When God is blessing us with happy times—when our relationships are going well, when we are succeeding at something, or when our family members are loving one another—we are as joyous as the Jamaican children and ask God for "More, more!" It's when things start to get harder and the "bubbles" of life begin to pop that we immediately whine and complain, forgetting to thank God for the bubbles he let us enjoy for a time. We forget that God doesn't have to give us bubbles, and that we definitely don't deserve them.

The Christian life isn't about being happy all the time or having everything go "right." There are many good times, and there inevitably will be many hard times. Let's remember to thank God for the bubbles, even in those times when all seem to have popped—for just as surely as other mission teams will go to Jamaica and blow bubbles with the kids, so also God will "blow bubbles" in our lives once again.

Prayer Focus: Thank God for those times in your life when he has blessed you, and pray for patience as you wait for times of blessing to come again.

February 5 ~ Seeing God in Unexpected Ways

Devote yourselves to prayer, being watchful and thankful.
—Colossians 4:2 (NIV)

I was in my dorm when a friend called me into her room to show me a web site she had found. The web page was called "Miracles by God," and I was curious to see what these miracles were. The site showed various pictures of clouds with what was said to be the face or body of Jesus in them. In another picture, there appeared to be the form of an angel within the clouds. The pictures truly looked real, and my first reaction was one of amazement and wonder. However, as I looked a bit longer, my cynicism kicked in, and I began telling myself that these couldn't be actual pictures—after all, this was the Internet! Next, a page came on the screen that displayed the different sizes and prices of each picture, including blurbs about what great gifts they would make. When I saw that, I immediately wrote the pictures off as fake, convinced that the web site's only purpose was to make money.

Later, as I thought more about the pictures, I wondered if my cynicism had robbed me of an encounter with our miraculous God. Whether or not the pictures on the web site were legitimate, they led me to an important realization. Often God reveals himself to us and we either don't have the eyes to recognize that it is God, or we simply don't believe it could be God and write it off as something of this world—as I did. God reveals himself to us every day—sometimes in ways we do not expect, such as in a stranger's hello, in booming thunder during a storm, or even in a movie theater.

We miss out on God's blessings when we refuse to be watchful and expectant of the things he wishes to show us. Be watchful today. Where do you see God?

Prayer Focus: Could God be revealing himself to you, yet you are too cynical to accept it? Or are you simply not watching for him? Pray for God to give you the eyes to recognize the awesome blessings he has in store for you.

February 6 ~ Seeing God in Our Labors

Therefore, my dear brothers, stand firm. Let nothing move you. Always give yourselves fully to the work of the Lord, because you know that your labor in the Lord is not in vain.

—1 Corinthians 15:58 (NIV)

A few summers ago I went to Colorado to backpack with some other students and faculty from my school. We began hiking early in the morning in order to reach the summit. I noticed that when we would stop to take a break, catch our breath, and enjoy the view, one of the girls in our group refused to turn around. When we asked her why, she said that she wouldn't look because she wanted the view from the summit to be absolutely incredible.

Needless to say, the view from 12,803 feet in the Colorado Rockies was incredible for those of us who had been seeing the view as we ascended; the view for the girl who had chosen not to look, though, was absolutely breathtaking. She had no idea how high we were, or how many different lakes, streams, peaks, and treetops we would be able to see.

45

In many ways, our Christian walk is like our walk up that mountain. Sometimes we may feel that we are always going uphill, not seeing the fruits of our labors for Christ. Other times, though, God gives us a glimpse of his "view"—of what he is doing through our labors. This view may come through seeing someone we've been witnessing to turn to Christ, or seeing God answer our prayers for a particular situation. Either way, if we keep walking, always looking upward to Jesus, nothing can compare with the view from heaven. Whether or not we saw glimpses of what God was doing on our way up, the view from the top is going to be beyond description, and that makes all our labors worth it.

Prayer Focus: Do you feel as if all your work for the Lord is fruitless? Pray that God will give you the perseverance to keep walking and the faith to know that when you get to heaven, you will see that all your labors have not been in vain.

February 7 ~ Seeing God in the Power of the Gospel Message

He said to them, "Go into all the world and preach the good news to all creation."

—Mark 16:15 (NIV)

A few years ago I took a trip to Costa Rica with SCORE International. Our purpose was to use soccer as a means for sharing the good news of Christ with the natives there. We had two games scheduled in a small town one afternoon, and when we arrived, there were only about thirty people there to watch our game. At halftime we shared the gospel, and to our surprise, by the end of our second game, there were some three hundred people there!

Later we discovered what had happened. The people who were there for the first game heard the good news and ran home to tell their families and friends. One Costa Rican woman told us, "What you sixteen girls did in two hours, we have been trying to do for the last three years." She and some other residents had been trying to get the rest of the town to come together to hear the word of Christ, and they had been unable to make it happen. As a result of that one day, many people accepted Christ into their hearts and the revival some had prayed for began!

46

What impressed me that day was how quickly the word spread through the town. It was amazing to see the excitement and eagerness on the Costa Ricans' faces as they listened to the Word of Christ, many for the first time.

You don't have to travel to a different country to encounter people who need to hear the gospel. They are all around us—in our neighborhoods, workplaces, schools, and even in our own homes. The challenge is taking that first step in sharing the gospel. When we choose to do so, we can have eternal influence.

Prayer Focus: Who around you needs to hear the good news? Pray that God would give you the opportunity to talk to them and the courage to speak the Truth.

February 8 ~ Seeing God in Difficult People

"If you love those who love you, what reward will you get?"
—Matthew 5:46 (NIV)

We all have difficult people in our lives—including coworkers, supervisors, children, teachers, or neighbors. You know the kind of person I'm talking about—the one who always has something negative to say, or who knows just how to get under your skin. Perhaps the most difficult thing about this person is that, no matter how hard you try, it seems he or she never appreciates you.

I had a camper one summer who fit this description perfectly. As soon as I met her, I knew it was going to be a long week. Not only was she mean to me and the other campers, but she also volunteered negative comments frequently. No matter what I said or did, it was clear that she was not going to change. I wanted to give up on her and stop trying to reach her, because every time I tried, I got hurt. God wouldn't let me, though. He kept urging me to pray, pray, pray. So I did.

In the end, the week I thought I would painfully endure became a week of surprising blessing as I saw the Lord work in her life. Don't get me wrong—it still was one of the hardest weeks of my life. Through prayer, though, God gave me a tenderness toward her. God helped me to truly love her for who she is—not for who I wanted her to be. It was only through that love that God was able to use me in ministering to her.

47

God wants to use you to reach those difficult people in your life; but it's only through love, not endurance, that he will be able to use you. Not until you love them with the love of Christ will you be able to see God tangibly working and making a difference in their lives.

Prayer Focus: Are there difficult people in your life you simply endure? Pray that God will help you to love them for the people he created them to be, not for the people you want them to be.

February 9 ~ Seeing God at Work in Frustrating Times

"You were wearied by all your ways, but you would not say, 'It is hopeless.' You found renewal of your strength, and so you did not faint."
—*Isaiah 57:10 (NIV)*

Being solely responsible for someone for an extended time is not an easy job. The first time I was faced with this task, I was completely overwhelmed. (Those of you with kids can relate to this, I'm sure.) One summer I was in charge of a mentally handicapped camper for one week, twenty-three hours each day—with one hour of free time. At times I was so overwhelmed with trying to take care of her and watch out for her while trying to meet my own basic needs (showering, brushing my teeth, and so forth) that I felt I was at the end of my rope. Sometimes I would get incredibly frustrated with my camper, but more frequently, I would get incredibly frustrated with my reactions to her.

Have you ever felt that way? You are frustrated at the outset. Then you react to someone in a way that is not Christlike, and that makes you even more frustrated than you were to begin with! It is in times like this that we need to stop what we're doing and go to God. Each time I sought refuge in his Word, the Holy Spirit was ever faithful to work in my life, renewing my heart and mind. Then I could return to my camper refreshed, with a better attitude.

Next time you are overwhelmed by responsibility or frustration, take a break with God and drink from his fountain of living water, contained in the Bible. If you are willing to let him, God will transform your heart and attitude. And through his transforming work in your life, God can use you as you venture back into the world.

February 10 ~ Seeing God When Our Efforts Go Unnoticed or Unappreciated

From the fullness of his grace we have all received one blessing after another.
—John 1:16 (NIV)

Have you ever given or done so much for someone, yet he or she doesn't seem to notice or appreciate what you have done? That's how I felt that week at summer camp when I was responsible for the mentally handicapped camper for twenty-three hours a day. From sunrise to sunset, I was never without her. If she wanted to swim, we swam together. If she wanted to canoe, we canoed together. If she went through her suitcase, I repacked it for her. If she made a mess, I cleaned it up. If she did something wrong, I took the blame. All that was okay with me, because I thought she understood that I didn't have to do it—I did it in hopes of showing Jesus to her. By the end of the week, though, I was exhausted physically, mentally, and emotionally. I felt that I had given everything I had to give to my camper.

The hurt came on the last day of camp when someone asked my camper my name, and she said, "I don't know." My first reactions were anger and pride. How could the one I had given so much of myself to not know my name? Did she think she deserved to be served in the manner I had served her?

But then the real question hit me: Couldn't Jesus ask the same of me every day? He has given all of himself to me; he watches out for me twenty-four hours a day, giving me blessing after blessing. I must think I deserve it, for I fail to thank him—and sometimes even to acknowledge that I know his name.

What about you? Do you give Jesus the praise and thanks he deserves for all he does for you? Or do you assume your blessings are the result of your own hard work and, therefore, you must deserve them?

Prayer Focus: *Do you give God credit for all he does for you? Pray to become aware of all the ways God works in your life and to have a thankful heart, recognizing these things as gifts of grace.*

February 11 ~ Seeing God in the Disappointments of Life

And we know that in all things God works for the good of those who love him.
—Romans 8:28 (NIV)

One summer my Bible study group took a trip to Colorado to backpack in the beautiful setting of Crested Butte. Carrying high hopes and heavy backpacks, we set off with nothing but an open trail ahead—that is, until we got lost. It wasn't even lunchtime before we found ourselves in the middle of the forest, being eaten alive by millions of mosquitoes and not knowing which way to go. At first we continued to have a positive outlook, but two days later, when we still hadn't found the trail and were bushwhacking our way through the dense forest, we began to get nervous. I thought that our entire trip was ruined and that we had wasted our time and money. However, God had a higher plan and purpose for our trip.

As our days unfolded, I realized that getting lost was the best thing that could have happened to us. God did some amazing things in our lives that I don't think could have happened had we been on the trail. It took getting lost in a completely alien environment to bring us out of our comfort zones, to help us realize that we are not in control of our lives, and to make us surrender completely to God.

Through this experience God made real to me the truth that he is in and through *all* situations, even the ones that seem disappointing or out of control. When you face circumstances that don't seem to fit the picture you had imagined, be patient and watchful. God may have something even greater in store for you, for he works in both the good and bad circumstances of life.

Prayer Focus: *Are you facing a situation that isn't exactly what you had hoped for? Pray that God will give you eyes to see his greater plan and purpose behind your circumstances.*

February 12 ~ Seeing God Despite Our "Stuff"

Listen, my dear brothers: Has not God chosen those who are poor in the eyes of the world to be rich in faith and to inherit the kingdom he promised those who love him?

—James 2:5 (NIV)

Jamaican infirmaries are the places where men and women, young and old, get dropped off—either because they are too sick for their families to take care of them or because their families are too sick of trying to take care of them. Unfortunately, it is usually the latter. The patients range from perfectly healthy blind men and mentally handicapped people to the old and dying. The men and women who stay in the infirmary live in utter poverty, owning but a few items.

Considering this, I was amazed one summer when I visited a men's infirmary to find that the patients were so joyous. After talking with a few of them, it was clearly evident that Jesus was in their lives. What struck me, though, was a statement one of my youth leaders told us after leaving. She said that, in the same way we Americans cannot understand how they could love God and be so joyous when they have nothing, the Jamaicans in the infirmary can't understand how we can love God when we have so much stuff.

I saw Jesus so easily and clearly in some of those men because they had no possessions or worldly things to come between them and the Lord. Our challenge is to not let our "stuff" distract or deter us from God. May we find a way to let Jesus be as evident in our lives as he is in the lives of the men at the Jamaican infirmary.

Prayer Focus: Can God easily shine his light through your life, or is all your "stuff" getting in the way? Consider whether Jesus is number one in your life, far ahead of your possessions.

February 13 ~ Seeing God in the Faith of Another

And the prayer offered in faith will make the sick person well; the Lord will raise him up. If he has sinned, he will be forgiven.

—James 5:15 (NIV)

The first time I visited an infirmary in Jamaica, I met a woman named Harriet. She was about thirty years old and had been hit by a bus when she was seventeen. The accident had caused her legs to be severely disfigured and intertwined, and she had lived at the infirmary ever since, unable to walk. I could tell that Harriet loved God, but little did I know how deep her faith was rooted until I returned to the infirmary the following year.

As I stood beside her bed, she said she had been praying that God would heal her legs and allow them to straighten out again. Then, she told us to watch what the Lord had done. With a look of determination and concentration, Harriet straightened her legs! Though she could hold them straight for only a moment, she looked up at us with a smile of pure joy. God had been faithful! Harriet believed that God would heal her legs, and a year later, the signs of healing were beginning to show.

So many times, I realized, I pray for something and believe in my heart God will answer my prayer; but when a long time passes, and I don't see evidence of my prayer being answered, I begin to lose faith. Harriet had prayed for over fifteen years and never once doubted that God would be faithful; and because of her faith, she is being healed. What an example of patient confidence Harriet is to us all.

Prayer Focus: Do you doubt God hears your prayers and wonder if he will prove faithful? Pray for the faith to believe and the patience to wait.

February 14 ~ Seeing God in the Generosity of Little Children

And he said: "I tell you the truth, unless you change and become like little children, you will never enter the kingdom of heaven."
—Matthew 18:3 (NIV)

I will never forget one year when I helped teach vacation Bible school at my church. We were in charge of the kindergartners, and every day we played games, sang songs, and did arts and crafts. Also, someone would come talk to the children each day about a charitable organization they could give an offering to. One particular talk really drew the kids' attention. A man explained that in the inner city, there were kids just like them who didn't have soccer balls and baseball bats as they did; instead, they played with rocks, sticks, or whatever they could find. One particular kindergartner, Jake, could not believe that every child did not have toys to play with.

The next morning, Jake walked in with a box full of coins and dumped them on the table. I told Jake that it looked like a lot of money and asked him what it was for. He responded, "It's my life savings," and he went on to explain that he wanted those kids in the inner city to get to play with toys like his.

I will never forget that day, because it was then that God used Jake, a kindergartner, to teach me what it means to give all you have to people less fortunate. He understood so easily what we adults seem to have a hard time comprehending. Unless we change and become like Jake, reaching out to those in need around us in trust and love, we will never enter the kingdom of heaven.

Prayer Focus: Is there someone around you who is in need—monetarily, emotionally, physically, or spiritually? Pray for God to give you a willing heart to reach out to this person, trusting that God will provide.

February 15 ~ Seeing God Through Answered Prayer

"If you believe, you will receive whatever you ask for in prayer."
                                              —Matthew 21:22 (NIV)

God has made himself so real to me this past year. Never before have I seen him working so tangibly in my life and the lives of those around me. One of those times God made himself and his faithfulness so clear to me was when a friend of mine came into my dorm room to talk. She was confused about life—about why some things had happened to her and why she felt so empty. As soon as she left my room, my roommate and I began praying for her, asking God to break her so that she would realize how much she needed to trust God and give her problems to him. A few minutes later, while we were still praying, our friend walked back in with tears streaming down her face; she began telling us of how God, just in those past few minutes, had made everything so clear to her. Everything my roommate and I had been praying for, God had done right then. For some reason, he had chosen not only to honor our prayers, but also to show us that he had answered them.

It is not every day that we get to see tangible results of our prayers as I did that day. We must always be confident, though, that God does hear us and will answer us, whether we recognize the answer or not.

Prayer Focus: Are you praying for something but not seeing the fruit of your prayers? Don't give up. God is faithful. Pray for perseverance in your prayers— and also for the eyes to see his answer.

February 16 ~ Seeing God Through Our Motives

All a man's ways seem innocent to him, but motives are weighed by the LORD.
—Proverbs 16:2 (NIV)

My senior year of high school, as I began to realize that it was my last year to spend time with those I had grown up with, I began to question why I did the things I did. While reflecting, I realized that much of my life I had done things out of habit, or because I felt obligated to do them, instead of doing things because they truly were what I wanted to be pouring my energies into. I had spent so much of my life doing things mindlessly, without considering what God really wanted for me—not to mention being completely unaware of the ways he may have been trying to direct me.

How true is that of our lives today? Sometimes we get so caught up in our hectic daily routines that we never stop to check our motives or to seek God's direction for our lives. Why do some of us wake up and do the same thing, day in and day out? Is it because that is our habit, or because that is truly what we want to do with our lives?

Jesus was constantly going to be alone with his Father in order to make sure he was always in the center of God's will, never doing anything in vain—never acting out of habit, a sense of obligation, or plain mindlessness. It is this example of Jesus that we should strive to follow in our daily lives.

Prayer Focus: Are you truly seeking God's will each and every day? Consider whether God is the ultimate motive behind all you do.

February 17 ~ Seeing God in the Mundane

Serve wholeheartedly, as if you were serving the Lord, not men, because you know that the Lord will reward everyone for whatever good he does, whether he is slave or free.

—Ephesians 6:7-8 (NIV)

54

One summer on a mission trip to Jamaica, my youth group volunteered to help a local man who needed to build the foundation for his house. There were two dump trucks' worth of rocks at the base of the extremely steep hill on which he was going to build. We lined up and passed buckets full of rocks from one person to the next until they reached the top. At first, we were excited and eager to help; an hour later, when we were still passing the buckets, which only seemed to get heavier, our work lost its sense of excitement and became mundane and boring. When we had finished, though, what we saw was amazing.

Each bucket of rocks had not looked like much as we were passing it up the hill; but after all of them were put together, the rocks had formed the whole foundation of the man's house! Seeing the foundation was so rewarding, and it made all our effort seem worthwhile.

This memory makes me think of what it may be like when we go to heaven. Though our everyday tasks look small when considered alone—such as going to work or school, giving someone in need a call, feeding our kids, writing a letter, or giving someone a word of encouragement—God remembers them all. When we get to heaven, all the small things we have done will amount to a huge reward.

God is in the mundane—the everyday tasks of life. Each grain of sand is small and seemingly insignificant by itself, but many grains together make miles of sandy beaches; so it is with the everyday tasks of our lives. Though to our human eyes they seem small, they are huge when considered together.

Prayer Focus: Do your everyday tasks seem to be mundane? Pray that God will give you patience and strength to continue, remembering that great is your reward in heaven.

February 18 ~ Seeing God Through Others

My message and my preaching were not with wise and persuasive words, but with a demonstration of the Spirit's power, so that your faith might not rest on men's wisdom, but on God's power.
—1 Corinthians 2:4-5 (NIV)

The band Ridgely sings a song called "My Elijah," and the lyrics to the song include these words: "Through your example, God my Father draws me near." God has used many people in my life to draw me to himself—not so much by their persuasive words, but by the way in which they live their lives. You know the kind of people I am talking about—those who have a sense of peace and joy about them that you know must come from God, or those who live their lives in a way that makes you want to live as they do. Whenever I spend time with people who truly love Jesus, I always leave with a desire to spend time with the Lord.

God uses the examples of others to draw us to himself. The question we should ask ourselves is this: Am I living my life in such a way that others could be drawn to God through my example? In other words, when others spend time with me, is my love of Jesus so evident and attractive that it encourages them to spend more time with God? Remind yourself of these questions throughout the day, for you never know when God may want to use your example to draw someone closer to himself.

Prayer Focus: Thank God for the people he has used to draw you to himself, and pray that your life may be an example for others.

February 19 ~ Seeing God in the Sunset

The heavens declare the glory of God; the skies proclaim the work of his hands.
—Psalm 19:1 (NIV)

Watching the sunset from an airplane is unlike seeing it from anywhere else. The golds seem more golden, the pinks seem pinker, and the rays seem to come from heaven itself. There is something about looking down on the clouds, instead of up at them, that makes you feel closer to God; after all, "Clouds are the dust of his feet" (Nahum 1:3 NIV). As I watched an incredible sunset while on an airplane a few years ago, I was inspired to write this poem.

Watch Me

I watch you all day long,
I get to see your every move.
I watch your still, peaceful eyes rest through the night.
If only you could be that still all the time.
But as soon as the alarm goes off, you are still no more.

I watch as you throw your clothes on and eat your
    breakfast as you run out the door.
I watch you work all day long—always moving from
    one place to another.

You're so busy.
There seems to be no time to simply be still.
Never time to think of Me.
But that doesn't seem to bother you.

At the day's end, I watch your sleepy eyes walk in the
    door.
I watch you sit to eat your dinner—but wait—did you just
    look up?

Yes—I think you see Me!
Look, through the window!
Do you see the clouds and all the colors?
Will you watch Me?

I know you're tired, but all you have to do is be still.
Just be still.
I'm painting this for you and you alone.
Will you watch Me?
I won't take long, I promise.
I just want to show you what I can do.
I want to give you a glimpse of what's to come.
Watch this . . .

Golden—just the way you like it.

Is that a tear?
I painted this for you . . .
Oh, you're welcome.
Thanks for watching.

Prayer Focus: *When was the last time you watched a sunset? Are you so busy
that you seldom take time to be still and allow God to bless your life?*

February 20 ~ Seeing God in the Random Thoughts of Life

And this is my prayer: that your love may abound more and more in knowledge and depth of insight, so that you may be able to discern what is best and may be pure and blameless until the day of Christ.

—Philippians 1:9-10 (NIV)

Yesterday as I was driving home from school, a friend of mine popped into my head for no apparent reason. I hadn't thought about her all day, but something told me not to discount it as just a random thought. Not knowing why I needed to, I picked up the phone and called her. As it turned out, my friend had just been in a fight with her mom and, through her tears, she told me that she had wished she had someone to talk to. There was no way I could have known that my friend was hurting, but God did; and he is the reason she "randomly" popped into my head.

Similarly, my grandmother called me once and said that, though she didn't know why, she felt that God wanted her to tell me that he loved me and that I needed to hang in there because I was going to make it. That was exactly what I needed to hear at that moment! The timing of her phone call couldn't have been any better. Her call made a huge difference in my life.

God uses so many ways to speak to us, even in the seemingly random thoughts we have. Have you ever thought about someone in the course of your day for no apparent reason? Don't be so quick to dismiss it next time; God may be trying to tell you something. It may be that this person needs prayer, a phone call, or a note of encouragement. Don't miss the ways God may want to use you; be aware that random thoughts are not always random.

Prayer Focus: *Pray that you will be aware and willing to act on the "random" thoughts God may be giving you.*

February 21 ~ Seeing God in Persistent Encouragement

Therefore encourage one another and build each other up, just as in fact you are doing.

—1 Thessalonians 5:11 (NIV)

It's funny how we can remember hurtful words people spoke to us years ago, yet we tend to store the compliments we receive in our short-term memory. I bet every one of us can pinpoint a time when someone hurt us—like the time a fellow fifth-grader spoke hurtful words to me about my face. Although that was years ago, I can repeat word for word what he said. On the other hand, I cannot even remember the compliments I received yesterday. However, there is one compliment that stands out in my mind even today.

I don't remember how or why it started, but a few years ago a good friend of mine began saying, "I love you, and I'm proud of you," every time we talked. It did not matter if we had spent a whole day together or only a few minutes, she always said it. Since I have gone to college, we cannot talk as much as we used to; but her words have stuck with me. At times when I have needed a little pick-me-up, I have always been able to go back to my friend and her kind words.

Because those words were repeated to me time and time again, they became ingrained in my memory, and I have never forgotten them. Maybe you have special sayings you hear repeated to you from your mother or father, your children, or your spouse. Or perhaps you repeat something to them. Either way, those are the words that will be remembered for a life time. Maybe that's why the word *love* is repeated 551 times in the Bible!

Prayer Focus: Are you persistent in your encouragement? Are your words of encouragement ones that people will remember? Pray that God will use your words for his glory, and also thank God for those people in your life he has used to encourage you.

February 22 ~ Seeing God in Our Words

The tongue that brings healing is a tree of life, but a deceitful tongue crushes the spirit.

—*Proverbs 15:4 (NIV)*

If you have ever tried to snowboard, you know that the first day is always the hardest and most frustrating. I tried snowboarding for the first time this past winter, and I could not go more than a few feet without falling. As I sat on the freezing ground and watched the more experienced snowboarders whiz past me with seeming ease, I became very discouraged. At one point I became so frustrated that I gave up, resolving to slide down the rest of the mountain on my backside. I was cold, tired, and bruised, and I just wanted to go home. Needless to say, I was in need of some encouragement.

A few minutes later, a friend of mine saw me and came to talk. He could tell I was upset, and he began telling me how great I was doing for my first day. Although I wasn't in the mood for someone to help me, the more he talked, the more I listened; pretty soon my spirit was restored, and I was back on the slopes. I may not have snowboarded any better than before, but I had restored confidence, which made all the difference in the world.

God has given us the amazing ability to build others up simply by doing what comes naturally to us: talking. It was through human words that God lifted my spirit on the slopes that day. Will you use your God-given ability to talk to help build up his kingdom, or to break it down?

Prayer Focus: Do you realize the effect your words can have on others? Pray that your words will be ones that bring hope and healing to those around you.

February 23 ~ Seeing God in Unexpected Places

Therefore, I urge you, brothers, in view of God's mercy, to offer your bodies as living sacrifices, holy and pleasing to God—this is your spiritual act of worship.
—Romans 12:1 (NIV)

I always smile when I think of the unexpected places where God has taught me a lesson. One of these places was a camp for mentally disabled children. My camper and I sat down at the arts and crafts table during one of the dances, with 'N Sync and the Backstreet Boys blasting through the speakers and people dancing all around. (Needless to say, I wasn't especially looking for God to reveal himself to me in that place.) Once we had the string ready to make a bracelet, my camper looked at me and said, "I need you to be my arm." You see, she had had a stroke during brain surgery as a child and, as a result, had little use of the right side of her body.

I agreed to "be her arm." Little did I know that for the next three nights we would not dance at the dances but, instead, would sit on a wooden bench for hours doing the same monotonous motions—up, over, and through. By the second night, it had become uncomfortable and boring, and I was becoming impatient. What a reward it was on the third night, however, to see her face when we had finally finished the bracelet—and it had turned out to be beautiful!

Isn't the question my camper asked me the same question God asks of us? Will we be his arms? Are we willing to let him use us in the monotonous and sometimes uncomfortable times of life so that, in the end, he can make something beautiful?

Prayer Focus: Jesus is asking you to "be his arms," even in the ordinary, day-to-day things of life. Are you responding to his call?

February 24 ~ Seeing God in His Wonders

"Listen to this, Job; stop and consider God's wonders."

—*Job 37:14 (NIV)*

There have been countless times in my life when God has literally stopped me in my tracks as I gazed upon his wonders. From a sunset, to a baby's laughter, to wedding ceremonies, to people reaching out in compassion—all are wonders that God has given us as gifts, so that we might see his majesty. Though we can see many of God's wonders, some wonders are so huge that we cannot see them with the naked eye.

For example, as Brennan Manning explains in his book *The Ragamuffin Gospel,* the earth is tilted at exactly twenty-three degrees. Had it been tilted any other way, the vapors from the ocean would cause new continents of ice to form. Had the earth's crust been a mere ten feet thicker, there could be no oxygen and, therefore, no life on earth. Similarly, had the oceans been but a few feet deeper, oxygen and carbon dioxide would have been absorbed into it, and there could be no plants on earth. And what about the enormous size of our galaxy? If we held up a dime at arm's length, the coin would cover up fifteen million stars—if we were able to see with that power.

Can we understand such precision? Such wonder? It is almost beyond our human comprehension. But God wants us to notice, for it is in things such as these that God may reveal himself most clearly. The next time you see one of God's wonders, don't just pass it by. "Stop, and consider God's wonders."

February 25 ~ Seeing God in Unexpected People

This is good, and pleases God our Savior, who wants all men to be saved and to come to a knowledge of the truth.

—1 Timothy 2:3-4 (NIV)

Do you know someone who, for whatever reason, you don't think will ever become a Christian? I have a friend I thought would never accept Christ. It wasn't because she was a "bad" person; in fact, she is one of the kindest, most loving people I have ever met. There were just certain details about Christianity that she didn't agree with. My roommate and I began to pray for her salvation at the beginning of the year; but after six months, when our prayers seemed to amount to nothing, I began to lose faith.

Then, at 2:00 A.M. on the morning before midterms, I heard a knock on my door. I went out in the hall to hear my friend tell me she had just accepted Christ! She and another friend had been studying in the hall and had started to talk. One thing led to another, and soon they were praying together. What if my other friend had chosen to ignore God's nudges because she had so much to learn for her exam the next day? What if she had been so concerned about her midterm that she chose to ignore the opportunity God gave her to talk with my friend? Instead, she obeyed God and focused on what was essential, instead of what was important.

Have you ever known that God wanted you to talk to someone, but you chose not to because you were too worried about what you needed to do or what you would say? Try to have an eternal perspective instead of a day-to-day one. It is only then that God will be able to work through you to advance his kingdom.

Prayer Focus: Is there someone you know who you think will never become a Christian? Pray for the faith to believe that he or she will come to Christ, and pray for the eternal perspective and obedience to take the opportunities God gives you to talk with this person.

February 26 ~ Seeing God in Scripture

"You will seek me and find me when you seek me with all your heart."
—Jeremiah 29:13 (NIV)

Scripture may seem like an obvious place to see God; more often than not, though, we read our Bibles for our own benefit instead of seeking to know God better. Many times I have gone to Scripture looking for a passage that will help comfort or encourage me—or a friend in need. Similarly, several times I have gone to Scripture looking for answers to defend why I, as a Christian, choose to live my life in the manner in which I do.

What do you go to the Bible looking for? Do you seek principles that may, in some way, help you make your life more successful? Or is it knowledge of the Scriptures you seek, so that at the right moment you will possibly know the right Bible verse to aid either yourself or someone around you? Or do you go to Scripture because of guilt, or because you feel that's what you *should* do?

Some of our reasons for going to Scripture are commendable, such as desiring to uplift a friend. Unless we go to the Bible looking for the author of all we read, however, we miss out. The most rewarding thing in life—more rewarding than being successful, being a good friend, or having biblical knowledge—is knowing God personally. So look for God in his Scriptures. Seek to know the author behind all you read, for you will find him when you seek him with all your heart.

Prayer Focus: Do you read your Bible for your own benefit, or do you truly seek the One behind it all? Pray that when you read Scripture, your ultimate end will be to know God better.

February 27 ~ Seeing God Through Christian Friends

Though one may be overpowered, two can defend themselves. A cord of three strands is not quickly broken.
—Ecclesiastes 4:12 (NIV)

Are there certain people in your life who you know will always be your friends, even if you are miles apart? I had a friend like that in high school.

Though we were complete opposites, we were the best of friends, and we always talked about how we would keep in touch when we went to college.

My friend and I kept in touch a little bit the first semester of college, but when we got together during the Christmas break, things were not the same. Whatever had held us together in high school was lost, and we now had no common ground to build upon. Though this experience made me sad, it helped me understand even more the importance of having Christian friends.

As I look back over my life, the friendships I have sustained have been the ones among my Christian friends. It does not matter if the last time I talked to one of them was last week or last year; our bond is never broken. Christ is the "third cord" in friendships between two Christians; and as Ecclesiastes 4:12 promises, "A cord of three strands is not quickly broken" (NIV).

God has blessed us with Christian friends we will have for a lifetime, no matter how many miles are between us. Cultivate those friendships, for it is through those people that God can hold us accountable, comfort us, and richly bless our lives.

Prayer Focus: Thank God for the blessing of your Christian friends, and pray for each one specifically.

February 28 ~ Seeing God in Your Changed Life

And we, who with unveiled faces all reflect the Lord's glory, are being transformed into his likeness with ever-increasing glory, which comes from the Lord, who is the Spirit.

—2 Corinthians 3:18 (NIV)

Difficult people, creation, hard situations, random thoughts, encouraging words, children—all of these are ways God reveals himself to us, if only we have the eyes to see. Regardless of where or how we see God, one thing is certain: once we have seen him, we are never the same. Seeing God radically changes lives.

Take Saul, for example, who devoted his life to persecuting Christians. When he saw God on the road to Damascus, his life was drastically changed, and he later wrote, "I have been crucified with Christ and I no longer live, but Christ lives in me. The life I live in the body, I live by faith in the Son of God, who loved me and gave himself for me" (Galatians 2:20 NIV). Talk about a changed life!

Moses is another great example of someone whose life, and even physical appearance, was transformed after recognizing the presence of God. The Bible says that when he descended Mount Sinai after being in the presence of God, his face was "radiant" with the glory of the Lord (see Exodus 34:29-35).

Recognizing God is a blessing that God offers to all, yet only those who are watchful may receive it. Since seeing God, has your life, and maybe even your appearance, been altered? You should be different in some way, for once you have seen him, you can never be the same.

Prayer Focus: Thank God for all the ways he has revealed himself to you, and pray that you will continue to "see" him every day.

March

LIVING ABUNDANTLY

Christian Coon

March 1 ~ Choose to Live Abundantly

"I came that they may have life, and have it abundantly."
—*John 10:10b (NRSV)*

Movies have a tendency to immortalize certain phrases—from Humphrey Bogart saying, "Here's lookin' at you, kid," to Arnold Schwarzenegger uttering, "Hasta la vista, baby." There was another phrase from the 1989 movie *Dead Poets Society* that caught the attention of millions of people: *Carpe diem.* Seize the day.

Some people need only this simple saying to help them live life to the fullest. You can also walk into a bookstore, find your way to the self-help section, and immerse yourself in countless variations on the theme of living up to your potential. It can be an overwhelming process.

Does Christianity have anything to say about this subject? You may wonder, since some Christians seem to talk more about life after death than the life we're living. But God wants us to have abundant lives now, lives that reflect God's fingerprints on the world. How can we do that? Over the next month, I'll suggest a few things for you to think about and, I hope, put into practice.

Our lives are filled with hope and joy, sorrow and despair. Our days are filled with the mundane and the magnificent. When we choose to live life abundantly, we discover that there is hope in the midst of all this. Our lives then have purpose and meaning and, in addition, honor and please God.

Prayer Focus: Ask God to help you discover new ways to live your life abundantly over the next month. Find a notebook or journal and, during the next few weeks, jot down experiences that are life-giving or help you sense God's presence.

March 2 ~ Discover Your Passion

Take delight in the LORD, and he will give you the desires of your heart. Commit your way to the LORD; trust in him, and he will act.

—*Psalm 37:4-5 (NRSV)*

The summer after my sophomore year of college, I had two very different kinds of jobs. First, I actually did something that would look good on a new graduate's resume: I wrote for the local weekly newspaper. Second, I also did something that future employers probably wouldn't care about: I washed dishes for the college cafeteria. I think my dad was happier that I had the second job because he always told me that those kinds of jobs would give me the incentive to get my degree. He was right. After my first day of suffering from pruned fingers, I knew pretty quickly that I didn't want to wash dishes for the rest of my life.

Too often in our lives we decide to stick with something that we don't enjoy doing, perhaps because we think we don't have a choice. It may be studying within a certain major, working at a job, or serving on a committee. We may do something because of a sense of duty *(If I don't do it, no one else will)*, because of external expectations *(Everyone expects me to follow this career path)*, or because it's the safe thing to do *(I really want to join the Peace Corps, but I'd better get a job because everyone else is doing that)*. We listen to societal voices instead of God's voice, which tells us something very different.

You may know that God gives us love and forgiveness, but did you also know that God gives us passion? Each one of us has something in the root of our being that brings us excitement and joy. When we don't actively seek that passion or when we ignore it to follow the path that is expected of us, we cheat both ourselves and God.

Your passion may be writing. Your passion may be washing dishes. Your passion is God-given and can be used to do amazing things in God's name. If you haven't found it, look for it and follow it.

Prayer Focus: Take some time to be honest with yourself and make a list of what gives you energy and excitement. If you have trouble with this, ask those who know you well to talk about their observations of what interests or excites you. You might look for a resource that helps you discover what your passion is (many books on spiritual gifts include personal inventories that might prove helpful). Talk to others about how you can use your God-given passion to serve others and God.

March 3 ~ Spend Time Alone

In the morning, while it was still very dark, [Jesus] got up and went out to a deserted place, and there he prayed.
—*Mark 1:35 (NRSV)*

A few years ago, my brother, Corey, came to visit. I live in a suburb of Chicago, and one of the things we always do when he visits is go to Wrigley Field to watch the Cubs play. I didn't plan ahead for this particular visit, however, and I failed to get tickets. So Corey, my wife, and I took the "L" train to try to find some tickets.

It was a beautiful June day, and there were thousands of people milling about. Needless to say, we could only find two seats together. My wife offered to miss the game, but I could tell by the look on her face that she was disappointed. Even though she's not a huge baseball fan, she loves to be around people and to be where the action is.

When you think about living life abundantly, you might believe that it's important to have constant adventures, like going to a major-league baseball game. But an abundant life is deeper than that. It also requires time alone.

That can be a scary thing. When we're alone and recognize that it's only us and God, we realize that we can't hide. That quiet time, however, is vital. Jesus often took time to be alone, pray, think, and renew. When we're alone and have nothing or no one interrupting us, we can be our true selves, the selves that only God knows and loves. Alone time allows us to reflect on our spiritual journey and seek God's guidance. God is there to forgive, inspire, and renew. Alone time is not a luxury afforded to today's hectic lifestyles. It's a necessity for abundant life.

Prayer Focus: Get out your calendar today and block out a couple of hours some-time this month to be alone. Be sure to plan a place where you can spend this time without being interrupted. Don't make an agenda for this time; just sit in God's presence and do whatever you feel called to do. Prepare yourself for this time by praying about it in advance, beginning today.

March 4 ~ Be in Community

Peace be to the whole community, and love with faith, from God the Father and the Lord Jesus Christ. Grace be with all who have an undying love for our Lord Jesus Christ.

—*Ephesians 6:23-24 (NRSV)*

Anne Lamott wrote a wonderful chapter in her book *Traveling Mercies* about why she makes her son go to church. Here she discusses one of those reasons, the power of community:

> I want to give him what I found in the world, which is to say a path and a little light to see by. Most of the people I know who have what I want—which is to say, purpose, heart, balance, gratitude, joy—are people with a deep sense of spirituality. They are people in community, who pray, or practice their faith; they are . . . people banding together to work on themselves and for human rights. They follow a brighter light than the glimmer of their own candle; they are part of something beautiful.

This passage highlights what happens when we're in community. Just as it is important to spend time alone, so also is it vital to be with others. Too often people in our culture believe you can be a spiritual pioneer, exploring the vast religious territories and staking your claim to a belief that fits your needs. They don't recognize how important it is to spend time with others.

When we are intentional about being in community, we grow in ways we didn't think possible. We come across opinions different from our own. We learn how to love others who may get on our nerves. We are held accountable for our own actions (or in-actions). We also get a glimpse of God through the eyes of others.

70

March 5 ~ Serve Others, Serve God

But be doers of the word, and not merely hearers who deceive themselves.
—James 1:22 (NRSV)

The actor Andrew Shue cofounded an organization a few years ago called, simply, Do Something, which encourages youth to get involved with their community and make a difference. I have read many articles stating that the "do something" philosophy rings true for young adults these days. Instead of the slacker stereotype we've been given, we members of Generation X are apparently quite interested in helping others. I often want to pat myself on the back for being a member of this generation, but then I have to ask myself, *Am I really doing something?* Am I, as it states in the Letter of James, a doer of the word?

One of the biggest challenges of serving others is being faithful in that service. I know plenty of people who think pretty highly of themselves because of their annual good deed. Although doing something charitable is certainly better than doing nothing, I think we're called to something a little more challenging.

A powerful passage is found in Matthew 25:31-46. In it, Jesus gives us an outline of whom we are to serve: the hungry, the thirsty, the strangers, the naked, the sick, the prisoners. We are called not only to do something for them, but also to be faithful in service. That's a challenge for us today, who live in a disposable society that honors cutting our losses rather than being committed.

When we serve others, especially "the least of these," we serve God. And when we commit ourselves to it, we discover that those we serve also serve us.

Prayer Focus: *Do you faithfully participate in an activity that helps those in need? Ask God to help you find something you truly enjoy doing, and then commit yourself to doing it. Your local church or United Way may be a good place to start.*

March 6 ~ Talk About Your Faith

So Philip ran up to [the chariot] and heard [the Ethiopian eunuch] reading the prophet Isaiah. He asked, "Do you understand what you are reading?" He replied, "How can I, unless someone guides me?"

—Acts 8:30-31a (NRSV)

I made a fantastic culinary discovery a few years ago when I went to visit my friend Steve in Birmingham, Alabama. I grew up in Iowa, and as a Midwesterner, I had not experienced the delectable joys of Krispy Kreme doughnuts until Steve introduced me to them. I was immediately hooked. I insisted that we keep going back there during my stay, and when I went home, I had to take a dozen with me. I told everyone I knew about these special doughnuts that, at the time, you could get only in the South. I was an evangelist for Krispy Kreme doughnuts!

Have you ever read or listened to or watched (or eaten) something that was so unique and different that you just had to tell people about it? You want others to share in the experience. Why is it, then, that we are sometimes hesitant to tell others about our faith? One reason, perhaps, is we don't want any of the negative stereotypes that often are given to "vocal" Christians. Stereotypes are hard to shake. And when we tell someone else that we're Christians and (gasp!) try to live out our faith, we may be misunderstood or even dismissed.

That's why it's so important to tell others—particularly those close to you—about your faith. Make it your mission to shatter any stereotypes. You might think you won't know what to say; but when you have the opportunity, God will help you start that conversation. An interesting thing then happens. When we talk about our faith with others, our own faith is strengthened.

Prayer Focus: *Take a minute to think of one person in your life who might be receptive to hearing or talking about your faith. Pray for him or her, and then watch carefully for opportunities to include faith in your conversation. Don't be* *overbearing; make sure that the conversation is natural and is authentic to who you are.*

March 7 ~ Be Quiet

He said, "Go out and stand on the mountain before the LORD, for the LORD is about to pass by." Now there was a great wind, so strong that it was splitting mountains and breaking rocks in pieces before the LORD, but the LORD was not in the wind; and after the wind an earthquake, but the LORD was not in the earthquake; and after the earthquake a fire, but the LORD was not in the fire; and after the fire a sound of sheer silence.

—*1 Kings 19:11-12 (NRSV)*

As a pastor, I spend lots of time focusing on the spiritual health of others, and so I have to be very intentional about focusing on my own spiritual well-being. Once a month I try to go out to St. Procopius Abbey, a Benedictine monastery outside Chicago, for a twenty-four-hour retreat. One of the rules at the abbey is that breakfast is eaten in silence. I had never been more conscious of a fork hitting a plate than I was the first time I had eggs at the abbey. When a room is so quiet, even little noises can reverberate like claps of thunder. After making many trips to the abbey, I'm finally to the point where I am thankful for the silence. It took me a while to get used to it, and it took even longer to sense God's presence in it.

We live in a sensory-overloaded culture. Brighter colors and louder noises constantly vie for our attention through computers, televisions, appliances, and even churches. Our attention spans have shrunk, but the need for silence, I believe, has increased.

It is difficult to get used to silence. The first time I took my city-raised wife to a farm in Iowa, she kept commenting, "It's so quiet, it almost hurts my ears." And yet silence can be a powerful opportunity for God to intervene. Like Elijah in today's scripture passage, we may be waiting for God to make a big splash; but sometimes God comes to us in the silence if we are patient and learn to embrace the wonderful noise of quiet.

Prayer Focus: *Sometime in the next day or two, try to put yourself in an*

73

environment where there is no noise—no appliances humming, no cars driving by. Sit with the silence. Listen to what God might be telling you, and pay attention to any images that come to you.

March 8 ~ Make Noise

Praise him with trumpet sound; praise him with lute and harp! Praise him with tambourine and dance; praise him with strings and pipe! Praise him with clanging cymbals; praise him with loud clashing cymbals! Let everything that breathes praise the LORD! Praise the LORD!

—Psalm 150:3-6 (NRSV)

One of my fondest college memories is Homecoming Week. Some professors were kind and realized that studies took lower priority that week, but others still scheduled tests and papers. It didn't matter. Students in residence halls, fraternities, and sororities all neglected their schoolwork and banded together to paint streets, create floats, and, on the night before the Homecoming game, yell like hell. That was the name of the final event: Yell Like Hell. Groups would create cheers complete with choreography as a way to inspire school spirit. I always enjoyed that event the most because it gave me permission to scream, dance, cheer, and generally make a fool out of myself.

I'd probably get a few quizzical looks if I suggested a "Yell Like Hell" event in church, but I think the psalmist in today's scripture knows where I'm coming from. Ecclesiastes 3 tells us that there is a time to keep silence; but there is also a time to speak, a time to laugh, and a time to dance. We need to take time to rejoice in the Lord and proclaim our praise for all God does for us in our abundant lives. It's a freeing feeling.

I've heard people say God must be pretty vain to insist on being praised. That's the wrong way to look at it. I think God knows that when we praise, we remember what truly gives us life. Don't be satisfied with a quiet "Thank you" or a reserved "Amen." Let God have it.

Prayer Focus: *Take an instrument and play it loudly—even if you don't know how to play! Sing a song at the top of your lungs. Find something to praise in your life; smile, and let that smile build to a laugh. You may feel corny or silly,* *but that's okay. Here's a rhyme to get you started: When we take time for praise, we break out of our malaise.*

March 9 ~ Talk to God

"But whenever you pray, go into your room and shut the door and pray to your Father who is in secret; and your Father who sees in secret will reward you."
—*Matthew 6:6 (NRSV)*

Despite all the ways to keep in contact with people in today's society, it's still a common occurrence for me to fall out of touch with friends. When I do get the chance to catch up with someone, and I realize it's been months or even years since we last talked, I wonder how I could have let that happen since I really treasure my friends and family.

Perhaps you have that problem, too. Maybe it's been a little too long since you called your mom or e-mailed your college roommate. As regrettable as these things are, however, it's even more difficult to have an abundant life when we neglect to talk to God. A more churchy way to describe this conversation is prayer.

It's a problem for many of us. We get too busy and have more important things to do. If we're lucky, we'll mumble a few words before a meal or before we go to sleep. Perhaps you're intimidated by prayer. Too often we believe that unless we have flowery words, God would rather not hear from us. Nothing could be further from the truth. As a friend said to me once, there's really no such thing as a bad prayer.

God wants to hear from us. God wants to hear how our day went. God wants to hear about how happy or frustrated we are with our jobs, relationships, and lives. God wants to hear the words "I'm sorry," and "I love you." Yes, you might argue, God knows all these things already. God wants to hear it anyway because it builds our relationship, just as we build a relationship with a special friend when we regularly keep in touch. God is our creator and redeemer, but God also should be our most important intimate friend. When you have a close relationship like that, you can say anything at all and be understood and loved.

Prayer Focus: If you can't find the right thing to say in prayer, start simply. Spend just a few minutes today talking to God as if God were your closest friend.

March 10 ~ Go to Church

Day by day, as they spent much time together in the temple, they broke bread at home and ate their food with glad and generous hearts, praising God and having the goodwill of all the people. And day by day the Lord added to their number those who were being saved.

—*Acts 2:46-47 (NRSV)*

You knew this suggestion had to be coming, didn't you? I'd be breaking the clergy code of conduct if I didn't do a little advertising for my fellow pastors. I think, however, I can speak for at least a few nonclergy types who would agree with me that going to church is important for abundant life.

It's no secret that going to church has changed dramatically in the last ten to twenty years. People have a plethora of choices. Whether you like contemporary or traditional music, a structured or very informal service, a sanctuary filled with thousands or a dozen, you can find something that fits your desires. Whatever you're drawn to, though, it's important to be a faithful part of that congregation. Why is it important? Here's a simple analogy.

I used to be able to go about two hours before my laptop computer battery would go dead. These days I need a new battery, because now I get thirty minutes if I'm lucky. The computer always beeps at me to tell me that I'd better shut down or find an outlet if I don't want to lose everything. It's pretty unforgiving that way. Once I do plug it in, however, it's like I get new life. I don't have to worry as much about losing my work, and I don't have to constantly look at the little icon that shows me how much juice my battery has.

The same thing happens when we neglect going to church and worshiping God in a community of faith. We can go for a while without it, and our faith might be fine. Sooner or later, however, our spiritual battery goes dead, and we might lose some things in the process like faith, hope, and joy—things that are integral for abundant life.

Prayer Focus: Make a promise to yourself and to God that you'll go to church for at least four weeks in a row. Make sure it's a place where you feel both comforted and challenged. See if you notice a difference, especially if you haven't gone for a while.

March 11 ~ Spend Time with Someone Who's Different from You

A Samaritan woman came to draw water, and Jesus said to her, "Give me a drink." . . . The Samaritan woman said to him, "How is it that you, a Jew, ask a drink of me, a woman of Samaria?" (Jews do not share things in common with Samaritans.)

—John 4:7, 9 (NRSV)

When I look back on the decisions I've made in my life, one of the best was to take a job in the Chicago area. Though I'll always have a soft spot in my heart for my home state of Iowa, most of that state is not known for its racial diversity. I had a very secure upbringing, but because of my lack of exposure to different cultures, I also was somewhat sheltered. That made moving to a major metropolitan area both exhilarating and frightening.

Suddenly, simple daily routines were filled with experiences with people who were significantly different from me—people of different races, religions, cultures, and sexual orientations. I was overly conscious about who I was and made every effort not to say or do the wrong thing. Yet I had very simple and somewhat naïve questions that I wanted to ask. What was it like to be black? Jewish? Asian? After a while, I established relationships with various people and felt more comfortable asking them to tell me their stories. Not surprisingly, many of my preconceived notions were shattered.

It takes some effort to spend time with people who are different from you. It's more comfortable just to stick with sameness. But then Jesus gets in the way. We read story after story of him eating with people, talking to people, praying with people, and healing people who were culturally taboo. That's an example we cannot ignore—nor should we want to. Part of living an abundant life means exploring the abundance of lives in our world. We get a glimpse of the power of God's creation and love when we're intentional about that.

Prayer Focus: *Pay close attention to the first impressions you have when you encounter someone who is different from you. Is that impression accurate, or is it created by something else? Pray daily to have an open heart and mind as you relate to all people.*

77

March 12 ~ Allow Yourself to Mourn

"Blessed are those who mourn, for they will be comforted."
—Matthew 5:4 (NRSV)

When I was in grade school, there was a television special that every teacher seemed to show. It was called "Free to Be . . . You and Me," and its objective was to encourage children to have the freedom to be who they really want to be. One of the segments, I remember, had the tough football player Rosey Grier singing, "It's All Right to Cry."

Like me, you may not recall ever being forbidden to cry, but too many of us still think it's preferable to keep a stiff upper lip than to show others we're vulnerable—or even sad. Countless books and articles, of course, tell us differently. If one is suffering some sort of loss, it's important to be able to express that. There are friends, family members, counselors, therapists, and clergy who can help us mourn, but it's also important for us to express our sadness and hurt to God.

Many of the psalmists had no qualms about doing that. They weren't afraid to let God know how they felt. Here's an example from Psalm 42:

> I say to God, my rock,
>   "Why have you forgotten me?
> Why must I walk about mournfully
>   because the enemy oppresses me?"
> As with a deadly wound in my body,
>   my adversaries taunt me,
> while they say to me continually,
>   "Where is your God?"
> Why are you cast down, O my soul,
>   and why are you disquieted within me?
>   (vv. 9-11 NRSV)

I find biblical witnesses like this enormously helpful when I am frustrated, angry, or sad. They give me the words to mourn. I don't always feel immediately better; but more often than not, I sense God's comforting presence, which is always life-giving.

Prayer Focus: *Read through a few of the psalms of lament and write verses that speak to you in a journal, on a notepad, or on index cards so that you will* *have them when it is necessary to mourn. A few examples are Psalms 22, 42, 43, and 77.*

March 13 ~ Savor Meals

Levi gave a great banquet for [Jesus] in his house; and there was a large crowd of tax collectors and others sitting at the table with them.
—Luke 5:29 (NRSV)

I like to consider myself a good listener, but there are times when I kind of tune everything out—like when I'm watching one of my favorite sports teams on television. My wife teases me about this, but she has her own weakness: cooking shows. I must admit that I find them interesting at times, too.

Unfortunately, fast food and microwave meals seem to be the sign of the times. I think Jesus would have a hard time understanding this cultural trend because he understood that sharing a meal together can be a wonderful time of fellowship.

If you read the Gospels carefully, you'll see that Jesus and his followers loved a good meal. Jesus did some important teaching during meals, but I can also sense that the time of communion with others was just as important to him. Jesus ate with strangers and outcasts; and he also took time to eat with his closest friends, especially when it was time to share his most important meal—when he broke bread and shared wine.

Whether you eat most of your meals in a cafeteria, in your small efficiency apartment, or in your first home with your family, don't treat these times lightly. Recognize them as opportunities to share your lives with others and to give thanks to God.

Prayer Focus: *Make it a priority to sit down and have a meal with someone. It could be someone close to you or a new acquaintance you want to get to know. Ask God to help you slow down and enjoy the communion of mealtime.*

March 14 ~ Fast Occasionally

The devil said to him, "If you are the Son of God, command this stone to become a loaf of bread." Jesus answered him, "It is written, 'One does not live by bread alone.'"

—Luke 4:3-4 (NRSV)

Pong was a simple game, but I was fascinated by it. There on the television screen were two "rackets" that weren't more than two inches long. You could employ something called a joystick and make these rackets move up and down. A small, moving square (the "ball") was also a part of the game, and you moved your rackets in order to hit the ball back to the racket on the other side.

Pong was one of the first video games. Of course, in this age where video games make life seem unrealistic, Pong is a relic from the past. You may think that fasting is in the same category—a relic that nobody takes seriously anymore. Sure, Jesus might have talked about fasting, and others in the history of the church might have encouraged people to fast; but we're not expected to go without food today, are we?

On the contrary, fasting is a spiritual discipline that is often ignored or forgotten, yet it is a powerful exercise. Our society triumphs consumption. Fasting is a strong statement that says, at least for a short time, my devotion is to God and God only. When we consciously go without a meal or without food for a day or longer, numerous things happen. It makes us just a little more sensitive to those who are truly hungry. It gives us some valuable time to be alone with God. And it reminds us of our true dependence—on God and not on "bread alone."

Prayer Focus: *Prayerfully prepare for a time of fasting. During your fast, use the time you would have spent eating to pray or read Scripture. (Note: Be sure you are healthy before fasting. If you are, start slowly. Maybe skip one meal. See how it feels. Eventually, try fasting for twenty-four hours. Remember to prepare several days beforehand by drinking plenty of water and eating well-balanced, nutritious meals. Also, be aware that fasting can have different effects on people, including a loss of focus or energy.)*

March 15 ~ Value Money

"No one can serve two masters; for a slave will either hate the one and love the other, or be devoted to the one and despise the other. You cannot serve God and wealth."
—Matthew 6:24 (NRSV)

I went a little crazy with the first paycheck I received from my first post-college job. It really wasn't much, but I thought I was loaded. I now had the confidence to take out a loan to buy a new car, and I also bought a new television. Reality hit soon enough. Student loans started coming due. I started paying rent. I found out that car insurance wasn't cheap. I was going paycheck to paycheck, and the thought of actually saving money was out of the question. For the first time I was learning the true value of money.

It's interesting that Christians spend so much time debating issues that Jesus really didn't say anything about (for example, abortion, homosexuality). And yet we shy away from discussions about money, which Jesus talked about a lot. He knew the traps that wealth could set. He knew the temptations of material possessions. He knew that little else in this world can separate us from God as obsession with money and things can. One contemporary word for this problem is "affluenza."

If you want to really challenge yourself and your faith, take a look at your checkbook or bank statement. How do you spend your money? What does that say about your priorities in life? Nothing makes me squirm more than when I do this myself.

Money itself obviously is not evil. Jesus encouraged the disciples to accept payment for their work, and the apostle Paul was dependent on benefactors for his mission. You don't have to look very hard to see that money can do wonderful things in our world. But it doesn't take much for money and material possessions to become our gods. Nothing can kill abundant life more quickly than when that happens.

Prayer Focus: Do some honest reflecting on your spending habits and priorities. Are your financial goals in conflict with your spiritual journey?

March 16 ~ Recognize the Power of Family

Elijah passed by [Elisha] and threw his mantle over him. He left the oxen, ran after Elijah, and said, "Let me kiss my father and my mother, and then I will follow you."

—1 Kings 19:19b-20a (NRSV)

When a couple asks me to be the pastor at their wedding, I insist on premarital counseling. They usually eagerly agree; but instead of talking specifically about topics such as how to communicate effectively or manage finances, we spend a lot of time talking about their families.

I don't think you can overestimate the influence of your family. For some, this is not a surprise, and, in fact, they celebrate that influence. For others, they'd rather not think about the impact of family because of different levels of emotional, spiritual, or even physical abuse. Even though a man and a woman pledge to be together for better or for worse, it is your family that truly knows the better and worse parts of you. This connection will never change, and it's important to recognize that.

Learning more about your family many times can answer a lot of questions about yourself. Why do I act this way? Why is it so difficult for me to do or believe certain things? When you research your parents, their parents, and all the siblings, cousins, aunts, and uncles involved, it is an invaluable insight into your own emotional and spiritual self. When you begin to recognize these things, you begin to have a better sense of yourself, which allows you to live an abundant life.

Your family may have traditions or behaviors that you want to keep. There are probably some things you'd like to change. God gives us the freedom and strength to explore all these things while also recognizing that it is God who is our true Parent.

Prayer Focus: One at a time, get together with your parents and/or grandparents, and ask questions about their upbringing, the relationships they had with their parents, how they related to other relatives, and how they related to God. Ask God to allow these conversations to give you great insight into your own life.

March 17 ~ Looking for God in All the Wrong Places

While they were talking and discussing, Jesus himself came near and went with them, but their eyes were kept from recognizing him.
—Luke 24:15-16 (NRSV)

Our church is a "partner" with a church in Pilsen, Czech Republic. I had the chance to visit that church two years ago, and I also took the opportunity to spend a few days in Prague. I stayed with my wife's cousin, David, a transplanted American looking to cash in on new business opportunities in this beautiful city. One of his ventures is running a night club called the Roxy. He took me to the club around midnight, and it didn't take long for me to realize that I was a little out of place wearing my basic knit shirt/jeans ensemble. David took me up to the stage behind the dee-jay, where I found myself among dozens of other sweaty bodies dancing to the techno music. As I stood there, kind of swaying back and forth, trying to soak in this cultural experience, a guy next to me asked if I was "that minister guy." He was a friend of David's, and when I confirmed his sus-picion, he broke into a big smile. "You know something? I think if Jesus were here today, he'd be in a place like this," he said, as he motioned with his arm toward the crowded dance floor.

I must admit my first reaction was to ignore his comment because I was-n't sure I wanted to get into a theological discussion with him at that time and place. But I quickly realized that maybe he was right. I also had a feel-ing of thankfulness that God's presence could be known to me in the last place I'd be looking. That experience helped broaden my narrow per-spective of the types of places where I might see the face of Jesus.

Prayer Focus: Where might be an unlikely place that you will see Jesus today? Ask God to help you see it.

March 18 ~ Pay Attention to God's Presence

God called to him out of the bush, "Moses, Moses!" And he said, "Here I am." Then he said, "Come no closer! Remove the sandals from your feet, for the place on which you are standing is holy ground."
—Exodus 3:4b-5 (NRSV)

Newlyweds quickly find that they each bring a lot of stuff into their mar-riage, both literally and figuratively. Each person has his or her own tradi-tions, habits, and expectations; and each person brings along physical belongings, as well. My wife, the English major, brought a lot of books, for which I'm thankful. Quite a few literary classics line our bookshelves, and I've tried hard to expand my reading list. It's difficult, however, because for every Jane Austen book I try to read, there's a John Grisham novel waiting in the wings.

But then along came a segment from Elizabeth Barrett Browning's poem *Aurora Leigh*:

Earth's crammed with heaven,
And every common bush afire with God;
But only he who sees takes off his shoes,
The rest sit round it and pluck blackberries.

This poem speaks volumes about the difference between the secular and the holy—that which communicates God's presence—in our society.

There are a lot of wonders in our world that many people appreciate: the natural beauty of our environment, the first gleeful sound from a baby, the strongly felt fellowship of friends. Although countless people can and do appreciate these things, how many people, in a sense, take off their shoes, understanding that they are in the presence of God, and assume an attitude of worship, holy awareness, and thankfulness? We are surrounded by God each day of our lives. We are called to open our hearts and eyes to this presence, to be led by God's voice, and to take off our shoes.

Prayer Focus: How do you respond when you experience God's presence in your everyday life? Ask God to help you take steps to have a thankful and worship-filled heart.

March 19 ~ Ease Your Anxiety

"And can any of you by worrying add a single hour to your span of life?"
—Matthew 6:27 (NRSV)

I am not a handy man. As a pastor, however, I've learned that I need to know a few things about maintenance, much to my chagrin.

Our church building has a flooding problem in the lower level that we still haven't figured out. When a plumber comes to investigate, I try to have him explain the problem to me, but I'm usually lost after a couple of minutes. I do know that when it rains heavily, I dread going into the church the next day because I know I may have to start bailing out the church—literally. It's one of those small aggravations in my life, and it's those aggravations that do more damage to my soul than I care to admit.

After one particularly hard rain, I was sloshing through the water when I discovered that another man from the church had come to help. I was very appreciative, but my attitude was still pretty grim. He sloshed along with me and then he stopped, turned, gave me a huge smile, and said, "You know, this is kind of fun, isn't it?"

My first reaction was to scoff at his sunshiny outlook. But before I said anything, his smile disarmed me; and as I thought about the water surrounding my ankles, I realized that God had graced me with a smile in the face of anxiety.

How do we live life abundantly when we encounter those small annoyances that cause such large anxiety? An insensitive roommate, an unhelpful boss, a parent who doesn't understand. Traffic jams, looming loan payments, a paper that's due.

We know that in the grand scheme of the world, these things don't matter, but often that doesn't alleviate our stress. On the contrary, small annoyances can paralyze us, making our relationship with God seem insignificant. Those are the times that we must have the faith to know that God will bail us out somehow, even when we least expect it.

Prayer Focus: I find it helpful to memorize a prayer or piece of Scripture when I confront anxiety. It can be as simple as, "Lord, have mercy," or, "Be still, and know that I am God." Doing this may help you to realize the bigger picture.

March 20 ~ Allow God to Guide You

Now as he was going along and approaching Damascus, suddenly a light from heaven flashed around him. He fell to the ground and heard a voice saying to him, "Saul, Saul, why do you persecute me?" He asked, "Who are you, Lord?"
—Acts 9:3-5a (NRSV)

If only we had that light from heaven. That's not asking for much, is it? It would really do a lot in furthering our relationship with God. Instead of having to wearily search for divine needles in secular haystacks, God could make things much easier if there were an occasional light from heaven. Granted, we'd rather not hear what Saul heard, but perhaps we can relate to what Saul immediately said: "Who are you, Lord?"

Unfortunately, we probably don't recognize the heavenly light as often as we should. But when we do, it moves us to changed hearts and lives, particularly when we have difficult decisions to make.

I had been out of college for four years and was faced with the decision of going back to graduate school or taking a different job. To make matters a little more interesting, I had to make this decision a month before I was going to get married, so I had to think of somebody else's life as well. If ever I needed a light from heaven, it was then. It worked out that my potential employer was located on the campus where I wanted to go to school. After I went through the job interview, I was emotionally exhausted. I walked across the campus, thoroughly confused about what step I should take. But then I came to a realization. As I saw other students with their bags slung over their shoulders, I thought about papers and late-night trips to the library and tuition bills; and despite all that, the thought of going back to school seemed to lift my burden. My light shone. It really came out of nowhere—just a feeling that going to graduate school was what I should do. I said a quick prayer of thanks.

Ask God for help in making decisions, and then watch to see where the light of wisdom might shine forth.

Prayer Focus: If you have a decision to make in your life, whether it's big or small, it pays to weigh the pros and cons and get feedback from people; but don't forget to spend time alone with God, too. Take a walk, go to a quiet place, write in a journal, and listen for God's direction.

March 21 ~ Recognize the Impact of Popular Culture

Do not be conformed to this world, but be transformed by the renewing of your minds, so that you may discern what is the will of God—what is good and acceptable and perfect.

—Romans 12:2 (NRSV)

There is a great scene in a movie about Michael Jordan that showed in IMAX theaters. Jordan is waiting by the scorer's table, ready to come back into the game. A ball boy, who couldn't have been more than eight years old, sat beside him and kept looking at him. Then Jordan changed his kneeling position while he waited. Two seconds later, the boy changed his so that he would be just like his hero.

Popular culture many times has that effect on us. We may ignore what we really want to do or wear or buy or think because someone more powerful or glamorous is telling us to do or wear or buy or think something different. That's what advertisers count on, anyway.

Because we are constantly overwhelmed by a barrage of images from the media, it's sometimes amazing that we can think for ourselves at all. That's why it's important to recognize the impact that popular culture has on your belief system and on your faith. It's so tempting to go with the popular flow without asking important questions: What is this message really trying to convey? What will it say about me if I go along with it?

One of the toughest challenges is to listen only to God's voice amidst the cacophony of mixed media messages, which tell us that we should be what they want us to be, rather than what God wants us to be. Once we hear God's voice, however, we know it distinctly. It is a voice of love and life.

Prayer Focus: Try this experiment. Pick a popular product, one that advertises through many mediums. Try to summarize what message this product is trying to convey and whether this is something that encourages or inhibits what you think God is trying to convey to the world. Ask God for discernment as you filter the messages of popular culture.

March 22 ~ Honor Ecumenism

Then Peter began to speak to them: "I truly understand that God shows no partiality, but in every nation anyone who fears him and does what is right is acceptable to him."

—*Acts 10:34-35 (NRSV)*

Ecumenism is one of those fancy-shmancy theological words that means the desire for unity among all Christians. It's an honorable goal that, I believe, can make significant progress in our generation.

I have heard some church experts complain that no one is loyal to his or her denomination anymore. It used to be that once a person was a member of a particular denomination, he or she always was a member of that denomination. That's not the case these days. On the one hand, I am concerned that some people are so open to different faiths or religions that they view the religious world as one big salad bar. There is a danger in that because a person may end up creating a religion that worships the self instead of God. On the other hand, you could look at this "lack of loy-alty" as an opportunity for unity.

Whatever faith tradition you prefer, make sure you at least learn about others. I myself have come to appreciate the insights of my brothers and sisters in Christ from different denominations. I find that when I worship with them, we are all moved by the same Holy Spirit. I discover that they, too, want to learn more about my tradition as I do about theirs. I don't think God wants all the same kind of worship or belief in this world; but God does want us to have one purpose: to love God and to love others. When we commit to that, it makes a world of difference.

Prayer Focus: Try to find a place where you can worship occasionally with peo-ple from other faiths. Taizé services (simple services of song and prayer) are very popular in larger cities and are ecumenical by design. Ask God to give you a spirit of unity toward all your brothers and sisters in Christ.

March 23 ~ Don't Ignore the Poor

"For you always have the poor with you, and you can show kindness to them whenever you wish."

—*Mark 14:7a (NRSV)*

Too often people assume that the poor live only in big cities, and, there-fore, poverty is an urban problem. I hope it's not surprising to you that the poor are all around us. I grew up in a town of about five thousand people located forty miles from what could be called a city—though that's a stretch in itself. There were probably more than a few poor people in my home-town, but it seemed pretty middle-class. The only person I knew was poor was a man named Lester. I have no idea if Lester was homeless. I do know he wandered around town a lot and would always show up at a church if they were having a potluck that day. He wore shabby clothes, didn't really say any-thing, and shuffled from place to place. I think I got used to Lester; he was a part of the town's culture, like the courthouse or the high school. That's familiarity-bred callousness, however, and perhaps that's even more dan-gerous than when some people get angry or disgusted with the poor.

Jesus' statement that the poor will always be with us does not mean we have to be resigned to that fact. Perhaps he knew that society will never be generous enough to make sure no one is left behind. Perhaps he meant it as a challenge, as well, to those who have the means to do something for the poor. Regardless, the one thing we cannot do is become hardened to the millions of people who struggle to find a meal and a place to sleep. It's especially sinful that our society allows countless children to grow up in poverty.

It's tempting to think only of ourselves. But living an abundant life does not mean worrying only about yourself. Abundance is meant to be shared.

Prayer Focus: Volunteering at a homeless shelter or a soup kitchen is always a powerful way to serve the poor, but it's also important to learn more about how our societal systems may stack the deck against the poor. Hold your governmental officials accountable on these issues, and begin to pray daily for the poor in your community and beyond.

March 24 ~ Keep the Sabbath

And on the seventh day God finished the work that he had done, and he rested on the seventh day from all the work that he had done.
—*Genesis 2:2 (NRSV)*

It is an amazing thing to think that God would rest. For those who believe (or actually take pride) in working seven days, seventy to eighty hours a week, it may be hard to comprehend this. How could God rest when creation was only six days old? Weren't there kinks to work out? Meetings to attend? Work to take home? A day of rest goes against a world that believes in busy-ness.

Honoring the Sabbath day is Commandment #4, found between not making wrongful use of the name of the Lord and honoring your father and mother. It may seem a little outdated, sort of like the command not to covet your neighbor's ox or donkey. More than ever, however, this commandment needs to be remembered and honored. Keeping Sabbath does not mean following a lot of rules about what you can and can't do. That defeats the purpose of the Sabbath, which is to worship God and to rest, intentionally taking time away from work.

In her book *Practicing Our Faith*, Dorothy Bass makes three Sabbath suggestions: refrain from work, refrain from shopping, and, as best we can, refrain from activities that may cause anxiety, like paying bills or making

89

to-do lists. An abundant life is one in which rest is built in to its schedule. We must fight the urge to think that the world will stop if we don't put in extra work. After all, if the Creator of the world rested, why shouldn't we?

Prayer Focus: Sunday is the natural day for keeping Sabbath, but some people's work schedules make that impossible. If that's your situation, make sure you choose another day to be your Sabbath and try to follow Dorothy Bass's suggestions about Sabbath activities. It's a wonderful day to enjoy God's creation or get in touch with loved ones. Pray for the resolve to keep the Sabbath.

March 25 ~ Care for Creation

Then God said, "Let us make humankind in our image, according to our likeness; and let them have dominion over the fish of the sea, and over the birds of the air, and over the cattle, and over all the wild animals of the earth, and over every creeping thing that creeps upon the earth."
—Genesis 1:26 (NRSV)

There are many people where I live who have great intentions when it comes to recycling. Every Monday night, they put out their green bins for the recycling company to empty the next morning. This process has a flaw, however. The bins don't have any kind of cover; so if it's windy, some of the refuse to be recycled becomes trash in the streets. This scenario sums up our society's attempt at taking care of creation. We sometimes make an effort, but we are far from perfect.

Today's Bible verse sometimes is misused. Actually, it's the word dominion that may be misused. Some interpret having dominion as our divine right to treat creation as a trash can. But having dominion should not be understood in this way. Biblical scholar Terence E. Fretheim explains in *The New Interpreter's Bible,* vol. 1: "A study of the verb *have dominion . . .* reveals that it must be understood in terms of care-giving, even nurturing, not exploitation. As the image of God, human beings should relate to the nonhuman as God relates to them. . . . This process offers to the human being the task of intra-creational development, of bringing the world along to its fullest creational potential."

Its fullest creational potential. What a wonderful phrase, because that is what God desires for us. That's what it means to have abundant life—to

90

fulfill this potential. If God wants this for us, how can we not work to bring this about for the rest of God's creation?

Prayer Focus: The opportunities to care for creation are plentiful. Here are three suggestions to get involved: Call Environmental Justice Resources through the National Council of Churches at 1-800-762-0968; read the book 101 Ways to Help Save the Earth *(published by the Eco-Justice Working Group); check out the websites and www.simpleliving.org. Prayerfully consider the ways you might care for creation.*

March 26 ~ Read the Bible

All Scripture is inspired by God and is useful for teaching, for reproof, for correction, and for training in righteousness.
—2 Timothy 3:16 (NRSV)

I'll never forget the first quiz I ever took in college. It was one of the most intimidating moments of my life. This was, after all, *college*, and I think part of me was expecting the quiz to be in Latin. The class was your basic History of Western Civilization requirement. My palms were clammy as the professor read off the first question. I was shocked, however, because I actually knew the answer. Next question, same thing. I quickly realized that I'd be able to handle the study load of college.

If you've never experienced something like college before and only have images of what it must be like, it can be intimidating to take those first steps. Some people see the Bible the same way, especially if they have little experience reading it. They may see it as a book of foreboding rules, hard-to-pronounce words, and outdated commandments. Others who do have experience reading the Bible might take it for granted. It's great for church or when you're in a bind and need an answer, but not for regular reading. Either approach is understandable, but it robs the individual of a richness that he or she can't comprehend.

God speaks to us in so many ways, but perhaps the most important way is through the Bible. If we truly want the abundant life that God can give us, it helps to keep open an important line of communication: God's Word.

Prayer Focus: Take a few minutes every day to read through a verse or two and meditate on it (as you're doing with this devotional). Imagine these are God's words to you and you only. In addition, try to make a commitment to taking a Bible study or other class about the Bible. It's a sturdy book and can handle your questions, doubts, and wonderings. More important, see the Bible as a treasure chest filled with the riches of life that God wants to offer to you.

March 27 ~ Be a Creator

All the skillful women spun with their hands, and brought what they had spun in blue and purple and crimson yarns and fine linen; all the women whose hearts moved them to use their skill spun the goats' hair.

Exodus 35:25-26 (NRSV)

Steven Soderbergh won the Best Director Oscar in 2001 for the movie *Traffic*. Instead of thanking individuals, as most do, he thanked other people: "I want to thank anyone who spends part of their day creating. I don't care if it's a book, a film, a painting, a dance, a piece of theater, a piece of music—anybody who spends part of their day sharing their experience with us. I think this world would be unlivable without art, and I thank you."

Just as we worship a creating God, I believe God wants us to create as well. You may disagree, thinking, "I don't have a creative bone in my body. I can't write or paint or draw. I certainly can't sing. How am I supposed to create anything if I don't have these talents?"

The key, I believe, is not in the finished product but in the ongoing process. Certainly some people have more obviously creative gifts than others. But if we refuse to allow ourselves to create anything because we are worried that the creation is inferior, we cheat God. Engaging in a creative process allows a totally different part of our personality to come alive, especially when we know that the only audience that counts—God—will burst into applause at the effort. At the same time, we allow ourselves a freedom of expression that seeps into other parts of our lives and affects how we relate to God and our neighbor.

Our creative process is an offering to God, just as it was for the creative women in today's verse from Exodus. So go ahead. Sing, even if you can't carry a tune. Paint, even if it looks like globs of color splattered on paper or canvas. Write, even if every word is misspelled. The important thing is to create, just as God has created and continues to create in our world and in our lives every day.

Prayer Focus: *If you have a hard time seeing yourself as a creator, start simply. Get some paper and a pen, some paints and a tablet, some fabric and a needle, some clay and water, some wood and a knife, some gardening tools and seeds, or anything else that strikes your fancy. Allow yourself to be creative with whatever tools you choose. Use them to express how you feel about God.*

March 28 ~ Love Your Enemies

"But I say to you that listen, Love your enemies, do good to those who hate you, bless those who curse you, pray for those who abuse you."
—Luke 6:27-28 (NRSV)

Love your enemies. These three words make up one of Jesus' most famous sayings—one that may have become too familiar. Think about the phrase for a minute and let its power sink it. This may be the biggest challenge in my own spiritual journey.

I can think of plenty of people in my life I'd rather not love. Difficult people. Annoying people. Stubborn people. Rude people. I admit that I certainly don't have these three words running through my mind all the time. When I confront insensitive people, my first thought usually isn't, *Love them, Chris, love them!* Instead, it's usually something like, *What jerks! Who do they think they are?*

But Jesus' words refuse to go away. "Love your enemies." I realized something not long ago that has made this commandment a little easier. As I looked at these three little words, I noticed that I had been reading them incorrectly. For some reason, I believed that to love those who are difficult to love meant that I needed to change them, as well. I would try to love them, but if they continued their difficult behavior, I'd get frustrated and angry, which would make the loving part even tougher. Changing the personality or behavior of someone who curses or abuses me is not my responsibility. Only God can do that, if the other person is willing to allow it. My only command is to love, which, though never easy, is what Jesus asks me to do. When I think about how I, too, am unlovable at times, I'm thankful that Jesus still loves me.

Prayer Focus: *Be very intentional about praying for someone in your life who just drives you crazy. Be patient and realize that this person may not change, but you will; and that's vitally important.*

93

March 29 ~ Befriend Death

For I am convinced that neither death, nor life, nor angels, nor rulers, nor things present, nor things to come, nor powers, nor height, nor depth, nor anything else in all creation, will be able to separate us from the love of God in Christ Jesus our Lord.

—*Romans 8:38-39 (NRSV)*

It may seem odd to include a devotion about death amidst other devotions about abundant life. It may seem even odder considering that this is a devotional for young adults, who probably don't think about death a whole lot. But if you're going to talk about life, sooner or later, you talk about death. And befriending death can help us lead a more abundant life.

You may have heard of the popular book *Tuesdays with Morrie* (New York: Doubleday, 1997), which chronicles the last weeks of a relationship between the author, Mitch Albom, and his college professor, Morrie Schwartz, who was suffering from ALS. Albom flew out to Schwartz's home for fourteen Tuesdays, and every week they talked about a different subject. One week they talked about death. Here are a few of Morrie's reflections on this subject:

> Everyone knows they're going to die, but nobody believes it. If we did, we would do things differently. . . . There's a better approach. To know you're going to die, and to be *prepared* for it at any time. That's better. That way you can actually be *more* involved in your life while you're living. . . . Do what the Buddhists do. Every day, have a little bird on your shoulder that asks, "Is today the day? Am I ready? Am I doing all I need to do? Am I being the person I want to be?"

Have you ever thought about your own death? Understandably, it can be a depressing subject. But once we are able to have the faith to trust in God and know that nothing separates us from God's love, not even death, we have an unbelievable freedom to cherish life's abundance.

Prayer Focus: *Do some reflecting on what your funeral might be like. Who would be there? What would they say about you? How can you live your life so that those in attendance would be moved by your example?*

March 30 ~ Repent

Now after John was arrested, Jesus came to Galilee, proclaiming the good news of God, and saying, "The time is fulfilled, and the kingdom of God has come near; repent, and believe in the good news."

—Mark 1:14-15 (NRSV)

New Orleans is one of my favorite cities, but I never know quite what to make of Bourbon Street, a location dedicated to helping tourists spend their money at bars, souvenir shops, and strip clubs. It's a place that teeters on the edge of sleaze and spectacle. The first time I was there was on a Friday night during a convention. Bourbon Street was, not surprisingly, crowded with people. In the midst of the crowd was a solitary man, walking slowly and carrying a sign that read, "Repent, for the kingdom of heaven has come near."

Even though I now have a deeper understanding of what repentance means, it is still an intimidating word; and the first image that comes to mind when I think of repentance is this man or others like him who berate people into giving up their evil ways and claiming Jesus Christ as their savior. Repentance is more than that.

The New Testament understanding of repentance comes from the Greek word *metanoein*, which means to change one's mind and life. For the early Christians, it meant the beginning steps of changing in order to follow the Christian faith. You may think repentance means only confessing all the things you've done wrong. That's a part of it. But it also means turning your life and mind to Christ so that your desire is to live as Christ would want you to. This process is explained well in the book *Beyond the Walls*, by Paul Wilkes. Wilkes writes about a conversation he had with a Trappist monk, who talked about what we should do in prayer before God. The monk said, "Be completely honest and forthcoming with [God]; that is enough. We know when we fail. The best thing is to be honest about it, right away, then pick yourself up and go on, with confidence and love, a bit more humble than before" (New York: Doubleday, 1999, p. 10).

Prayer Focus: *Repentance is an ongoing process, a continual turning away from behaviors and attitudes that lead to spiritual death and a turning toward God, who offers us spiritual life. Make a promise to God today that you will begin committing to repentance.*

March 31 ~ Choose Life

I call heaven and earth to witness against you today that I have set before you life and death, blessings and curses. Choose life so that you and your descendants may live, loving the LORD your God, obeying him, and holding fast to him; for that means life to you.

—*Deuteronomy 30:19-20*a *(NRSV)*

We are faced with choices every day of our lives. Some are inconsequential *(Do I wear the green or blue sweater?)* and some are more significant *(Should I quit my job? Where should I go to school?)*. God also gives us a choice every day: Should we choose to live our lives in Christ? It's a choice that we probably aren't conscious of, and yet all our other choices affect that decision. Should we live our lives in Christ?

Today's Bible verse is in the midst of a covenant or promise that God makes with the Israelites. It's a simple proposition. God says, if you follow my guidelines and love me and your neighbor, you will live a life of abundance. It seems simple, doesn't it? How could anyone not say yes to that arrangement? And yet we, like the Israelites, may say yes with our lips, but our hearts eventually stray to other things that we think will give us bigger, better, happier lives.

Choosing life in Christ is actually not a simple choice. It requires us to look at our behaviors and attitudes, and sometimes it challenges us to change them. That's uncomfortable. Choosing life in Christ means living an alternative lifestyle, one that many times goes against the societal grain. It means doing really radical things like loving your enemies, caring for the poor, forgiving others, taking a break from the rat race, and spending time with God. Choosing life in Christ is not a simple choice, but it's a joyous one. If we do indeed choose life, the abundance we receive will change us forever.

Prayer Focus: During the past few weeks, you have been given some suggestions on how to live an abundant life. You can probably think of a few ideas yourself. Take some time to prayerfully consider other ways that you can choose life. You might even make a list.

April

DECISIONS, DECISIONS, DECISIONS

Harriet P. Willimon and William H. Willimon

April 1 ~ A Decision to Follow Jesus

As Jesus passed along the Sea of Galilee, he saw Simon and his brother Andrew casting a net into the sea—for they were fishermen. And Jesus said to them, "Follow me and I will make you fish for people." And immediately they left their nets and followed him.

—Mark 1:16-18 (NRSV)

All the Gospels begin with Jesus calling disciples. With a simple "Follow me," he beckons ordinary people to change direction in their lives, to come forward, to walk down a road with him. Whatever work Jesus is sent to do, he needs us to help him do it. Jesus does not work alone. He calls disciples—invites ordinary people (like us!) to follow him.

Jesus is presented by the Gospels as a decision to be made, a path to be taken. Thus, a relationship with Jesus begins with a choice. Some people choose by saying, "No, I don't want to be part of anything related to Jesus." Others walk another path simply by choosing not to choose—by just allowing their lives to drift along without any particular sense of direction.

Jesus' narrow way of discipleship requires a verdict, a decision for or against him. Yet to those, like you, who dare to come forward, say "yes" to his invitation, and do your best to follow after him, he promises life abundant.

In reading this meditation, in studying scripture, in focusing your life on this path, you are busy following Jesus. You are being a contemporary disciple. You are saying "yes." You are allowing Jesus to have his way with your life—to take you someplace you would not have gone if you had been left to your own devices.

Godspeed for the journey.

Prayer Focus: Pray for the courage, the insight, and the wisdom so that, when Jesus invites you to walk his way, you will be able to say "yes."

April 2 ~ Be Prepared

Be strong in the Lord and in the strength of his power. Put on the whole armor of God, so that you may be able to stand.
—Ephesians 6:10-11 (NRSV)

Maybe there was a time, a time before you got where you are today, when being a Christian was the normal, natural, expected thing to do. Home, school, and job all conspired with the church to make being Christian seem like the most natural way in the world.

But no more. In countless ways—at school, in the dorm, at work, and in social settings—your generation has been impressed that to be a Christian is to find oneself swimming against the stream, marching to the beat of a different drum. You may have friends who do not understand why you go to church. You work with people every day who can't imagine what would drive you to read a book like this one!

The apostle Paul ends his Letter to the Ephesians with a strong admonition to a struggling band of early Christians to "put on the whole armor of God" (Ephesians 6:11 NRSV). Paul uses military metaphors in order to indicate that Christians in his day were in a kind of war. "Do not go out there unarmed!" he seems to say. Poorly equipped, weak Christians are no match for the attacks of the world, Paul says.

Perhaps that is one reason you are reading these meditations. You have the good sense to know that being a Christian today requires study, reflec-

98

tion, self-knowledge, prayer, Bible knowledge, and a whole host of other defensive armaments that enable Christians to resist, to survive as disciples, even to triumph.

I know someone who is training for a decathlon. He knows that he will have some stiff competition from many good athletes. One of his greatest challenges will be himself—his own fatigue, pain, and commitment. So he trains every afternoon after work. And on weekends, he is biking, jogging, pumping iron, and all the rest. With enough work like this, he will be prepared.

In a way, his story is a parable of what it's like to be a Christian today.

Prayer Focus: Examine your own preparation for the demands of Christian discipleship. In what ways do you need Christ's help in being better fit for those demands?

April 3 ~ Forgiveness: The Basis of Bold Living

"I tell you, her sins, which were many, have been forgiven; hence she has shown great love. . . ." Then he said to her, "Your sins are forgiven."
—Luke 7:47-48 (NRSV)

A friend of mine who counsels students tells me that the primary cause for depression and anxiety among them is "conflict between two possible alternatives."

"It almost never fails," he says. "When students walk in my office for counseling, complaining that they are depressed or having difficulty coping, I am tempted immediately to ask, 'What decision must you make?' Invariably, they answer that they want to break up with their boyfriend/girlfriend, but he/she is a really nice guy/girl and they don't want to hurt him/her—something like that."

Tough decisions can make you sick! Choosing between two conflicting alternatives is particularly tough when one alternative is not clearly better than the other, and when there is some pain connected with one of the choices. We become paralyzed, unable to move forward or backward. Fearing that we will make the wrong choice, or that the choice we make will be unbearably painful, we become depressed, stuck at a fork in life's road.

Protestant reformer Martin Luther once advised Christians of his day to "sin boldly." What he meant was that we Christians, being called and forgiven by Christ, are free to act courageously, freely, and boldly without overly concerning ourselves with acting in the absolutely right way. We make our decisions as best we can; then we put our lives in the hand of God. We do not have to make the world turn out right. That is God's business. Our business is to live, to act, to serve as best we can, to ask forgiveness, and to accept that forgiveness when it is given.

Prayer Focus: Pray that Christ will give you the grace to feel that you do not always have to make the right decision.

April 4 ~ Choosing the Right Burden

"Take my yoke upon you, and learn from me; for I am gentle and humble in heart, and you will find rest for your souls. For my yoke is easy, and my burden is light."

—Matthew 11:29-30 (NRSV)

The statistics are in. Americans are working longer hours than ever. Particularly when starting a first job, a person can work the longest hours of anyone in the office. After all, he or she must prove to be a good, hard-working employee. Americans also have less vacation time than workers in the rest of the industrialized world. So when Jesus promises his disciples "rest," our ears perk up. We all need rest from the grind of daily labors.

But note that Jesus has something rather peculiar to say about his promised "rest." "Take my yoke upon you," he says. "My burden is light." A yoke is what they put around the necks of farm animals so that they can work together. And a burden, even if light, is still a burden.

Jesus offers his tired disciples not a vacation, a respite from all labors, but rather another burden, a different kind of yoke. Perhaps in life the question is not, *Will I be burdened?* Rather, the question is, *Will the burdens I bear be worth it?*

Consider our burdens. Many of us are burdened by work. We neglect our health and forsake our friends all in the service of money. Cars, big mortgages, the latest computers—we busily burden ourselves with all the stuff, working night and day for the next new gadget that will make our lives more exciting. These are the heavy burdens that we call "freedom," "a better lifestyle," or "a great opportunity."

Jesus does not promise us a life free from all burdens. Rather, he promises us a burden worth bearing, a yoke worth wearing. Jesus lifts one burden off our backs so that he can give us another—abundant life, discipleship, obedience to the call of God.

Prayer Focus: Think over your life at this moment. What are your chief burdens? Ask Jesus to give you what you need to willingly assume his burdens of discipleship so that you might truly "find rest for your soul."

April 5 ~ Decisions for Christ

Jesus departed with his disciples to the sea, and a great multitude from Galilee followed him; hearing all that he was doing, they came to him in great numbers.
—Mark 3:7-8 (NRSV)

Sometimes you hear people speak of the Christian faith as if becoming a Christian were a one-time thing.

"Since I accepted Jesus as my Savior . . . ," they say. "Now that I have decided to follow Jesus . . . ," they declare.

True, there must be a decision to walk the way of discipleship. At some point in our lives, there must be that decisive moment when we say "yes."

But that's not the end of it. The first steps of faith are far from the last. It is fine that, at some dramatic or soul-stirring moment, we are able to declare, "I have decided to be a disciple of Jesus." But that is the beginning of the journey, not the end. There will be more steps along the way, more decisions, more growth—the deepening of a relationship once begun. In fact, some of the most difficult days of discipleship are after that initial enthusiasm—when we must keep at discipleship, even when it doesn't feel fun to be faithful.

The Gospels present the life of Jesus as a journey. Jesus is always on the move—always moving from here to there. With a simple, "Follow me," Jesus invites us to walk that journey with him. We haven't arrived yet; still, we're on the way. None of us ever gets so smart, so sure in our walk with Jesus, that there is no need to grow. Along the way there are many decisions, many choices to be made; and in the walking with him is the growth—and the way, the truth, and the life.

April 6 ~ First God's Forgiveness, Then Our Courage

"And forgive us our debts, as we also have forgiven our debtors."
                                        —Matthew 6:12 (NRSV)

She had about the saddest case of indecision I've ever seen. For the life of her, she just couldn't make a decision. All sorts of daily dilemmas became excruciatingly difficult for her; they were magnified all out of proportion, making her miserable. She would weigh all possibilities, attempt to make a move, come to a conclusion, and decide. Then she would sink back into a quandary. She procrastinated, so fearful was she to move toward a decision.

Her life became so difficult with all these unresolved dilemmas that she sought out a therapist for help. After meeting with him a few sessions, she discovered the source of her indecision.

"My therapist says I don't believe in myself enough to take charge of my life. I think she is right. I just can't bear to make a mistake. I guess my parents set me up for that. They were so critical of me when I was growing up. School was hard for me. It shook my confidence. If I can't learn to forgive myself when I mess up, I'll never move forward."

Hers was a great insight. Forgiveness is somehow inextricably linked to the ability to move, to decide, to go forward. Don't attempt anything in life that's large, risky, or important unless you can forgive yourself. Perhaps that's one reason we often say the Lord's Prayer when we gather for worship. Jesus taught his disciples to pray this prayer by heart. Whenever we pray this prayer, we are reminded of the gracious willingness of God to forgive.

Courageous decisions rest upon the rock of forgiveness.

Prayer Focus: Pray the Lord's Prayer. Then pray that Jesus will help you to forgive those who make wrong decisions—particularly yourself.

April 7 ~ Grow Up

Then I said, "Ah, Lord GOD! Truly I do not know how to speak, for I am only a boy." But the LORD *said to me, "Do not say, 'I am only a boy'; for you shall go to all to whom I send you, and you shall speak whatever I command you."*

—Jeremiah 1:6-7 (NRSV)

How many times have you been told, through the years, "You need to grow up"?

Then there's the line, "You are just being immature." Now you are a young adult. You are no longer a youth. It's been years since you were a teenager. Yet you still sometimes get the feeling that, when people are dealing with you, the emphasis is always on the *young* in "young adult." And sometimes, you feel that way about yourself. In your first job, first apartment, first serious relationship, there are so many decisions to make, so many mistakes to be made, and so many lessons to be learned.

It's funny, isn't it? All those years you wanted to make your own decisions, to go your own way, to be free and independent. Now sometimes you wonder if it would be good to go back again.

Young adult Jeremiah felt a call of God upon his life. He heard God calling him to be a prophet, to tell the truth to Israel. His response? I am too young. I don't know how to make a speech. I'm inexperienced.

God's response? God told Jeremiah that he would be with him. God had confidence in the young Jeremiah. "You shall speak whatever I command you." In other words, the Lord told Jeremiah to go ahead and grow up.

As you go forward into adulthood, God goes with you. God gives gifts, support, and encouragement to those whom God calls. As you stride into tomorrow, know this: You journey not alone. God goes with you, and God promises to give you what you need in order to grow up as God wills.

Prayer Focus: *Focus upon one area of your life in which you currently feel inadequate, inexperienced, or immature. Ask God's guidance and presence to help you grow to meet this challenge.*

April 8 ~ Being Alone

I did not sit in the company of merrymakers, nor did I rejoice; under the weight of your hand I sat alone.

—Jeremiah 15:17 (NRSV)

Loneliness is a painful thing. Sitting alone in your apartment on a Saturday night when everyone else seems to be at a party—that's painful. We are social creatures who crave fellowship, togetherness, and community. Loneliness is the pain of separation, and who among us desires that sort of pain?

And yet the prophet Jeremiah speaks of the loneliness that occurs not because someone has forgotten to invite us to the party, or because our friends have forsaken us; rather, he speaks of the loneliness that comes because of "the weight of [God's] hand."

Sometimes faithfulness to the way of Christ can make us feel very much alone. Sometimes, out of obedience to Jesus, we are required to march to the beat of a different drum than that of the crowd—to swim against the stream.

In such moments, we can feel very alone. Yet to be unable to stand against the crowd and speak out, despite the will of the crowd, is to be unfaithful. Sure, as Christians, we love others, crave community, and value friends; but sometimes we must decide to go against the desires of others out of our desire to be a faithful disciple of Christ.

Do you have the strength to brave the will of the crowd, to do the right thing, even though everyone else seems to be going in a different direction?

This is loneliness that is close to godliness—loneliness as a necessary aspect of faithfulness.

Prayer Focus: *Pray for the strength to know when to go against the will of the crowd—when to be willing to be alone in order to be faithful to your convictions.*

April 9 ~ Not to Decide Is to Decide

"I know your works; you are neither cold nor hot. I wish that you were either cold or hot."

—*Revelation 3:15 (NRSV)*

In 1943, the French philosopher Jean-Paul Sartre wrote *Being and Nothingness*. In the book, Sartre asserts that the thing that makes us truly human is *our ability to choose*. In every circumstance in life, we have the freedom to decide. Even when we don't realize that we are choosing, we are, says Sartre.

At one point in the book, Sartre is having a conversation in a French café. Across the café sits a couple, talking and drinking coffee. The young man reaches across the table and puts his hand on the hand of the woman. She does not pull her hand away. She glances briefly at his hand touching hers, and she continues to talk.

Sartre says that in that moment she has made a decision. She does not think about it; she does not agonize over it. But she is entering a relationship with this man through her actions—or lack of actions. Even not to choose is, therefore, to choose. Through our choices we are becoming certain sorts of people. We are shutting doors and opening others.

Much of our lives, says Sartre, is an attempt to evade responsibility for our lives. We make excuses for ourselves, saying, "This is the only thing I could do in this situation." But that is usually self-deceit. What we are saying is, I chose this alternative because it was the easiest, or would cause less pain, or required less risk. Still, a choice was made.

In the Revelation, the last book of the Bible, the voice of God says to the church in Laodicea, "I wish that you were either cold or hot." God wants us to stand somewhere, to burn bright, or to run cold. Sometimes, even when we think we are avoiding a decision, just drifting along, we are deciding. Sometimes, not to decide is to decide.

Prayer Focus: *Ask God for the wisdom to see the decisions that you are avoiding and the strength to face them.*

April 10 ~ Here I Am, Send Me

Then I heard the voice of the Lord saying, "Whom shall I send, and who will go for us?" And I said, "Here am I; send me!"

—Isaiah 6:8 (NRSV)

We don't know much about King Uzziah. Yet it is interesting that the prophet Isaiah signifies the date of his call from God as "the year that King Uzziah died" (Isaiah 6:1 NRSV).

When a ruler died in ancient times, there was inevitable crisis, insecurity, and instability in the country. Here was a young adult, Isaiah, entering the temple for prayer during a time when the world seemed to be falling apart, shifting on its axis. Things were out of control. Or, as Isaiah put it, it was "the year that King Uzziah died."

And there, amid a difficult, tumultuous time in his life, Isaiah got a vision of God. He heard a voice: "Whom shall I send?"

"Here am I; send me," he said.

So we must be attentive, particularly during life's inevitable times of instability and crisis. Perhaps we are particularly open to a vision during times in our lives when we are in crisis and, therefore, are vulnerable. In such times, an old world may be ending for us—a new world beginning to be born. That day in the temple, in "the year that King Uzziah died," Isaiah saw heaven open, heard his named called, and said, "Here am I; send me."

In one of his short stories, John Updike speaks of a man who was like a lobster between shedding his old shell—still soft, vulnerable, exposed—and waiting for a new shell to be formed. It was a time when he could either be the victim of something terrible or receive some new existence.

It's in those in-between times for us that an old world may be dying and a new one awaiting birth.

Prayer Focus: *Pray for the insight to hear the call of God upon your life. Then pray for the courage to say, "Here am I; send me."*

April 11 ~ Keeping at It

"So I say to you, Ask, and it will be given you; search, and you will find; knock, and the door will be opened for you."

—*Luke 11:9 (NRSV)*

An acquaintance of mine gives this as the reason that he does not go to church: "I just don't feel like it," he says. "I think it would be hypocritical of me to be there when I can't understand what all the fuss is about."

He has the idea that religion is mostly right emotions. You either feel it or you don't. Yet some things in life—often the most important things—are best not left to mere feelings. Your relationship with God, like any important relationship, requires time, patience, effort, and persistence.

At least that is what Jesus implied in the parable of the friend at mid-

106

night. At midnight, a man realizes that he has no bread. He knocks on the door and asks for a loaf. The neighbor tells him, in effect, "Drop dead."

But the man is persistent. He keeps knocking until his neighbor finally gets out of bed, opens the door, and gives him the bread. This is the way we ought to pray, said Jesus. This is the way we ought to yearn for God.

You have found, no doubt, that friendship takes time, patience, and persistence. You need time to be together—time just to hang out with one another. Friends who are not often together, who do not keep finding time for their friendship to grow, don't stay friends long. You have to make time. You have to keep at it.

Some folks say they no longer feel close to God—no longer hear the voice of God in their lives. Perhaps the problem is that *they* are absent from God.

So it is important to decide to keep at it—to keep going to church, keep reading your Bible, keep praying, keep reading these meditations! Knock, and the door will be opened; search, and you will find.

Prayer Focus: *Think about the practices, habits, and rituals that keep you close to God. Then pray for God's help in keeping at it!*

April 12 ~ Cocreators

Then God said, "Let us make humankind in our image, according to our likeness; and let them have dominion."
—Genesis 1:26 (NRSV)

"Let there be light," and there was. God is the Creator who makes something out of nothing—a world out of formless void. Creatures are created to fill the world, including the creatures called humans.

But then, in a stunning act of divine graciousness, God gives two of the creatures, the woman and the man, a role to play in creation. They are to be "fruitful and multiply"; they are to be coworkers in God's good garden. Thus, creation is not only something that God does, but also something that we do. Out of God's great love for us, in an act of great confidence in us, God allows us to cocreate.

God's world is not yet finished, not yet complete. God allows us to consider, to decide, to fabricate, and to create. In our work, we are graciously allowed to join in some of God's creative activity. As we move in the world and make our choices and decisions, we mirror some of God's creativity.

Why, just yesterday, I heard someone say, "Even though he has hurt me and done wrong to me, I've decided to forgive him, to see if we can start over in our relationship, to begin again."

Thus a new world is created; something is added to creation that would not be here without a courageous act of creation. We get to obey God by being fruitful and creative. It is as if an ordinary, mortal human gets to participate in some of the fun that God had in creating the world—as if we got to say, "Let there be light," and into the darkness, there is light.

Prayer Focus: What do I need to do to contribute to God's creation? What creative responsibility has been entrusted to me?

April 13 ~ Life Is What Happens When You Are Making Plans

Build houses and live in them; plant gardens and eat what they produce. Take wives and have sons and daughters; take wives for your sons, and give your daughters in marriage, that they may bear sons and daughters. . . . Seek the welfare of the city where I have sent you into exile, and pray to the LORD on its behalf, for in its welfare you will find your welfare.
—Jeremiah 29:5-7 (NRSV)

"Life is what happens to you when you are making plans," somebody said.

I woke up in my late twenties and realized that I had this image of myself as temporary. I was just temporarily here in this place, doing this work at this time. I was waiting for my next move, for the next door to open, for the next good break. I had been living in this apartment for two months and had not hung any pictures or hooked up the TV. What was I thinking?

I was thinking that I was here temporarily, just passing through, on my way somewhere else. Yet here I was. This was my home—as much my home as anyplace would ever be. The average American moves every four years. If we wait to settle in somewhere until we permanently dwell there, forever, we will be forever drifting and never really *be* anywhere. Exiles.

108

But exiles are not always on the move. Exile is also a place, and that place can be home, if we will make it home. The prophet Jeremiah speaks a word to Israel in exile. What were the people of God to do now that they had been uprooted, cast a thousand miles from home in Babylon? *How can this foreign place possibly be a home?* they must have asked themselves.

Jeremiah hears a word from the Lord: *Take root. Settle in. Be where you are. Make this your home for however long you happen to be here. Home is not where you will finally land when you are forty. Home can be wherever you are with God.*

Prayer Focus: *Pray to God for the creativity and the courage to be where you are, to put down roots in the place where you currently find yourself, to seek the presence of God here, now.*

April 14 ~ A Way When There Is No Way

I have set before you life and death, blessings and curses. Choose life so that you and your descendants may live, loving the LORD your God, obeying him, and holding fast to him.

—Deuteronomy 30:19-20 (NRSV)

One of the most moving books of the twentieth century was Viktor Frankl's *Man's Search for Meaning*. Viktor Frankl was a distinguished psychotherapist who was uprooted and put in a Nazi concentration camp. He was separated from his wife and family, as were many of his fellow prisoners. Many of his fellow prisoners fell into complete despair. They had lost everything, had been stripped of their human dignity, and had been treated as the lowest of the animals by their cruel Nazi guards.

Little wonder, then, that some prisoners simply sat down and died. Frankl noted the deaths of a number of prisoners who were not particularly ill, or ill-treated. They simply stopped living. They saw themselves as utterly powerless. With little hope of escape from the prison, they died rather than lived. Their deaths were hastened because they gave up and quit.

Frankl took another way. Each day, while being marched out to the work site, he thought of a book that he had been writing. He composed the book in his mind, one chapter at a time. He thought of his wife. He pictured their good times in the past; he fantasized about the future they would have together. Thus Frankl survived. God certainly had a hand in bringing Frankl through a horrible situation; however, Frankl's survival was also due to his own conscious efforts—his own choice to find meaning in a place of terrible meaninglessness.

Maybe our freedom to choose, our ability in every situation to decide, is one of God's greatest gifts to us. Perhaps we are not as trapped as we think. Even when there appears to be no way, there can be, by God's grace, a way.

Prayer Focus: Think about those areas of your life in which you feel caught, trapped, out of control. Now bring those areas to God in prayer, asking God to help you to live courageously and boldly, to decide, to choose to take charge.

April 15 ~ Pain That Precedes Newness

This one thing I do: forgetting what lies behind and straining forward to what lies ahead, I press on toward the goal for the prize of the heavenly call of God in Christ Jesus.

—Philippians 3:13-14 (NRSV)

The word *decision* says it all. It comes from the Latin word meaning literally "to cut off." That's one of the reasons that life's decisions can be so difficult, so painful. Decisions require that we make a break—that we cut off one aspect of ourselves in order to move into some new manner of existence.

In any decision, therefore, we wonder, *What am I leaving behind?* We also wonder, *What will my life be like on the other side of this decision?*

The word *decision*, cousin of the related word incision, suggests the painful, almost violent quality of some of our decisions. In deciding, something is being cut off, cut away, amputated from our former life.

Yet there can be no new life without our severing ourselves from the old. There will be no fresh beginning without a break from the past. Nothing can be fully embraced without our first letting go of that to which we previously clung. Decision—the severing, the breaking, the letting go—is a necessary, even painful prelude to the new. Birth tends to be painful.

The apostle Paul, in his letter to the church at Philippi, speaks of his own determination to forget what is past, to strain forward, to press on

110

toward that fresh new future toward which Christ is calling us. Let us also have the faith to let go, to press forward, confident that Christ is calling us.

Prayer Focus: Is there some difficult decision that you are avoiding because you fear the potential pain involved? Pray for the strength to make tough decisions.

April 16 ~ Stepping into Life

When they had brought their boats to shore, they left everything and followed him.

—Luke 5:11 (NRSV)

Jesus confronted James and John while they were fishing. And they left everything and followed him, venturing forth on the basis of nothing but Jesus' words: "Follow me." Here is a dynamic at the heart of the Christian faith. We cannot know Jesus simply by thinking about him. We must follow him in order to know him.

Philosophers in the modern world have noted the development of what they have called "the onlooker consciousness"—that attitude in which we assume the detached stance of the tourist who is just passing through. The modern way of knowing tends to stress detachment—objective, dispassionate, intentional distancing of the knower from that which is to be known. Want to understand something? Then step back, detach, coolly consider; don't get emotionally involved.

Lately we are learning what a limited, narrow way of thinking the "onlooker consciousness" really is. Something can be learned by stepping back from what we are trying to think about. Yet something—perhaps the most important things—also can be learned by *stepping in.* For instance, if you want to understand the Bible, it is best to step into the text, to identify with the characters, to put yourself into the action of the story. In fact, the whole purpose of the Christian faith is to get us into the act, to move us from the sidelines to the center of the action. Jesus asked people to *follow* him, not just think about him!

Are you drifting? Are there areas in your life in which you are playing the part of the tourist, just passing through?

Sometimes the only way to figure out whether a relationship is right for you is to get into the relationship, try it on, experience it. Sometimes the best way to get to know Jesus is to go ahead and follow him. There are some things you can know only by experiencing them from the inside.

Prayer Focus: Have I been avoiding involvement, engagement, in some area of life? Is there some relationship that I need to pursue, rather than simply to observe? Is there some specific commitment that I need to make to Christ in order to be a more faithful follower?

April 17 ~ Preparing for Life's Decisions

Happy are those who do not follow the advice of the wicked, or take the path that sinners tread, . . . but their delight is in the law of the LORD. . . . They are like trees planted by streams of water, which yield their fruit in its season.
—Psalm 1:1-3 (NRSV)

English philosopher and novelist Iris Murdoch, in an essay on ethics, noted that the majority of the ethical work we do takes place before we're faced with a decision. By this she meant that our decisions are not momentary, detached, ad hoc events. Our decisions arise out of who we are; they detract from or contribute to our sense of self.

Recently, when I was talking with a young woman about her decision to marry a young man of my acquaintance, I asked her, "What sort of process did you go through in order to make this important decision?"

She responded, "Didn't have to. I've been preparing myself for this decision for the last twenty-two years."

She is twenty-two. And she was right. In a sense, she has been in preparation for making the promises of marriage almost every day of her life. Her decision will stick, will have significance, on the basis of her character. Who she is will make significant that which she has decided to do. One is able to keep one's decision to be faithful only if one is already a faithful person. Every day of your life, you are busy becoming the sort of person who can be depended upon to keep your promises, to behave in a responsible way, to be worthy of another's trust.

Some people think that the Bible is mostly a book of rules for behavior. However, you may have noticed that the Bible is mostly stories, sayings, literature of no immediate ethical content. The good life is more than wise decisions; it is also a matter of character. Character has been defined this

112

way: it is who we are and how we act when no one is looking.

Think of reading this meditation and praying this prayer as the cultivation of Christian character, as preparation for the next big decision you must make in life.

Prayer Focus: What new disciplines—daily Bible reading, daily prayer, work in some community service project, leadership in your church—do you need to assume so that you might cultivate your Christian character?

April 18 ~ Regret and Forgiveness

"Forgive, and you will be forgiven; give, and it will be given to you."
—Luke 6:37-38 (NRSV)

Poet Dylan Thomas says that men close doors more gently after they turn forty.

Now that I'm well past that age, I can see the poet's point. Life involves the closure of so many doors, the conclusion of so many dramas, the end of so many journeys. You take this road, but not that one. You choose this option rather than the other. So I will tell you what one day, not too long from now, you will experience for yourself. By age forty, there is bound to be some regret that some bridges were crossed, that some dear places and fair faces were left behind.

Regret is an unavoidable by-product of life and life's decisions. Perhaps that's one reason Jesus talked so much about forgiveness. God forgives us and thereby enables us to forgive ourselves. Because of forgiveness, we are not forced to carry on our shoulders the great burdens from the past. We can go on, we can begin again despite the past. Forgiveness is the great antidote to regret.

You are still relatively young, yet I expect that even you have some regret that some things in your life didn't work out as you had planned, some roads were not taken, some decisions did not turn out differently. We are not gods. We cannot make the world always work the way we want. Therefore, there is always regret.

Yet know this: Because of the gracious gift of God's continuing, relentless forgiveness, you can breathe, begin again, let go of your regret, close

113

those doors, and go ahead and live. If it weren't for the gift of Jesus' gracious forgiveness, the regret would kill us.

Prayer Focus: Think about any regrets that you may have. Ask God to help you find the grace to forgive yourself for those regrets.

April 19 ~ Deciding to Break the Barriers

But Ruth said, "Do not press me to leave you or to turn back from following you! Where you go, I will go; . . . your people shall be my people, and your God my God."
—Ruth 1:16 (NRSV)

It's a touching story, the story of Ruth and Naomi. Ruth had married into Naomi's family. Ruth was from a different tribe, a different race and religion. When Ruth's husband died, her mother-in-law, Naomi, told her to go on back to her country and her people. Perhaps there she would be able to survive.

Then Ruth said something to Naomi that surprises us: "I want to go where you go." It is a verse that is sometimes sung at weddings today: "Your people will be my people."

It is a touching story about two women who decided to reach out to each other across racial, family, and religious barriers. Ruth decided to link her life with that of an older woman. Naomi decided to accept Ruth into her world. Together they survived and even prospered. Ruth was a great-great-grandmother of King David. And King David was the great-great-grandfather of Jesus. Thus, in linking their lives together, in reaching out to each other across great barriers, these two women played a role in the great, grand story of God-with-us, Jesus.

We are born to live behind certain barriers of race, religion, and family. Yet through our faithful, courageous decisions, we can step over those barriers, reach out to each other, link our lives to those different from us, and thus be part of the great, grand story of God-with-us.

Prayer Focus: Honestly think about some barrier that separates you from another person. Picture yourself reaching across or stepping over that barrier. Pray for the grace to imitate the barrier-breaking decisiveness of Ruth and Naomi.

April 20 ~ Take Heart

They were terrified. . . . And they cried out in fear. But immediately Jesus spoke to them and said, "Take heart, it is I; do not be afraid."
                                                                    —Matthew 14:26b-27 (NRSV)

Life may be smooth sailing for you right now. But you know that it will not be so always. And what then?

Jesus commands his disciples to get in a boat and move out by themselves onto the sea. A storm arises. The wind and the waves beat against the boat, and "they were terrified."

Then, in the middle of the storm, in the dark of night, they spot a figure in the middle of the waves. "It is a ghost!" they cry. But no, the figure speaks, "Take heart, it is I; do not be afraid." Jesus is with them on the sea. At the sound of his voice, the waves and the wind cease, the storm passes, and there is peace.

It is a story about what it's sometimes like to be a disciple of Jesus. In any life, no matter how well-lived, there are bound to be storms. And when there is a storm, there is fear. In the middle of the night, in a storm, we feel very much alone.

But then, in the darkness of the night, when we think we are about to go under, sometimes there is a voice, a presence in the middle of the storm: "Take heart, it is I; do not be afraid." And then there is dawn and peace.

Next time you find yourself in a storm, remember this Bible story. Jesus is the Savior who comes to us in the middle of the storm, speaks to us, tells us not to be afraid; and there is peace.

Prayer Focus: *Thank God for the times when you have felt the presence of Christ during storms in your life. Ask God for the grace to sense the presence of Christ the next time you are experiencing rough sailing.*

April 21 ~ Temptation

The devil said to him, "If you are the Son of God, command this stone to become a loaf of bread."
                                                                    —Luke 4:3 (NRSV)

As a young man, Jesus was led into the wilderness. His life work was beginning, but before his first day on the job, he went into the desert. There he came face-to-face with the devil. There, the devil said to him, "If you are the Son of God, turn these stones into bread . . . seize political power . . . do some spectacular miracle."

To all these tempting offers, Jesus said, "No."

Note carefully what Satan said. "If you are. . . ." Satan's was a question about identity. It is a peculiarly appropriate question for young adults. At this time in your life it is typical to ask, "Who am I?" This was the question that the Tempter put to Jesus. Who are you?

Most of the time, when we think of the word *temptation*, we think of doing something we shouldn't do—that extra piece of chocolate cake, that questionable behavior with someone on a date, some indiscretion with finances. But here, in Jesus' wilderness experience, the temptation is quite specific. It is not so much a matter of doing what you shouldn't do; rather, it's a matter of being who you shouldn't be.

When we arc just starting out—when almost every day we must decide which path to take, which way to turn—that's when we are most likely to meet the devil, according to this story of Jesus' temptation. When we are young, that's when we are tempted to be who we are not created to be, to turn aside from our God-given vocation.

Jesus refused not only to do what Satan wanted him to do but also to be who the devil demanded. Jesus would follow the will of God above all.

That is the good news behind the story of Jesus' temptation. Jesus resisted the temptation to be who he was not meant to be. With his help, so can we.

Prayer Focus: In what way do you feel tempted to be who God has not called you to be? Pray for the strength to resist this temptation.

April 22 ~ The Peril of Overchoice

For to me, living is Christ and dying is gain. If I am to live in the flesh, that means fruitful labor for me; and I do not know which I prefer. I am hard pressed between the two: my desire is to depart and be with Christ, for that is far better; but to remain in the flesh is more necessary for you.

—Philippians 1:21-24 (NRSV)

The apostle Paul was caught between two difficult alternatives. On the one hand, he was willing to die, to go ahead and be with Christ in eternity. On the other hand, he still had important work to do among the churches. "I am hard pressed between the two," he confessed.

Back in the 1970s, futurist Alvin Toffler wrote his bestseller *Future Shock*. In a book that attempted to predict our future, Toffler spoke of "the peril of overchoice." Noting that modern life presents humanity with a plethora of choices and possibilities—at least in highly developed technological societies—Toffler predicted that some of us would, when faced with so many possibilities, simply become numb. We would be paralyzed by the prospect of the myriad of options, the multiple paths. Overchoice.

Many of us have found that Toffler's predictions were on target. Some days our problem is not that we have nowhere to turn; rather, there is a dizzying array of possible turns to take—so many that we cannot move. There is that difficulty when we have only one path to take. Yet there also is that difficulty when we have so many possible paths, so many alternatives, that we don't know which way to turn. We freeze.

Christians believe that God gives us the grace to turn our lives into a pilgrimage, a journey with God. God gives us possibilities so we may fashion our lives in such a way that, when our lives are all done, they will be a credit to the God who gave us life. Therefore, we don't have to fear the future, for the future is in God's hands. We need not always make the absolutely right choice at every turn in the road. Our God forgives our wrong choices and enables us to begin again.

Prayer Focus: Lord, help me to do the best I can with all the possibilities that life presents me, and to leave the rest in your hands.

April 23 ~ The Seduction of Dreams

But the LORD was with Joseph and showed him steadfast love.
—Genesis 39:21a (NRSV)

My first year of college, the dean gave a speech in which he retold a story from *The Odyssey*, the ancient Greek tale of how Odysseus and his men had to sail past the island of the sirens. The sirens were those alluring women whose songs were so beautiful that sailors who heard them forgot their sailing and dashed their ships on the rocks.

The dean asked us, "What songs did the sirens sing?" What song was so alluring that it drove these sailors off their appointed course?

I expect that the song is different for each of us. We make the decision to move toward a certain goal. But then there is the allure of money, comfort, popularity, or sex. And we find that we have been seduced, led on some detour from our chosen path.

You have your dreams, your goals. But then comes the siren song, and dreams are deferred, laid aside, or forgotten—victims of the allure of some lesser goal.

In Genesis, Joseph was noted for his dreaming. Joseph, despite his older brothers' enmity toward him, was convinced that God had great things in store for him. Joseph's life was a story with lots of twists and turns, lots of opportunities for detours and deviations. Yet through it all, Joseph was convinced that God had a claim upon him, had plans for him. Four times in the Joseph saga, the narrator repeats the phrase, "But the LORD was with Joseph." Joseph held on to his dream.

Or should we say that, in his dream, God held on to Joseph?

Prayer Focus: Think about your dreams. Now think about your "siren songs" that threaten to turn you away from the path that your dreams have made for you. Ask God for the strength to resist such seduction.

April 24 ~ There Was Nothing Else I Could Do

What are human beings that you are mindful of them, mortals that you care for them? Yet you have made them a little lower than God, and crowned them with glory and honor. You have given them dominion over the works of your hands.
—*Psalm 8:4-6 (NRSV)*

"There was nothing else I could do," he said to me, "I had no other choice."

This is often the way we describe our lives and explain ourselves. I had no choice, no way out. There was nothing else to be done. I was caught.

Our lives are constricted and constrained by a web of necessity and determination. Isn't that what we have learned from our studies in the

118

social sciences? We are not really living our lives or determining the course of our destiny. Rather, we are caught in a web of psychological determination. Our parents did it to us. We are mere pawns of impersonal, unavoidable economic forces. Or blame it all on our DNA.

Of all the things I hear when people explain themselves, this is the most popular reason: *I had no other choice. I had no alternative.* In other words, I am the sum, not of what I decide or choose, but of my gender, class, race, economic background, social location, and genetic heritage.

Really, despite our protests, there is something quite comforting and reassuring in thinking of ourselves as caught, unable to choose or decide. That way, life is easier for us. We are mere puppets—controlled by strings that are pulled by forces over which we have no control.

The Bible, while admitting our innate human limitations, also has a high view of our ability to shape our destinies. While we are not gods unto ourselves, able to do anything we want, we are created a little less than God, sharing some of that divine ability to choose, to decide, to make, and to create. God has graciously left something for us to do.

We may be more free than we dare to admit.

Prayer Focus: Think of those areas of your life where God may be asking you to take responsibility, to use your God-given freedom to choose.

April 25 ~ Traveling Light

The Lord appointed seventy others and sent them on ahead of him. . . . He said to them, " . . . Carry no purse, no bag, no sandals."
—Luke 10:1-4 (NRSV)

How are you at packing? One of the tough aspects of taking a trip is deciding what to take and what not to take. A tennis racquet? A Bible? An extra pair of socks? After enough travel, one often learns to travel light. Overstuffed suitcases, dragged from here to there, crammed with things that you probably will never need, make for difficult travel.

When Jesus sent out his disciples, he told them to travel light. He told them not to take a bag, a purse, or extra sandals. He did not want them to be overburdened with lots of useless baggage. He wanted them to be free to do the work that he called them to do, unburdened by needless care.

119

As a young adult, you are now on a journey that requires careful packing. As you move into your new job, your new course of study, or your new relationships, you will want to take with you your cherished values, your sense of who you are, your gifts from God. But there is also much that you ought to leave behind. Any life transition requires that you let go of some old things in order that you might embrace new things. There are some people who carry around unnecessary baggage throughout their lives and pay a heavy personal price for their inability to travel light.

Past hurts must be left, in order that there may be healing. Resentments, injustices, and fears that characterized our lives in the past—all must be cast aside. It will be tough to go forward unless you are able to decide what not to take with you.

Prayer Focus: Make a list of two or three things that you need to leave behind as you grow in the coming years. List three things that you need to take with you. Ask God for the courage to travel light.

April 26 ~ We Try to Get It Right

In the beginning when God created the heavens and the earth, the earth was a formless void and darkness covered the face of the deep, while a wind from God swept over the face of the waters. Then God said, "Let there be light."
—Genesis 1:1-3 (NRSV)

We try to get it right. We take all factors into account, carefully consider all relevant circumstances, weigh alternatives; but sometimes things just don't turn out as we had planned. Sometimes we mess up because of our own weaknesses. It is our own fault. At other times, things don't turn out right because of factors beyond our control. We can't know everything. Despite our best efforts, what we think is the right path to take sometimes turns out to be a wrong turn.

And what then? What's to be done when things don't turn out right, when our carefully considered "right thing to do" becomes the wrong decision?

Church reformer Martin Luther said, "God can ride a lame horse and shoot with a crooked bow." God is able to take our mess, our wrong, and turn it into God's good. In our mistakes and wrong turns, therein is our

120

hope. We do not have to get everything right. Indeed, we cannot get it all right, and that is all right.

Fortunately, the future is not solely in our hands; the last chapter of the story of our lives will not be written by us. Genesis, the first book of the Bible, begins, "In the beginning when God created the heavens and the earth. . . ." The original Hebrew could be translated more accurately, "When God began creating. . . ." The creative work of God does not end with Genesis. God continues to create, to bring light out of darkness and creation out of chaos.

Prayer Focus: Pray about those wrong turns, mistakes, and bad decisions that you have made. Ask God to continue God's gracious, creative work in your life.

April 27 ~ When We Come to Ourselves

"But when he came to himself he said, 'How many of my father's hired hands have bread enough and to spare, but here I am dying of hunger! I will get up and go to my father. . . .' "

—*Luke 15:17-18 (NRSV)*

A great moment occurs in Jesus' story of the prodigal son. Jesus says that the young wastrel, in degradation in the far country, "comes to himself." He literally returns to himself so that he may return home. He remembers his home, his father; thus, he remembers himself, who he is and is meant to be. It is a great turning point in the plot of the story, as well as a revelation of one of the most important truths of life.

The great challenge of most decisions we make is the newness of it all. In some decisions we are asked to go away from our safe and secure places and move into some new place. Yet there are other decisions where we are asked to turn and return to a very old place: home. In remembering, we recall who we really are. We realize that we somehow lost our way, forgot who we were meant to be. We come to ourselves.

In our young adult years, it is important for us to leave home, to go to college, to take a job somewhere else, to venture forth. Venturing forth is developmentally important. Yet sometimes, in venturing forth, we get lost. Then, by the grace of God, we "come to ourselves." We remember that we are not orphans. We have a parent, a home. We can turn and return.

Augustine said, after his conversion to Christ, "I knew, but until then, I didn't know that I knew." His life in Christ felt like a return home. He had come back to himself.

Prayer Focus: Ask God to help you, amid the sometimes confusing clamor of life, to turn and return to yourself, the one God intends you to be.

April 28 ~ When We Did Not Decide

But when God, who had set me apart before I was born and called me through his grace, was pleased to reveal his Son to me, so that I might proclaim him among the Gentiles.

—Galatians 1:15-16 (NRSV)

We Americans are big on freedom of choice. That's why we have supermarkets where you are able to choose between a dozen different types of grapefruit, and cornflakes done fifty ways. At home, we have 120 cable TV channels. And there are fast food restaurants featuring hamburgers any way you want them.

I choose, therefore I am.

The modern world gave us a host of different choices. In the new world, no longer did you have to be a blacksmith merely because your father was one. One could choose.

Yet, if we are honest, we must also admit that many aspects of our lives, often the most important aspects, are matters over which we have little choice. The color of my skin, my name, my parents, and my country are all crucial aspects of my identity over which I had no choice.

Therefore, much of our lives becomes a matter, not of choosing and deciding whether to take this road or that one, but a matter of *making the best out of that which we did not decide.*

"Necessity is the mother of invention," is the old slogan. And sometimes necessity is also the mother of creativity, courage, and a host of other great virtues. When things are outside our control, beyond our power to decide, then we must find a way to make the best of what we have been given, to go ahead and be who we are, even when we may not have decided to be who we are.

As he looked back on his life, Paul felt that he had been called "before

I was born." He had been given a mission, an assignment by God. We make our choices, but God also chooses. In relating our lives to the plans of God, therein is true freedom.

Prayer Focus: Take a moment and list all those things in your life that make you who you are. Then ask God to help you both to accept and to work with those things in order to be all that you ought to be.

April 29 ~ Who Am I? What Should I Do with My Life?

And when Jesus had been baptized, just as he came up from the water, suddenly the heavens were opened to him and he saw the Spirit of God descending like a dove and alighting on him. And a voice from heaven said, "This is my Son, the Beloved, with whom I am well pleased."
—*Matthew 3:16-17 (NRSV)*

Two of the biggest questions young adults often ask are these: Who am I? What am I supposed to do with my life?

In his early thirties, Jesus was baptized. At his baptism, the heavens opened and there was a voice, saying, "This is my Son, the Beloved. . . ." This was the beginning of his ministry, his life's work, his vocation. That fateful day of his baptism, the voice from heaven made clear who Jesus was and what he was meant to do.

Wouldn't your life be easier if, when you ask those two big questions, there was an unmistakable voice from heaven? Perhaps you have experienced such a voice, such a vision. For most of us, the matter of "Who am I and what should I do?" is less certain, even conflicted. We have hints, glimpses, suggestions from friends, and other subtle leadings. Yet who is to say that such subtle leading is not a voice from heaven?

Someone has said that wherever the deep needs of the world intersect with the gifts that God has given you, there is your call from God, your summons, and your vocation. Perhaps your call will come like a dove descending, like a voice from heaven. More likely, your call will come as a growing, gradual sense of what God wants you to do and who God wants you to be. Friends may be helpful. Sometimes those who know us best have the best sense of what we ought to do. Trial and error, guidance counseling, and prayer all can be means whereby God gets our attention, speaks, summons, and calls.

123

So listen. Be attentive to your life, particularly at this time in your life. God knows you, loves you, and has plans for you.

Prayer Focus: What would you say is your vocation from God? Where is God calling you? Who does God want you to be?

April 30 ~ Stepping Over the Threshold

"The LORD is with us; do not fear."

—Numbers 14:9c (NRSV)

After their sojourn through the wilderness, the Hebrews at last stood on the threshold to the promised land. One small problem: the land was already occupied, crawling with Canaanites. Scouts were sent out to reconnoiter the land. After a few days, the explorers returned. There was a majority report, followed by a minority report given by Caleb and his band.

"We looked like grasshoppers next to the giants who are over there!" said the majority report.

Then Caleb said, "The land is rich. God is with us. Do not fear; we can take it!" As a young adult, you're on a threshold of sorts. How does the land look from where you stand? Who shall name the future—the fearful majority, or the faithful minority? Every journey consists of a number of thresholds. Will you open the door, cross over the threshold, and step into tomorrow?

The key to Caleb's positive view of the land on the other side was his conviction that the land, Israel's future, was a gift. "God is with us." With that conviction, we are able to move with confidence into even the most daunting tomorrow. The future is not your fearsome task. The future is a gift of God, God's promise. Knowledge of that enables you to take heart, to stride with confidence over the threshold.

God is with us! Let us go forth.

Prayer Focus: Identify two or three thresholds you must cross over in the next few months. How do you feel about those thresholds? Ask God to help you walk into tomorrow with confidence.

May

GOD'S WORK OF RENEWAL

Mitch McVicker

May 1 ~ Forever Changed

He who began a good work in you will carry it on to completion until the day of Christ Jesus.

—Philippians 1:6 (NIV)

September 19, 1997, will always be a benchmark in my life. That was the night my closest friend was killed, and my life was forever changed. For two years, I traveled with Rich Mullins, doing concerts and writing songs with him. When we were not traveling, we were roommates. Then I was involved in the car wreck that took his life. I spent a month in the hospital recovering from broken bones, collapsed lungs, and a coma. I was released, but my recovery went on for a few years, and my questions persisted.

I was unable to understand the situation, and I could not figure out why it had happened. Many doubts and fears arose within me, and I longed for God to fill me in on what was going on. God did not do that.

However, I have learned that God brings good from tragic events. I have also found that my idea of what "good" is does not always coincide with God's idea. Yet I know that good exists in the world because of God. Jesus will use whatever we encounter to bring us to him. He will complete the work he began in us no matter what comes down life's road. We encounter good in the most unlikely situations.

God takes the "not good" and brings good from it. The path we are on is made new, and we are forever changed by the good that God works. This month we'll consider how God is continually at work in our lives, renewing our souls and bringing us hope.

Prayer Focus: Thank God for working on you. Ask God to change you and make you new by working good in all life's situations.

May 2 ~ The Hits Keep Coming

Be joyful in hope, persevere in hardship; keep praying regularly.
—Romans 12:12 (NJB)

There seem to be many instances in life when it is hard to be hopeful. How does the guy sleeping under the bridge in a cardboard box find any hope? Where is the hope for the woman struggling through an unwanted divorce? How can someone whose brother just committed suicide be hopeful? When things repeatedly go wrong, the question looms even greater.

When life hits us time and time again, we often become tough. We get calloused souls so that nothing affects us or touches us or hurts us. However, just as raw meat is tenderized when it is pounded, we too can be shaped and made tender when life beats us down. It's just like God to take despairing situations that are rough, hard, and hopeless and use them for our benefit.

It seems the only ones who are able to get through to those who have been made tough are those who have gone through similar hard times and have become tender. It is the tender one who can get the tough one's attention and say, "There is a reason to have hope; hold on; don't lose heart."

As we look to God, even though we're beat down by life, we become tender. We are able to provide hope to those who are toughened by life's poundings. We all are in this together; and though the hits keep coming, hope springs anew.

Prayer Focus: Look to the Lord during rough times so that you will become tender and hope will overflow from you to those around you.

May 3 ~ The Green Pastures of God's Presence

He makes me lie down in green pastures, he leads me beside quiet waters, he restores my soul.

—*Psalm 23:2-3a (NIV)*

My legs are tired. My lungs burn. The journey has been long and steep and, at times, rough. However, there is a clearing up ahead. Let us stop and rest. Set down your pack and take a load off.

This psalm talks of being guided along the path of righteousness. It is not surprising that this path would pass through such a peaceful place.

Can you hear the wind brushing over the long-stemmed grass? Can you hear the gentle bubbling of the stream? The world around us is murmuring with quietness. Listen.

How can we not hear what God is doing? Our souls are being restored, and the incessant spinning within us is stilled. A strong and tender silence comes sweeping in as we lie back in the green pastures of God's presence, enjoying the tranquil brook that flows alongside the path we will soon continue downward.

But here, in these green pastures, rest begins to seep into every crack that the journey might have made in our souls. Here we are restored and renewed so that we may keep going. And who knows what lies ahead, what surprises God is guiding us toward?

Through the murmuring, we are replenished. Through the bubbling and brushing, we are strengthened. We are made new through the gentle silence of God's presence; we are enabled to continue along the path with ears wide open.

Prayer Focus: *Ask the Lord to be your rest and your peace. As you lie down in his presence, he will restore your soul.*

May 4 ~ What Counts

Neither circumcision nor uncircumcision means anything; what counts is a new creation.

—*Galatians 6:15 (NIV)*

I go bowling once or twice a year, and each time I go I am convinced that I should be good at it. For some odd reason, I get frustrated when I do not bowl well, and I cannot understand why my score reflects my lack of experience and practice.

I have become enamored with keeping score. I love neatly packaged ways to measure my life and gauge how I am living. But it seems my life's scorecard, like bowling, is rarely as I want it to be. Even so, it doesn't matter if I roll a strike or a gutter-ball in life. God does not keep score. In fact, the apostle Paul says, "Neither circumcision nor uncircumcision means anything." Therefore, our attempts to claim goodness through our actions are meaningless.

God is unconcerned with our scorecard, no matter how good or bad it happens to be. And God is unimpressed with our efforts to perform well. So our initiative and striving have no bearing on our stance before God at all. The only thing that counts, according to Scripture, is being a new creation. Yes, the only thing that counts is completely out of our control. God makes us new.

Yes, God is unimpressed and unconcerned; yet God is completely and crazily in love with us. God's love is so great that we become a new creation, and that is what counts.

Prayer Focus: Ask God to help you lay down your attempts to impress him and, instead, to focus on how God is making you a new creation.

May 5 ~ "Are You Jesus?"

We serve in the new way of the Spirit, and not in the old way of the written code.
—Romans 7:6 (NIV)

Five men were racing through the train station after a long day's work. They were trying to catch the last train that could get them home in time for supper. As they whipped around the corner and hustled to board the train as it was pulling off, they knocked over a table full of apples that a young boy was selling.

Four of them barely made it onto the train and were summoning, prodding, and rooting the fifth man to join them. But he stopped and yelled that he would catch the next train.

He turned around and walked over to the boy. He saw that many of the apples had been bruised, and he felt he needed to make things better. He picked up the apples, pulled a twenty-dollar bill from his pocket, and gave it to the boy. He said, "I hope this can repair some of the damage. I hope we didn't ruin your day."

He didn't know that the little boy was blind and was selling the apples to help pay his way through school. As he turned to go wait for the next train, he heard the frail voice of this little blind boy call to him and say, "Sir, are you Jesus?"

The person who serves in "the new way of the Spirit" is the one who is seen by others to be like Jesus. Will others see Jesus in you today?

Prayer Focus: Pray that someone, sometime, will notice the Lord in you as you serve him and the world he loves in a new way.

May 6 ~ Resolutions

Create in me a clean heart, renew within me a resolute spirit.
—Psalm 51:10 (NJB)

I used to make New Year's resolutions. I would vow to pray more, work out more, or stay away from sugar. I would do just fine for a few days, a few weeks, or, if I was lucky, a few months. But in the end, I would fail and all would seem lost. I would not remember the times I had done what I set out to do; I could see only that I had faltered.

From time to time, I have also been very resolute in becoming good or holy. I have planned to make myself clean by whatever means necessary, darn it. However, the psalmist knew that the only way his resolutions would hold up was for God to make his *spirit* resolute.

My determination never stands the test of time; yet, where determination gives out, God's forgiveness picks up. God is continually scrubbing our hearts clean, and God has made a lasting commitment to keep doing so. That is the only way we can ever become holy.

Our determination always will seem spineless and our resolutions flimsy, unless they are held up by forgiveness. Real determination and real resolutions happen only as God makes our spirits resolute and our hearts clean.

129

May 7 ~ The Soil of the Soul

"Every plant that my heavenly Father has not planted will be pulled up by the roots."

—*Matthew 15:13 (NIV)*

God is tirelessly tending the gardens of our souls. God is the master gardener who is always planting and looking after life and seeing to it that it grows. When a seed sprouts and breaks through the soil, the whole garden becomes new. When a plant grows to completion, the whole garden is finally what it was intended to be. Yet it is the individual plant and the newness it brings to the garden that has had God's attention. After all, God cared enough to plant it, and the Scriptures say that God's eye is on every flower.

However, scripture tells us that if a plant is growing that shouldn't be, God will pull it up by its roots. When something is pulled from the soil of our souls, it undoubtedly will hurt. Often things have taken root deep within us and have wrapped themselves around our innermost places. So, this process is not smooth.

Still, as these unhelpful plants are removed, more room is made available for God's planting. Then, growth happens, and the garden again becomes new. Yes, God is the Master Gardener.

Prayer Focus: *Ask the Lord to make your soul more fertile so that what God plants will grow; and pray for the removal of anything growing there that shouldn't be.*

May 8 ~ Sea of Love

When they landed, they saw a fire of burning coals there with fish on it, and some bread.

—*John 21:9 (NIV)*

Hollywood loves the story of a wreck at sea. *Gilligan's Island*, *Titanic*, and the more recent *Castaway* are all tales in which the sea wrought havoc, leading to tragedy, hardship, and perseverance.

Much of Jesus' activity also revolved around the sea. Yet in his life, the sea was like a canvas used to display his miracles, his teachings, and his compassion. Jesus taught the crowds from a boat that was just off shore. Jesus walked upon the waves. Jesus calmed the raging sea. And Jesus made breakfast on the beach as his best friends were coming in from a morning of fishing. It is comforting to know that Jesus, whose miracles and teachings confounded and awed the masses, was interested in what appeared to be a trivial act of cooking for those he loved.

Acts of kindness are never more profound, and service is never more moving, than when motivated by love. Jesus is constantly going out of his way because of his love for us.

It's not surprising that much of Jesus' life involved the sea. Heaven itself cannot even contain the sea of Jesus' love.

Prayer Focus: *Pray that your actions will be motivated by love, and that love will flow out of you like water.*

May 9 ~ Alive and Kicking

I will give you a new heart and put a new spirit in you; I will remove from you your heart of stone and give you a heart of flesh.
—*Ezekiel 36:26 (NIV)*

When I was young, *The Wizard of Oz* was shown on television every year. Everyone came to know the story and the characters whether they wanted to or not. The film was a part of the culture, as it seemed everyone could relate to it in one aspect or another.

I was always drawn to the tin man. He would knock on his chest but hear only a hollow echo. He felt he was missing a heart, so he set out to find one.

We, too, go in search of ways to "fill" ourselves. We are hoping that pleasure, work, excitement, or people might take up the empty void we feel inside us.

In the Scriptures, God promises to come to our rescue by giving each of us a new heart. We often turn our hearts to stone with sin, selfishness, and our attempts to keep ourselves busy. We lose feeling and convince ourselves that there is nothing inside us.

However, God will remove our hearts of stone and replace them with hearts of flesh. God does not replace our hearts with some kind of ethereal, fairy-tale hearts, but with real, living, beating hearts.

Our new hearts make us fully human and return us to what God intended us to be. And, once again, we are alive and kicking.

Prayer Focus: Ask to be led away from that which turns your heart to stone. Ask God to give you a new, living heart of flesh when yours becomes hard and stony.

May 10 ~ Staring into the Light

But those who hope in the LORD will renew their strength. They will soar on wings like eagles; they will run and not grow weary, they will walk and not be faint.

—Isaiah 40:31 (NIV)

As legend has it, when an eagle is injured, it stares at the sun. It doesn't move. It just looks into the light until it is healed. No matter how long the healing takes, the eagle's eyes are fixed on the glow of the sun. Scripture tells us that our strength will be renewed, and we will be like eagles. God will heal us and revive us, and we will soar.

When our strength has been renewed, we fly high. God also promises that we will not grow weary as our faith settles and we begin running. And once we begin walking by faith, we are told, we will never tire. When our bodies grow weary and tired, our spirits will not.

So, will we stare into the light and trust that our strength will be renewed? Will we be still enough to wait for God to intervene, trusting that faith will eventually move us to leap? It is then, in God's timing, that we find ourselves soaring like eagles, running without growing weary, and walking tirelessly. All we need to do is stare into the light—stare at God and wait on the One who makes our spirits soar.

Prayer Focus: Pray for the ability to stare at the Light and wait for God to bring renewal and revival to your spirit.

May 11 ~ Pocket Change

He put a new song in my mouth, a hymn of praise to our God.
                                                    —*Psalm 40:3 (NIV)*

It is such a treat for me when I am at a restaurant and I find some change in my pocket. I love to go to the jukebox and pick a song or two. Most of the time, I select something I have not heard for quite a while.

The song is always new to me, though it has been played on the jukebox many times before. It could be any number of years old, but it is music to my ears. The record player is simply doing what it was designed to do— merely going through the motions. But the song is fresh.

David reminds us that God has placed a new song within us. It is a tune that is unaffected by the world. It is a melody that soars high above our lives. It comes from beyond our human lungs.

Sometimes we take for granted the fact that we have a song to sing at all. We merely go through the motions like so many times before, simply because the right buttons are pushed.

However, when we open our mouths, a new song is there because God has made it so. God has saved us from the mundane. All it takes is a little pocket change for God to do a new miracle within us.

Prayer Focus: *Remember that God has given you a new song to sing with each new day. Pray that the song will send you soaring high above the temptation to simply "go through the motions."*

May 12 ~ Sparkle, Gleam, and Shine

He saved us, not because of righteous things we had done, but because of his mercy. He saved us through the washing of rebirth and renewal by the Holy Spirit.
                                                    —*Titus 3:5 (NIV)*

When I wash my car, it is as if it becomes new to me all over again. The old dirt and grime are whisked away, and just because there are more miles on the odometer than ever before doesn't mean that it shines any less. Never before has it been in its present condition. It has never had this combination of gleam, sparkle, and life.

As a Christian musician, I am often asked why I have faith and why I am

133

a Christian. I explain that I have faith because it was given to me. I am a Christian not because I have achieved a high level of spirituality or attained a certain level of "goodness." I am a Christian because I am incapable of ever attaining or achieving this "goodness," and I need to be rescued from myself. I do not make myself a Christian. Jesus makes me one. I am a Christian simply because God is faithful and merciful.

In the Scriptures, Paul talks of the Spirit of God being poured out over us, washing and renewing us. Just because there are some miles on our "odometers" does not mean that we shine any less. It is the Spirit that makes us sparkle, not what we have done or will do. The old dirt and grime have been whisked away, and thanks to God's mercy, we gleam like a new van just driven off the lot.

Prayer Focus: Ask God to take away your dirt and grime and make you shine. Pray that you will remember your newness is God's doing and not your own.

May 13 ~ On Top of the Pile

And you have put on a new self which will progress towards true knowledge the more it is renewed in the image of its Creator.
                                                        —*Colossians 3:10 (NJB)*

I have a T-shirt I have enjoyed wearing since I was fifteen. I love to wear it, and the more I do, the more comfortable it seems to become. I often wear it several times before I wash it. The washing machine cleans it, but it comes out stiffer, less comfortable. So I have to wear it a while before it's comfortable again. And each time I put it on, it seems to fit better. In a way, the shirt takes on my "image" the more I wear it. Whenever it's time to put on a shirt, it is always on top of the pile.

God has given us a "shirt" to wear. The shirt fits God perfectly, yet God is gracious enough to share it with us. The more we wear it, the better it fits and the newer we become.

In the Scriptures, Paul calls this shirt the "new self." The more we wear it, the more we progress toward "true knowledge" and become our true selves. The more we put on the new self, the more comfortable it gets.

When we wear the shirt God has given us, we are renewed as we take on the image of our Creator. It is always there, waiting for us on top of the pile.

May 14 ~ Forever Strong

My glory will be for ever new and the bow in my hand forever strong.
—Job 29:20 (NJB)

Not many of us today own a bow, and hardly any of us who do own one use it as a way of providing food for ourselves or our families. But scripture says God will keep the bow in our hand "forever strong."

Should this mean anything to us, or should we dismiss it as ancient? Maybe it means that God will keep whatever we use to provide and sustain life in better condition than we ever could. God might be telling you that your computer or your camera will be kept forever strong. Maybe it is your books, or your mind, for that matter. God is keeping my guitar and pen, which I use to write songs, forever strong. Whatever we think depends on our own elbow grease actually is kept strong by God.

Job says that our glory will be new always. But how can we remain new as we live life? God must be renewing us constantly. But how?

Jesus said Spirit gives birth to spirit. Paul talked of being led by the Spirit. Therefore, as the Spirit leads us, we are born. Yet, since we have already been born and cannot actually return to the womb, this birth comes from God. God renews our glory, which is what makes us who we are. Yes, as we are led by the spirit through life, God renews us.

God will use our experiences to renew us, and God will keep us, and whatever we use to do our jobs, forever strong.

Prayer Focus: Thank God for your gifts, skills, and abilities. Pray that you will remember that your strength comes from God and not your own elbow grease. Ask God to lead you and to renew your glory and your spirit.

May 15 ~ At the Threshold

See, I have placed before you an open door that no one can shut. I know that you have little strength, yet you have kept my word and have not denied my name.

—Revelation 3:8 (NIV)

When I would go places with my family as a child, I remember I would stop at doors and wait for my dad to open them for me. If I wanted to pass through the door, I was completely dependent upon someone stronger than I to push or pull it open. Even though I was not strong enough to open the door, I could do what was needed to get to the threshold. If I took the proper steps to get there, stopped, and waited, the door would open.

Scripture tells us that God understands that we are not very strong, yet God can see us as we take the proper steps—or, in other words, as we keep God's commandments. When we enter into a new phase of life, we might be able to do what it takes to get there, but we are unable to open the door ourselves. The door is opened only because God chooses to and is strong enough to do so. And there is no one who can close it!

Will we keep God's commandments in order to put ourselves at the threshold? Will we wait there for God to open the door? Or, will we try to do it ourselves? Only God can open the door of newness for us. And there is no one strong enough to close what God has opened.

Prayer Focus: *Pray that you will come to know what God has opened and closed; pray that you will place yourself at the threshold and trust God to act.*

May 16 ~ A Confidence Not My Own

We have confidence to enter the Most Holy Place by the blood of Jesus, by a new and living way opened for us.

—Hebrews 10:19-20 (NIV)

Not everyone will get into heaven. According to scripture, drunkards, liars, adulterers, and those who have been mad will have no part of the kingdom of God. Neither will those who have been greedy, nor those who have been envious.

I don't know anyone who isn't included in that list, who doesn't fall under one of those categories. So, we're all in trouble. Something we have done sometime, somewhere keeps us from entering the "Most Holy Place." Based on the lives we live and our misguided actions, we are unable to find our way there. Yes, apart from Jesus, we are in trouble.

However, scripture also says that a "new and living way" allows us to enter confidently into the holy place. Yet, when I look in the mirror and think of myself entering the kingdom of heaven, many words other than *confident* come to mind. My admittance to heaven does not make much sense to me.

Paul says it is the "blood of Jesus" that provides us with a new way of entering the Kingdom. The blood of Jesus overshadows all our inadequacies, covers all our sins, and is beyond our need for things to make sense.

We will have no part in the kingdom of heaven based on our own merit. We could not find the Most Holy Place if it were merely left up to us. Yet, somehow, someway, Jesus makes this possible by giving us a new way to get there, and a confidence that is not our own begins to grow within us.

Prayer Focus: *Look to Jesus to provide you with a way to enter the Kingdom— and with confidence.*

May 17 ~ Soul by Soul

Do not conform any longer to the pattern of this world, but be transformed by the renewing of your mind.

—Romans 12:2 (NIV)

Once when I was introduced to someone, my new acquaintance asked me, "What are you going to do to change the world?" I didn't know how to respond. I'm not sure what gave her the impression that I was *trying* to change the world. I have my hands full just making sure that when I walk out the door in the morning, my hair is not sticking up, my fly is not down, and I don't have anything hanging out of my nose! But change the world? I hadn't thought about that.

Paul says we should not be conformed to the world but be transformed by being renewed. Instead of focusing on the world and how it needs to change, maybe we need to look at how we need to change ourselves.

If we have any hope of changing the world, we need to let God do a transformation on us. The world will inevitably change soul by soul.

137

John 3:16 talks about God loving the world so much that he sent his Son to save it. It seems that God's love is the only thing that could bring about a change in the world.

As we are renewed, we have the opportunity to extend that same love to the world around us. And the world will inevitably change soul by soul.

Prayer Focus: Pray that God will change you so that you can do your part in changing the world.

May 18 ~ Holy Breath

Send out your breath and life begins; you renew the face of the earth.
—Psalm 104:30 (NJB)

My favorite time of the year is spring. I am moved by the new life I see around me. Trees begin to bud, flowers start to bloom, young bunnies begin to hop, and baby birds try out their first songs. Just a few days earlier, the long nights seemed unbearable, and the cold days seemed to cut through our much-too-thin skin. Then, just in time, we are renewed by the breath of God as it covers the world.

Our hearts are no longer heavy. Our breath no longer freezes as we walk down the street with our eyes fixed on the tops of our shoes. The fields are no longer dormant, so why should we be?

Our breath is now free to sing spring's new song, and our hearts are lifted as they join in the melody that is floating all around us. Our eyes can now look upward and around us, as they no longer share the same blank stare with the face of the earth. We now feel a warm gentle breeze blowing across the fields.

God's breath has been sent out. Only *that* is able to renew us and renew the whole earth. God has once again reminded us that we have been made alive by life itself. We have an unbridled hope that comes from the source of all hope. And we, along with the entire world, have been renewed by God's very breath.

Prayer Focus: Ask for God's breath to fill your lungs and bring you to renewal.

May 19 ~ Less Cool

Therefore we do not lose heart. Though outwardly we are wasting away, yet inwardly we are being renewed day by day.
—*2 Corinthians 4:16 (NIV)*

I went through a phase when I bought three jackets over a span of just a few months. I purchased a fleece jacket from one of the trendy stores at the mall, bought a lined jean jacket from an outdoors shop, and picked up a loose fitting beatnik coat from a used clothing store. I had all the bases covered. I could feel stylish and contemporary, rugged and natural, or cool and "hippyish."

I was able to make myself look and feel different, but inwardly I was still as debilitated as ever. I was losing heart without even knowing it, and there was not a coat to fix that.

I was getting older and becoming less cool, but I was going to fight it. If I was going down, I was going to go down swinging. It took me a while to realize that I was taking a step toward the god of appearance and a step away from the God who holds the real remedy for my condition.

Outwardly, we are wasting away, yet our souls are being renewed and our hearts are being revived. God is constantly at work within us, and that is where our true selves lie.

Prayer Focus: Ask God to revive your heart and renew your soul. Pray that you will trust your true self to God rather than trust in outward appearances.

May 20 ~ Beyond Expectation

"Be perfect, therefore, as your heavenly Father is perfect."
—*Matthew 5:48 (NIV)*

I recently made a point to say "hello" to every person I passed while I was jogging. I figured this probably would be the only time I would ever see these people, and this could be my way of praying for them and asking God's blessing on their lives. I just didn't want to pass them by as if they weren't there. After doing this for several days, I quickly learned that I was bad at loving without expectations. I *expected* a response from each person after my greeting. If I did not get one, it infuriated me.

Jesus calls us beyond expectation to perfection. I had always thought this to be impossible, because I thought that perfection meant being flawless. But I discovered that my understanding of perfection was off track. I realized that Jesus calls us to be perfect immediately after he asks us to do one thing: love our enemies—those whom it is hard to love and those who don't deserve our love. Jesus is calling us to love not because of what we can get out of it, but because it is what we were created to do. Through loving others, through doing what we were created to do, we are brought by God to a perfection that is beyond flaws. Not only does our loving benefit those around us, but it also benefits us. You see, God works through our loving actions to make us into what we are meant to be.

Prayer Focus: Ask God to help you focus more on loving than on being perfect. Ask to be made perfect in God's eyes.

May 21 ~ A Big Clump of Grass

"While you are pulling the weeds, you may root up the wheat with them."
—Matthew 13:29 (NIV)

I remember when my dad asked me to weed the yard when I was a young boy. I was supposed to pull the weeds up by their roots and then mow the lawn. When I would try to pull up the weeds, however, many times I would pull up a big clump of grass. I soon would become frustrated and would revert to just mowing the lawn. When the lawn was all neat and trimmed, you could not see the weeds. But a week later, they would be back again, and I would try to avoid my dad's gaze.

Jesus tells a parable similar to this. He tells of a field of wheat that contains many weeds. The workers ask the field owner if they should pull up the weeds; but the owner fears that in doing this, they will pull up the wheat as well. He tells them instead to *separate* the weeds from the wheat after harvesting.

Many times I "yank at myself" in haste, trying to get rid of what looks like a weed. I fail to realize that what is new or good is often growing closely to what is not. Before I know it, in my impatience, I have pulled a big clump of grass from my soul. If only I had taken time to carefully dig out the weed instead of yanking at it impatiently. I must learn determination and patience, trusting that, in God's time, the old will be separated from the new.

Prayer Focus: Pray that you will not miss out on the wheat growing in your soul because of the weeds. Ask God to help you get rid of whatever you do not need in due time.

May 22 ~ Shrunken to Newness

"No one sews a piece of unshruken cloth on an old cloak; otherwise, the patch pulls away from it, the new from the old, and the tear gets worse."
—Mark 2:21 (NJB)

As children we were told to keep our clothes nice. The only way I can think of accomplishing this is for a child not to wear the clothes, or not to fully "live" while wearing the clothes.

In today's scripture, Jesus refers to the patching of an old cloak. A cloak is able to fully function as a piece of clothing again because it is patched by another cloth. The patch is new not in the sense that it is "fresh" or has its whole "life" ahead of it, but in the sense that it is shrunken. It is new because it is something it never has been before. With each turn of life, it is closer to being able to perform its function. Sure, it used to be in better shape—more pleasing to the eye. But it has never been more new.

The cloak is made whole again and "better" because the piece of cloth has been shrunk, has become smaller. The piece of cloth's newness does-n't come from keeping itself uncontaminated and pristine; rather, it's newness comes because it has given of itself. Its identity is found in its function—in becoming a part of the whole.

Becoming new isn't a one-time event. It happens throughout life. Are we willing to be "shrunk" in order to be equipped to perform our function? Are we willing to be made smaller by God at every turn in order to discover and follow our calling?

Prayer Focus: We are made new not because we have kept ourselves uncontam-inated, neat, and fresh, but because we are becoming. Are you willing to be made "smaller" in order to be made new?

141

May 23 ~ Good Things

He contents you with good things all your life, renews your youth like an eagle's.
—Psalm 103:5 (NJB)

As I was writing these meditations, I read a few to a friend of mine. She consistently responded by telling me they were "good." She said that she needed to use another descriptive word, however, because "good" didn't do justice to what I had written.

We commonly use superlatives and other descriptive terms for things or concepts, assuming that "good" merely means somewhere above average. Yet really there is nothing better than saying something is good.

Scripture says that God will give us good things all our life. Think about it. Nothing is better than that. Jesus thwarted a man's attempt to call him good, telling the man that he didn't even know what the word meant, and that only God is good. God contents us with good things. Yet often we look past that promise without it having much of an impact on us.

For the most part, we are bad at being content. Society tells us to keep striving and achieving. There always seems to be something better, and it's hard for us to believe that God could ever provide us with all that we need. God offers us what should end our pushing and striving, and make us content.

In giving us good things, God offers us the best. Nevertheless, we are not content. We fail to take God up on the offer. God stands before us with an armful of blessings, and there is nothing better.

Prayer Focus: *Give thanks for the good God has given you. Pray that you may see the good in your life and not focus on what you think you should have.*

May 24 ~ Eternally Fresh

As Christ was raised from the dead by the Father's glorious power, we too should begin living a new life.

—Romans 6:4 (NJB)

It seems that whenever the electricity goes out, I stumble through the dark to no avail. I fumble around until I finally get my hands on a flashlight. Yet when I flip the switch to turn it on, nothing happens.

142

The flashlight is not broken. It still works. It is perfectly capable of lighting up the room; however, its batteries have died. Without a source of power, it is unable to do what it was intended to do.

Scripture says that the "Father's glorious power" enables us to live a new life. Many times we flip our switch on, intending to light the darkness around us, without recognizing that the only reason we can shine is because God's power gives us the ability to do so.

The same power that raised Jesus from the dead makes us able to live a bright, new life. We have eternally fresh batteries.

At times, life is dim, and we stumble and fumble around; but because of God's glorious power, we still shine. Our new lives glow with a brilliance that is not our own, and the darkness cannot overpower it.

Prayer Focus: Pray that you will turn to God for "energy" whenever you set out to be a "light." And ask to remember that you can do so only because God's power has made you new.

May 25 ~ Right Behind Us

Whether you turn to the right or to the left, your ears will hear a voice behind you, saying, "This is the way; walk in it."
—Isaiah 30:21 (NIV)

Isaiah mentions a voice that simply says, "Walk this way." But I ask, *which* way? I can really get caught up in the logistics of a given situation. *When?* Is it God's will for me to do this now or later? *Where?* Is it God's will for me to go to this college or that one? *Why?* Should I take this job over the other? *How?* Should there be something happening differently in my life?

In essence, the voice Isaiah heard was saying that our questions, our focus, and our attention to details are worthless. The important thing is simply to walk—to walk with God day by day. If we walk with God, God assures us that *either* the path to the left *or* the right will be fine.

You see, it's *hearing the voice* that makes the path the right way to go. Direction is not as important. We should concentrate more on hearing God's voice and put less of our focus on detail. We should trust that God is working in all situations. God brings about the good, and we should rest assured that it will happen whether we walk to the right or the left.

143

Of course, this doesn't mean we are to walk carelessly or recklessly. It means that if we listen for God's voice each day, God will direct our steps. Heading in a new direction can be scary, but if we sincerely seek to follow God, God will bring about good. And God will be right behind us the whole way!

Prayer Focus: *Pray for the ears to hear God speaking to you. Ask God to help you be more concerned with hearing his voice than with analyzing directions and details.*

May 26 ~ World on End

"New things I declare; before they spring into being I announce them to you."
—*Isaiah 42:9 (NIV)*

Leave it to God to turn our world on end. The kingdom of God stands in direct contrast to the messages we get from TV commercials, billboards, and magazines. Many times, Jesus' descriptions of the Kingdom, his message, and his promises defy our reason and our ability to understand.

Jesus says that the poor in spirit and the pure in heart are blessed. God promises to turn the darkness into light and make the rough places smooth. This blows our minds, and we cannot make heads or tails of it.

But God is declaring "new" things. It's no wonder that the kingdom of God seems to go against common logic and is so surprising to us. God has made us new creations—has revealed the Kingdom to us—but our old selves are unable to make sense of it.

The kingdom of God is a dinner party that nobody wants to go to, yet we are invited. The kingdom of God also is like a lamp that keeps getting covered up. We just need to uncover it and stand aside so that it may shine.

So, all we need to do is show up with open hands and open hearts, get out of God's way (let God work), and behold the new things that God is revealing. God is turning our world on end—and turning us into new creations to fit within it.

Prayer Focus: *Pray that you will live in God's kingdom today. Though it is different from the world around you, you will become accustomed to the newness as God makes you new.*

May 27 ~ No Expiration Date

For you have been born again, not of perishable seed, but of imperishable, through the living and enduring word of God.

—1 Peter 1:23 (NIV)

I have finally started to notice the dates printed on milk cartons. I have learned the hard way that I prefer fresh milk to spoiled milk. Also, milk seems to be much more nourishing when it tastes good—when it's as it was intended to be.

Much of what I think is important and holds value is perishable. I put too much trust in that which will not last. Things around me seem to be spoiling all the time, and I cannot keep track of all the expiration dates.

When things are new in life, we get excited, as if we are returning from the store with a carton of milk to pour over a bowl of cereal first thing in the morning. Many times we depend on "new" things for our vitality, but inevitably they lose their freshness, never staying as they were intended.

According to scripture, God has placed within us an ingredient that ensures we will never spoil and will always be fresh. The Word of God keeps us from being anything less than what we were intended to be. God is nourishing us with something that is imperishable. God makes us new, and we have no expiration date.

Prayer Focus: *Thank God for making you fresh and new, and for not allowing you to spoil. Turn to God to be the person you are intended to be.*

May 28 ~ Smoke and Flames

Make us come back to you, Yahweh, and we will come back. Restore us as we were before!

—Lamentations 5:21 (NJB)

Something is done in my home state of Kansas in the spring that I think is beautiful. The dead, brown, and dried-up grasslands are burned so that new grass can grow. Before long, the pastures are black and charred, but soon little green blades of grass begin sprouting. Life begins to spring out of what appeared to be dead.

In the Scriptures, we are told that God will restore us and make us what we were before. Just as God restores the fields, so also God restores us. Lamentations says that if we are "made" to come back to God, we will. God brings us back—by force, if necessary.

It hurts to be burned, but the good news is that not only are we being restored, but we are also being remade into what God would have us become.

On the other side of the smoke and flames, there are little green blades of grass growing. We are rid of what we don't need anymore as God replaces the old with the new. We are restored. Yes, life often comes from what appeared to be dead.

Prayer Focus: Ask God to revive and replenish you, even if it means going through the flames of renewal.

May 29 ~ In Plain View

So for anyone who is in Christ, there is a new creation: the old order is gone and a new being is there to see.

—*2 Corinthians 5:17 (NJB)*

I am really bad at being able to see the hidden images in those 3-D pictures. You are supposed to stare at the picture as a whole and let your eye muscles relax so that you are not really focusing on anything at all. When you do this, an image emerges from what appears to be visual nonsense. But I never can seem to do it, and I walk away frustrated. Just because I can't see the hidden image, however, doesn't mean that it's not right in front of me.

Life is often that way. I can't even begin to imagine how many things I miss in general. Perhaps I'm focusing too hard, or not taking time to view the whole often enough. Scripture tells us that Jesus has made us a new creation and has done away with the old. There are new creations all around us, but often the newness becomes covered up by layers of dirt and dust. Yet, for those who remain in Christ, the stuff that gets in the way and keeps our newness from being in plain view is being removed. Jesus is cleaning away the debris and is putting us directly in the world's line of sight so that all may see our newness.

May 30 ~ Past the Present Confidence

But if we hope for what we do not yet have, we wait for it patiently.
—Romans 8:25 (NIV)

I once played a concert at a home for boys who had committed some fairly serious offenses but were too young to go to prison. After the concert, I ate dinner with the boys and spent some time with them. They just wanted someone's attention; they wanted to be listened to. They wanted to be with someone and to be loved. Most of them suffered from a sense of hopelessness and despair without even knowing it.

Sadly, there's not much separating those boys from most of us. However, this is the good news: There's hope in despair. Jesus comes to our rescue. He just wants our attention and wants to be listened to. He wants to be with us, to love us, and to be loved by us.

Still, it's so hard for us to find hope when we're in the midst of a desolate situation. Often tragedy sneaks up on us when we least expect it and lays waste to whatever we hold most dear. And when the "house" we have so carefully constructed begins to crumble and fall, it's difficult to notice the hope that waits past the present.

Though it's hard to see, just beyond the dust-cloud and debris, beyond the crashing and tumbling, a new house is being built for us by a pretty good carpenter.

Prayer Focus: Place your hope in the Lord. Pray that you will be able to look past the present and trust that God is preparing something better than you have known.

May 31 ~ Sweeter Than Chocolate

Like newborn babies, crave pure spiritual milk, so that by it you may grow up in your salvation, now that you have tasted that the Lord is good.
—1 Peter 2:2-3 (NIV)

I remember having milk in the afternoons in elementary school. I always looked forward to it and always asked for chocolate milk. I craved it. It was such a welcome break from worksheets.

I'm not sure if it was the milk or the passing of time or both, but I have grown a lot in the years since then. And I'm thankful that my parents and teachers gave me nourishing milk as a child.

In the Scriptures, Paul talks of craving pure spiritual milk. We are told that it makes us grow up in our salvation. So, not only does milk do a body good, but it also is good for our spirits.

As spiritual newborns, "milk" was what sustained us and got us on our spiritual feet. We may have come a long way since then, but we're still as dependent upon God to feed us now as when we were young in the faith.

Paul goes on to say that the Lord tastes good. As we grow and mature and continue to turn to God for our nourishment, we will find that the Lord is even sweeter than chocolate milk.

Prayer Focus: Depend on God for your spiritual nourishment. Ask God to continue feeding you so that you may continue to grow in hope and become the new creation you are intended to be.

June

LIVING FAITHFULLY

Julie O'Neal

June 1 ~ Timing Is Everything

For everything its season, and for every activity under heaven its time.
—Ecclesiastes 3:1 (NEB)

We complain about not having enough time in our busy schedules today. Considering that most of us are juggling school and/or work, a social life, family, and other responsibilities, it's no wonder that we wish we had more time to relax, have fun, and even sleep. As we wish for more time, we start prioritizing things that need to be done; and, unfortunately, spending time with God often becomes lower and lower on the list. We may realize that this is something we should do, and we may feel guilty about not doing it more often; yet often we simply make a mental note that we need to make a change.

Part of making God a more important and apparent part of our lives is being intentional in the way we manage our time. Although things such as work and school are significant, we must realize that what is truly important is making sure that in every single thing we do, God is right there, as much a part of it as we are. When we keep our minds set on God at all times, then any time becomes "God time." When we continuously transform ordinary time into "God time"—in every activity of the day—we come much closer to living faithfully. Being open to the ways that God is directing us, we create a communion with God. Being intentional about

149

making an effort to include God in all the decisions we make, in our actions, and in the words of our speech brings us into harmony with God.

This month we will consider what it means to live faithfully. I invite you to find time to re-center yourself in God's presence each day. Spending time with God is an important first step in learning how to live faithfully. Setting our minds on God nourishes our souls and creates within us a deep inner peace so that we may be able to live both faithfully and fully.

Prayer Focus: Is my mind set on God at all times of the day, in all my activities? How often do I set aside time just for God? How can I truly make God a priority in my life?

June 2 ~ Faithfully Discerning

"I know what I am planning for you," says the LORD. "I have good plans for you, not plans to hurt you. I will give you hope and a good future."
—Jeremiah 29:11 (NCV)

We experience much transition during our young adult years. Some of us are searching desperately for the path that God wants us to take. There are so many possibilities vying for our attention that it is difficult to decide which one to follow. Even if the path seems clear, discouragement and feelings of hopelessness can settle in when things don't go as planned. When you fail the exam you spent all week studying for, or when someone else is chosen for the job you worked so hard to get, it is as if detour signs go up, redirecting every step. All the while you're wondering where God's plan fits into the whole scheme of things. It's easy to give up and feel there is no purpose in what is happening. Frustration sets in, and you can't remember the last time things "felt right."

The good news is that God has a plan for each one of us, even though we may not know it—and especially when we don't believe it. God's plan is like a gift that is waiting to be unwrapped. God is just bursting with anticipation, ready for us to "open" the plan and take full enjoyment in it. Yet there is a time when it should be opened. If it is opened too soon, then it will spoil the period of hope and anticipation. If it's never opened, then its potential and purpose are wasted.

150

As the old saying goes, "Patience is a virtue." Knowing and believing deep down inside that God has something so wonderful, so awesome, so incredible for us makes the waiting a little more tolerable. During the hard, frustrating, almost unbearable times of wonder and uncertainty, remember: God is waiting for the right time to give you the gift. Trust in the timing and the certainty of the good plans God has for you.

Prayer Focus: Today I will ask God for patience and serenity as I wait for God's plan to be revealed to me.

June 3 ~ Spiritual Radios

"Be still, and know that I am God!"
—Psalm 46:10a (NRSV)

When I'm driving in my car, I usually have the radio on; but when my car radio was stolen, I was left with the sound of silence. As a result, I ended up hearing the radios of others around me. There was quite a diverse selection, which I might never have experienced had I not been given the gift of silence.

On a spiritual level, it's important for us to occasionally turn off our life "radios" and listen to the "radio" of God. Oftentimes our radios are going full blast with things we have to do, assignments we must prepare for, and groceries we must buy. It's times like these when we need to turn down our radios and tune ourselves in to what God is trying to tell us. Focusing on the stillness brings us one step closer to living faithfully with God.

Prayer Focus: How can I be more "in tune" with God?

June 4 ~ A Grateful Heart

Give thanks to the LORD, for he is good; his love endures forever.
—Psalm 107:1 (NIV)

I have lived near a very wealthy part of town, and I have lived in a very poor part of town. Most people in the wealthy part of town live in very expensive houses, drive only the finest cars, and wear only designer labels. The majority of people in the poor part of town struggle to make ends meet, wait for their monthly food stamps, and wear clothing from the local donation center. There is a deep sense of wrong priorities when these two extremes can be found in the same city.

In a culture that is wrapped up in greed and desire, we are called as Christians to live by a different standard. To pride ourselves because we gave a few dollars to this charity or that cause is not enough. In God's eyes, whenever we have given to "the least of these" (Matthew 25:45 NRSV), it is good. Our efforts of giving must come from our gratitude and blessings, which God has bestowed upon us. It's the attitude we have when we think about material wealth that makes a difference.

Having an abundance may not be a bad thing; how you use the wealth that God has given you is what counts. Do you immediately spend your money on things you could really live without? Do you give any portion of it back to God? Is your focus on getting what you don't have rather than on appreciating what you do?

I like the analogy of the tree that bears much fruit in order to give it away to those who don't have any. The point is not about the tree's loss of fruit, but about the generosity from which it gives. The way we use our money reflects the condition of our hearts.

Prayer Focus: Today I will thank God for the blessings in my life. How can I bless others? How can I constantly live in the attitude of gratitude?

June 5 ~ The Gift of Friendship

"Where you go I will go, and where you stay I will stay. Your people will be my people and your God my God. Where you die I will die, and there I will be buried."

—Ruth 1:16-17 (NIV)

When we are asked to name the people who are closest to us, most of us usually name family and then friends. Especially during the years of transition, bonds of friendship can go through many experiences. Some are

152

broken, weakened, or barely maintained, while others are strengthened so deeply that, regardless of difficult times, they will endure.

We can gather friends from many aspects in our lives: school, jobs, church, or groups that we're involved in. Whether right next door or a thousand miles apart, friends can feel bonded to each other. In dramatic life-changing events or simple everyday activities, friends are supportive, caring, joyful parts of our lives.

God has blessed us with people with whom we can share our hopes and dreams, our deepest secrets, the things that make us laugh, and the things that cause us pain. God also listens as we express our weaknesses and our triumphs. God's friendship, like others, is a bond that helps us get through life's fumbles and highlights. It's important to maintain our friendship with God, just as it's important to maintain our bonds of friendship with others. Our friends help us become closer to one another and closer to God, who is our ultimate friend.

Prayer Focus: Today I will thank God for those special people I call friends, remembering why they are blessings in my life. I will rest in God's true friendship and live in the assurance of God's ever-present love.

June 6 ~ Sabbath

By the seventh day God finished the work he had been doing, so he rested from all his work. God blessed the seventh day and made it a holy day, because on that day he rested from all the work that he had done in creating the world.
—Genesis 2:2-3 (NCV)

Several days ago I was up quite late working on a paper that was due the following morning. I had worked on it little by little the week before, but that was still not enough time to complete it. I ended up staying awake until the early hours of the morning. I finished the paper, got a few hours of sleep, awoke, and began my day. Although I was functional, I could tell that I was not in the same shape that I would have been with a few more hours of sleep.

In the same way, our lives can become so tired from our everyday activities and duties that we start to recognize a change taking place. Although we can function through each day, the quality is lacking. Rest and nourishment are essential not only for our health, but also for our well-being. Our moods, actions, thoughts, and conversations can be affected if we don't take time to rejuvenate and renew ourselves.

This renewal can come in various forms for each of us. Whether it is reading a book, relaxing outside, or spending time in silence, it is important to clear our minds of the clutter of the week in order to refresh our souls.

One of the Ten Commandments is to remember the Sabbath and to keep it holy. How often do we say that we're too busy or don't have enough time? God realized the need and importance of rest. It was important to God, so let it be important to us. Not only one day of the week but every day, let us remember to take time to rest in God's loving presence.

Prayer Focus: In what ways do you observe the Sabbath? How can you renew and refresh your soul?

June 7 ~ Divine Imagination

I am confident of this, that the one who began a good work among you will bring it to completion by the day of Jesus Christ.
—Philippians 1:6 (NRSV)

Imagine, if you will, a blank sheet of paper representing my life. The first lines I will draw come from my faith foundation. There are some straight lines representing all my years of being a pastor's kid, attending church, and going to Sunday school. There are some squiggly lines representing my confirmation into the church. And there are some curved lines representing my participation in my church youth group. Together these lines form a pattern. Some overlap each other while others never touch at all.

After I draw the lines, I pick up the crayons and add some color—colors representing my school, my work with church boards and agencies, and the places where I've traveled and experienced God's love. Some colors stand for my involvement with campus ministry and my passion for ministry with young people. Some colors are hard for me to add, for they represent some of the difficult decisions I've made in my life. Yet I have been greatly blessed by all the hues I have experienced thus far.

Now I pause, for I don't know which crayon to pick up next. I am listening for what will follow. Do I stop coloring? Do I change my medium and switch to markers or watercolors? Although I am unsure where I am headed, I am open to wherever God is leading. I may encounter struggles, but I know that one day my picture will be complete. I have so much confidence in the divine imagination of God that I know that my picture will contain brilliant and unique hues my eye has never seen. All I need to do is be patient and receptive so that God may lead me to the next step in completing my picture. I can't wait to see what will follow!

Prayer Focus: How do I see my life-picture developing? What makes up the splashes of color? Today I give thanks for the divine imagination of God working in me!

June 8 ~ Reconciliation

Restore to me the joy of your salvation.

—*Psalm 51:12 (NIV)*

In our violent world there are many struggles and painful experiences. Circumstances and disappointments get us down. Tiredness and stress wear us out. Anger and conflict tear up our souls. It's easy to give up and sink into depression and mediocrity. But we must not be discouraged. We have to remember that we are not alone. Whether we realize it or not, God works in all situations in our lives. When we are overwhelmed, God gives us strength and wisdom to grow from the changes taking place around us. Confusion is replaced by understanding; despair is replaced by hope.

Webster defines reconciliation as "restoring a friendship or union; to make consistent; harmony." As Christians, reconciliation is a turning away from something bad and, even more important, a reunion with God. In the depths of disappointment, reach for the healing hope of God. Let your will join the will of God. Allow the Holy Spirit to breathe a restoring breath of life into your soul. Allow yourself to turn toward the light before the hole you're sliding into gets any darker or deeper. Rely on the reconciling love of God to redirect your life.

Prayer Focus: As I look to the light of God, I pray that he may restore the joy of my life and bring me out of the darkness I feel.

June 9 ~ God's Provision

They asked only one thing, that we remember the poor, which was actually what I was eager to do.

—*Galatians 2:10 (NRSV)*

Oftentimes my family will donate to a local charity that collects clothing, toys, and other household items. This happens after we have gone through our closets and have found things that we no longer wear or find useful. One time I came across an item of clothing that still had its price tag attached. I had not worn the item even once, yet it had hung in my closet a long time. Finding it made me sharply aware of the materialism and greed that permeate our society.

Homelessness and extreme poverty exist not only in far-off counties but also right in our own cities. Too often we are not satisfied with all the material blessings that God has given us. We tend to be shallow and complain about not having enough TV channels, the latest DVD, or an expensive car. Instead, we can be grateful for the abundance we have and the many ways God has provided for us.

Prayer Focus: *Today I will ask God to help me rely on his provision. How can I live more simply?*

June 10 ~ Habits

Teach me your way, O LORD, that I may walk in your truth; give me an undivided heart to revere your name.

—*Psalm 86:11 (NRSV)*

There are many kinds of habits, such as making our beds, biting our nails, or going about our daily routines. Some habits can be good and beneficial. Washing our hands, for example, can lead to good hygiene. Exercising can lead to good health. Other habits can be harmful or damaging. Lying, for example, is destructive, and not setting limits can be wasteful. When we get into the habit of doing something, this means that a particular action manifests itself repeatedly to the benefit or detriment of ourselves and others.

Living faithfully involves certain habits that allow our faith to grow and flourish. When we attend worship, we are in fellowship with others. When we pray regularly, reflect on scripture, and tithe, we develop habits that help nurture our souls. Developing these habits takes time, but the foundation they build is strong and sure. And when we maintain these habits, we incorporate God's ways into the routines of our lives. Faithful habits can lead us toward truth and life. Maintaining these habits can strengthen a joyful heart and a giving nature and bring us closer to God.

Prayer Focus: What habits have I developed that are keeping me from being close to God? What habits bring me into harmony with God? Help me to revere you, God, with all my heart, soul, strength, and mind.

June 11 ~ God's Forgiveness

But you are a forgiving God. You are kind and full of mercy.
—Nehemiah 9:17 (NCV)

We all make bad decisions from time to time, and when we do, we usually regret the course of action we took and hope the situation will be resolved in a timely manner. Usually, we experience the consequences of our bad decision soon after we've made it—or, in some cases, possibly not until later. But, if we're wise, we admit that it wasn't the wisest of choices, we recognize any circumstances that contributed to our impaired judgment, we see how things might have been done differently and might have turned out better, and we vow to learn from the experience.

Yet in all our decisions, God is faithful to us in the way we approach the situation as well as in the outcome. No matter how bad the decision, God is there, reminding us that we are God's children and that, through Jesus, our sins are forgiven. This doesn't mean that we should ignore the wise advice of those around us; rather, we should listen for the voice of God in others, in scripture, and in prayer. When we make mistakes and fall flat on our face, God is there to remember the good and forgive the bad.

We will make bad decisions; that is inevitable. But we are equipped with the promise that God is with us, reminding us that forgiveness is a very inevitable part of life as well.

Prayer Focus: I will allow God to help me choose wisely in all my decisions, and I will give praise for the reassurance of God's promise to comfort me.

June 12 ~ Idols

"Of what value is an idol, since a man has carved it?"
—Habakkuk 2:18 (NIV)

What is an idol? When we hear the word, we often think of some sort of large statue of a powerful godlike image to which one bows down and worships in a humble manner. One example might be a huge golden cow. Certainly for Aaron and others in the wilderness, this was their image. But this is the twenty-first century! That sort of image is rare and uncommon. Or is it?

Idolatry may not be expressed today in bowing down to golden statues, but it is often expressed in trusting one's own power or the things one has made or created. Through this form of idolatry, the act of creating and sustaining takes hold of one's idea of who's in charge. Does the "I can do it myself" attitude sound familiar? Have you ever taken matters into your own hands, rather than trusting that God is in control? This sort of attitude can lead to self-idolatry.

We also have the problem of worshiping "things" we have rather than the One who has blessed us with them. Have you ever said the words "I would die if I lost this," or "I just could not live without . . . "? In many ways, our possessions can be so controlling that they actually have the power to make us think we can't live without them. This idolatry can be damaging to our relationship with God, stealing away our trust and loyalty.

We are to trust and be loyal to God, not to the idols we create for ourselves—for this is what God wants. Instead of "carving" images to worship, let us allow God to carve our hearts.

Prayer Focus: *Is there anything, other than God, that has power over me? How can I get rid of the attitude of idolatry?*

June 13 ~ Building a Heavenly Home

And I shall dwell in the house of the LORD my whole life long.
—Psalm 23:6 (NRSV)

On a recent visit home from school, I reflected on the way a house can become a home. The house that my parents own has been our house for

158

over nine years. We have lived in the house—every evening, slept, and eaten in the house for this long period. It is where we carry out the practical skills of life, but it also is where we encounter many joys, endure many pains, experience precious moments, and struggle with life's hard situations. This is what makes a house a home. When memories are made, not only about the house itself but also about the relationships and experiences within the house, the house becomes a familiar place.

In the same way, we have a home with God. We can build our heavenly house by maintaining habits of prayer, nurturing our fellowship with other Christians, and tending our souls through scripture. When we build our house on the foundation of Christ, God makes the relationship we have built into a home. Our memories and moments with God make an impression that allows us to dwell in God's house forever. In all the rooms, we are invited to come and take part in the living that gives everlasting life and hope in the community of God.

Prayer Focus: *How can I build a heavenly house to reside in? What moments have already been created in my home with God?*

June 14 ~ Worshiping God

"Woman, believe me, the hour is coming when you will worship the Father neither on this mountain nor in Jerusalem. . . . But the hour is coming, and is now here, when the true worshipers will worship the Father in spirit and truth, for the Father seeks such as these to worship him."

—John 4:21-23 (NRSV)

I have many close friends I met in our church's youth group. Back then, we saw one another only during our youth group activities; but as time passed, our friendship soon extended outside those settings. Some of us have graduated from high school and college and have gone our separate ways. Yet despite these changes, we have remained close friends.

One thing in most of our lives that has seen the effect of time and transition is church attendance—or rather, the lack of it. I've had many discussions with friends about why they don't attend church regularly anymore, what inspires or dissuades them from attending, and what they think about church in general. Some find God in the high church liturgical styles of worship, while others really connect with God in a more contemporary praise and worship service. Some fall in between these extremes and can find God just about anywhere.

In today's scripture passage, Jesus notes that it is not the place of worship but our response to God's gift of himself that is important. It matters not where we worship but that we keep God as the center of our praise and adoration. Focusing on God does not excuse lack of involvement in the act of corporate worship, but it points to the real reason that we come together for worship.

Wherever we may worship God, let us worship in spirit and truth.

Prayer Focus: What do I find appealing about corporate worship? Unappealing? How can I worship God in sincere spirit and truth?

June 15 ~ "I'll Pray for You"

Pray in the Spirit at all times with all kinds of prayers, asking for everything you need. To do this you must always be ready and never give up. Always pray for all God's people.

—Ephesians 6:18 (NCV)

"I'll pray for you; I'll keep you in my prayers; my prayers are with you." Has anyone ever said these phrases to you? Sometimes we hear them when we are going through a tough time, when we do not understand the reason for events, or when we or family members are ill. But what does it mean to keep someone in prayer? Is it enough to lift up a name during a worship service, a Sunday school class or group Bible study, or a private time of intercessory prayer? And what do we say when we pray? Do we ask for God to wrap his arms around them and bring them comfort and security? Do we ask for patience and healing for the wounds that they have? Do we ask for strength and strong faith so that they don't stray from God's love? The answer is yes, all of the above, and more!

God hears all our prayers, regardless of what they're for. When we pray, we are to take time to talk with God about the needs of others as well as our own joys and concerns. Lifting others up in prayer helps us grow closer to God as well as to those around us. Through intercessory prayer we invite God to intervene in human affairs, allowing us to discover the beneficial process of prayer.

160

June 16 ~ "Who Says?"

Be an example to the believers with your words, your actions, your love, your faith, and your pure life.

—1 Timothy 4:12b (NCV)

In this age of technology, there are many "authoritative sources." Music, movies, television, magazines, tabloids, and radio all compete for our attention and our time. They bombard us with information that we are to process. We get various points of view, depending on how much we want to believe what is being said and our capacity for critical thinking. Do we listen to a song because we like the beat, or are we really listening to the ideas that the words promote? Where are we finding our authority? Is the source trustworthy? Is the topic credible and worthy of our attention?

The authority of God, Scripture, reason, and (Christian) tradition are the basis of our spiritual nourishment. These things fill us with the knowledge and wisdom of knowing more about God, who is all-powerful and everlasting. These things give us authority for filtering what we read, hear, watch, and observe.

In biblical times, some people were chosen by God to be prophets, to bring a message to the people. Today we read and hear the words of Christ, which give us guidance and a clearer picture of faithful, righteous living. May we continue to live in the authority of Christ as an example to all God's children.

Prayer Focus: Today I will thank God for the authority that guides my life. I will ask for the ability to exude the love of God to others as an example of the true source of light and life.

June 17 ~ "Did You Hear . . . ?"

I may speak in different languages of people or even angels. But if I do not have love, I am only a noisy bell or a crashing cymbal.

—1 Corinthians 13:1 (NCV)

Have you ever been in a situation where someone begins to say something derogatory about another who is not present? Not knowing exactly what to say, maybe you stammer something about not knowing that person. Or maybe you politely excuse yourself from the conversation. Or maybe, against your better judgment, you enter the conversation.

Gossip can arise out of nowhere, whether we are in a social or business setting, and it can be harmful to all involved. Gossip can take the form of malicious, envious clatter or meaningless, idle talk. Either way, engaging in gossip is talking about someone in a destructive manner when, instead, we should be uplifting and supporting that person in a Christian attitude.

Because of the nature of gossip, there can be a fine line between talking about someone with mean intentions and talking about someone out of genuine care and concern. Making someone else's pain or concern part of your own business is all right when you intend to help or alleviate that hurt; it's not all right when you do not plan to give encouragement or support. As members of a faithful community, we must be careful when we begin to talk about others. Asking ourselves if it is something God would want us to discuss can be a good reminder.

Next time we enter a situation where gossip could erupt, let us remember to say and do all things in a Christlike spirit.

Prayer Focus: When was the last time I felt the urge to gossip about others? How can God help me to turn a conversation from gossip to genuine care and concern?

June 18 ~ Lifetime Guarantee

The LORD is good. His love is forever, and his loyalty goes on and on.
—Psalm 100:5 (NCV)

"Lifetime Guarantee." How many times have we seen that promise on a product or service? What quality and craftsmanship must be present in order for something to last a lifetime? How many things actually have the capacity to last a whole lifetime?

There aren't many things that have the ability to endure the trials of time and wear and tear. In fact, there are few things durable enough to last a few years, let alone a generation or two. Many nonmaterial things also pass away in time, things such as minor problems, bad days, successes, and joys. But one thing that won't fade is God and his promises to us. The promise that God will be with us is a guarantee—a guarantee that will last not only for a lifetime but for all of eternity. The things of this world can hardly compare to that.

Regardless of what trials we face and what errors we make, God is here. In our times of celebrating and praising, God is here. In our times of struggling, searching, and questioning, God is here. God will always be here. We don't have to worry about God disappearing or fading away. We can depend on God. Now that's a promise that will last a lifetime.

Prayer Focus: In what ways is God's promise that his love will endure forever comforting to me? How have I experienced this enduring love?

June 19 ~ New Beginnings

Anyone who is joined to Christ is a new being; the old is gone, the new has come.
—2 Corinthians 5:17 (GNT)

Spring, butterflies, a sunrise, toddlers taking their first steps, freshly cut grass, dandelions, new babies, buds on trees, longer days—these things hold promise, hope, and encouragement for a fresh start. They are signs of new beginnings—each open to the inspiring, refreshing, amazing, sustaining, life-giving presence of God. All around us are wild possibilities of God's newness, reminding us that we are new creations, each unique in our own way.

When we choose to live faithfully, we choose to loosen ourselves from the grip of old things, damaging things, and destructive things. Darkness in our lives can be brought on by being stressed or fatigued, not spending time with God, or making bad choices. Renewing ourselves spiritually, mentally, emotionally, and even physically brings forth the joy of new life. We choose to enter into a life that is abundant with grace, forgiveness, and everlasting love. God has promised these things to us when we are joined with Christ. Being free allows us to live with such passion and enthusiasm that each day becomes a new beginning to live faithfully.

Prayer Focus: Today I will celebrate the new life that I have been given. I will look for ways that my life is plentiful with God's blessings.

June 20 ~ "But What Can I Do?"

He has told you, O mortal, what is good; and what does the LORD require of you but to do justice, and to love kindness, and to walk humbly with your God?
—Micah 6:8 (NRSV)

There is a popular saying that goes something like this: "One person can make a difference." What are the odds that one person out of all the billions of people in the world can really make a significant difference? Actually, they're pretty good! Just think about people such as Gandhi, Mother Teresa, and Abraham Lincoln. They were just ordinary people who did extraordinary things. Their motivation wasn't self-glorification; rather, they felt compelled to answer the call for justice.

We, too, are called to act for justice wherever we see injustice being done. Being involved in our local communities, keeping current with the news near and far, and acting upon our convictions are ways that we can help justice to flourish. Sticking up for the underdog, being a good steward of the earth's resources, or campaigning for an important cause allows us to feel the call to justice. God may press upon our hearts the need to act in a particular situation, moving us with courage or compassion. Yes, one person *can* make a difference, no matter how insignificant it may seem. God's purpose is in all things, working for good.

Acting justly, loving kindness, and walking humbly with God constitute social action and morality that are rooted in religion. When we combine these three, we worship God through serving and sticking up for others.

Prayer Focus: *Are there areas in my life, community, or church where I or others are acting justly—or unjustly? How can I become involved in doing justice?*

June 21 ~ Forgotten

I will not forget you. See, I have inscribed you on the palms of my hands.
—Isaiah 49:15-16 (NRSV)

Sometimes we forget things. The things we forget are usually not as drastic as leaving a child somewhere or leaving something on a hot stove; generally they're things such as an appointment at the dentist's office, something we were supposed to buy at the grocery store, a friend's birthday, or even directions to the library.

We may not realize we've forgotten something until it's too late—or until we are sharply reminded. But the sinking feeling is always the same. So we try to remember things by writing them down, repeating them, scribbling them on our hand, or associating them with other things.

Sometimes we're the ones who are forgotten, and it's not a fun feeling either. When someone forgets to meet you for lunch, or when no one remembers your birthday, it leaves you with a rotten, unworthy feeling.

God did not forget the Israelites, his chosen people, even when they felt forgotten. He reminded them that regardless of their trials and struggles and their feelings of hopelessness and restlessness, he did not forget them. In fact, he reassured them by saying he so wanted to remember they were his people, and were important enough not to forget, that he inscribed their names on his hand.

We are bound to forget things, and we hope it won't happen too often. But we can be assured that God will never forget us. What comfort and security that brings. How wonderful it is to be remembered by God!

Prayer Focus: Are there important people in my life whom I've forgotten? How can I let them know how much they mean to me?

June 22 ~ Third Rock from the Sun

We brought nothing into the world, so we can take nothing out.
—*1 Timothy 6:7 (NCV)*

I recently began a recycling program in my dorm. We recycle plastic, cardboard, paper, and other materials. My desire to do this comes from growing up in a city that implemented a recycling program, knowing that we live in a wasteful society, and wanting to take care of the earth. I know that all the materials we have come from God, and a way to give back is to be a good steward of the earth on which we are privileged to live.

By our conscious acts may we always be mindful that we are only in this world for a short time, and that the decisions we make regarding the resources we have affect not only those around us but also future generations. Accumulating goods, hoarding possessions, and having a wasteful greediness are dangers implied by today's verse. The verse isn't saying that we should neglect our normal physical needs; rather, it means that we should be cautious about how we use what God has given us. By giving back and recycling the limited amount of resources we have, we gain the satisfaction of knowing we are making rightful use of God's world.

Prayer Focus: In what areas of my life can I be a better keeper of God's world?

June 23 ~ I've Got the Joy

"I have told you these things so that you can have the same joy I have and so that your joy will be the fullest possible joy."

—John 15:11 (NCV)

Joy, rapture, amazement, happiness, excitement, delight, elation—these are emotions we have when something good happens to us. We scream, shout, jump up and down. We can hardly contain ourselves.

I've always been amazed by the miracle that God performed in Jesus Christ and by what his resurrection meant for believers—not only those who lived in his day, but us today as well. Just think how Mary, the mother of Jesus, must have felt when she encountered him after he had risen from the dead. She was the one who gave birth to him and stayed with him until his death on the cross. She must have been devastated by the events that led to his death. Her grief must have been overwhelming. Yet all of that changed when she found out that her son was raised from the dead. Her heart must have been ecstatic! Her spirit must have leapt for joy! Only God could have provided this inexplicable joy despite the events that had happened.

In the same way, we can celebrate and have an ineffable joy at the idea of this divine miracle. Being thankful is a faithful response to God's love. Our praise and elation for God is pleasing to our souls and is music to the ears of God. As a good friend of mine says, "Embrace the joy!"

Prayer Focus: Today I will give praise and thanks to God for the great things in my life, for those around me, and for the gift of Jesus Christ who gives me joy.

166

June 24 ~ Extra Baggage

Trust in the LORD with all your heart and lean not on your own understanding; in all your ways acknowledge him, and he will make your paths straight.
—Proverbs 3:5-6 (NIV)

When I was young, my family took many vacations during the summer. Some places we drove to; some we reached by airplane. With six members in the family, my father always said, "Only pack what you can carry." That way we all could manage our own bags, and he wouldn't get stuck carrying heavy bags that he didn't pack. I also think he said this because he was cautioning us from over-packing. We asked ourselves, *What things are essential to our trip, and what things can be left behind?* We were equipped with only the necessary items that would enable us to fully enjoy our journey.

God also wants us to pack only what we can carry, filling our hearts and minds with spiritual disciplines, caring attitudes, and a joyful spirit. This way we will be equipped when we have to face adversity, discouraging times, and painful moments. We can trust that God will show us what will be necessary and what we can leave behind. With careful preparation and God's help, we can enjoy the most awesome trip we've ever had.

Prayer Focus: Am I holding on to extra "bags"? What things can keep me from trusting God?

June 25 ~ Man in the Moon

To have faith is to be sure of the things we hope for, to be certain of the things we cannot see.
—Hebrews 11:1 (GNT)

In college I was required to take an astronomy course. We learned about comets, stars, and galaxies, but my favorite part of the course was the section about the moon. It was fascinating to discover the reason for the craters, the phases of the moon, and its influence on the earth. I love being able to look at the moon through a telescope and see its beauty magnified. I feel so close to God, and I marvel at the beauty and harmony of creation.

167

The phase of the moon that amazes me most is the new moon. This occurs when the earth is between the sun and the moon, casting a shadow on the moon. Although we are unable to see the moon while it is in this phase, we know that it is still there.

This constant presence reminds me that God will always be with us. Whether life's struggles cast a shadow on his presence or the clear skies illuminate it, God's promise to be with us overwhelmingly abounds. It's comforting to know that in a culture where seeing means believing, God transcends all proof and allows trust and faith to flourish.

Prayer Focus: Today I will remember that whether seen or unseen, God's presence is always with us.

June 26 ~ Fine Print

In reading this, then, you will be able to understand my insight into the mystery of Christ.

—Ephesians 3:4 (NIV)

On her way to church one day, a friend of mine passed various road signs. First she passed a large billboard for a nearby restaurant. The next one she passed was a medium-sized sign advertising a golf range. Then came a small sign, with words written in large letters, advertising a garage sale. Despite the different sizes, all of the signs had small print at the bottom. The large billboard had its address at the bottom so that people would know how to get to it. The medium sign stated the rates for golfing. At the bottom of the small sign was the address of where the sale was taking place. In each case, the reader had to look a bit closer at the sign to understand the entire message.

In the same way, God is in the small print of our lives. We are like a giant billboard that people may see from far away. The things we do each day show who we are, what we like or dislike, and how we treat others. In order for people to see our faith and whose we are, they must look at the fine print of our lives. With this close examination, they will be able to see where and how our faith and devotion to God manifest themselves in our lives. They will see that the big things make sense after reading the stuff below.

168

May our lives be an example for others, so that they can understand that God works in the fine print of our lives.

Prayer Focus: What areas of my life display the fine print of God?

June 27 ~ Bread of Life

Jesus said to them, "I am the bread of life. Whoever comes to me will never be hungry, and whoever believes in me will never be thirsty."
—*John 6:35 (NRSV)*

Food, nourishment, cuisine, grub, chow, groceries—whatever you call it, it's all the same. We all need food to nourish our bodies and survive. We eat at many different times throughout the day, whether we're eating three square meals or grabbing a bite here and there. The way we eat varies as well, from enjoying a seven-course meal to scraping the cupboards. But no matter how full our stomachs may be, we still may be lacking in "spiritual food."

Fasting, serving food at a soup kitchen, and donating food to a food bank are ways that we can help others meet their daily needs. Just as spending time with friends allows us to nourish those friendships, spending time with God allows us to nourish our souls. The love God has for each of us is enough to fill us so that our cup runs over. We will be fed plentifully if we live faithfully for God. As today's scripture indicates, our spiritual appetites will never go hungry with divine provisions.

Prayer Focus: How I am being spiritually nourished? In what ways am I "going hungry" spiritually?

June 28 ~ Is Anyone There?

"I will be with you always, even until the end of this age."
—*Matthew 28:20b (NCV)*

Have you ever called out in a cave or down in a deep ravine? "Hellooo," you call, listening as your voice echoes for quite some time. Usually the only sound you hear is the same one that you sent. When you are feeling lonely, this echo can seem to go on forever, without any sign of hope for an answer.

Loneliness can creep up on you without notice and leave you feeling empty and upset. It covers you with an insatiable emptiness that puts you into a funk. Its grasp can seem so strong that daily activities become dull and your attitude becomes dejected. You don't feel like doing anything when days seem gloomy, dismal, and disconsolate. Your mood is pensive and melancholy.

It is during these lost, lonely, desperate times of sadness and emptiness that God is quietly yet amazingly at work. God is growing us, strengthening us, and encouraging us so that we may recognize his bountiful grace, his loving arms, and his eternal love. His presence catches us, puts us back on our feet, and renews the disparities in our lives. All we have to do is ask, and it is ours. God's generosity overflows, and his promises are constant.

God's calming peace, which surprises us, is a means of grace. It arrives to gently announce God's presence. God is with us. God has never left us. Though we may have felt we were alone, the truth is that we are never truly alone. And when we are in tune to God's presence, we have faithful hearts, ecstatic laughter, and joyful spirits.

Although human companionship is wonderful, God's companionship is even better. Through Jesus, God has promised to be with us—always, forever, until the end of time.

Prayer Focus: *Today I will pray for those who may feel alone.*

June 29 ~ Picture Perfect

"Be still, and know that I am God; I will be exalted among the nations, I will be exalted in the earth."

—*Psalm 46:10 (NIV)*

Not too long ago I began a scrapbook project that involved pictures, scissors, and various shapes, sizes, and colors of paper. As I looked at each set of pictures, I not only thought about how I wanted to place them on the page and what colors of paper would coordinate, but I also recalled when and where the pictures were taken. The pictures captured moments

170

when I was enjoying time with friends or family—laughing, playing, and having a good time. Sometimes it would be a special occasion, a holiday gathering, or simply a night of hanging out at home. I cherish and treasure these moments, for they were times well spent.

God gives us time to enjoy each moment of our lives. Whether talking with a five-year-old or going to a baseball game with a parent, we should enjoy the opportunity and live in the moment. Time is a precious commodity. We need to be thankful for the occasions when we gather together, as well as those when we are alone. Rather than rushing through time or thinking about what is on your to-do list, reflect on what is going on—right now in this moment. Invite God's presence to enter your time. Listen to what God is saying to you. Hear God speaking to your soul. Let each moment be a picture in your mind and on your heart that will be treasured for time to come.

Prayer Focus: What "pictures" are significant to you? Focus on where God is in these moments.

June 30 ~ Tell Me That Old, Old Story

Since you were a child you have known the Holy Scriptures which are able to make you wise. And that wisdom leads to salvation through faith in Christ Jesus. . . . Using the Scriptures, the person who serves God will be capable, having all that is needed to do every good work.
—2 Timothy 3:15, 17 (NCV)

My siblings and I always enjoyed listening to our grandparents' stories of the childhood days of our parents and aunts and uncles. It was neat to hear about the tricks they played on each other, the things they did while growing up, and the way that those things are echoed in our own behaviors today. We loved for them to tell us those stories over and over while we imagined what it would have been like to have been with our parents at that moment in time.

In the same way, understanding the history of Christian traditions can be just as fulfilling and enriching. Finding out that there were people who were similar to us in many ways, hearing of the great battles and struggles they went through, and understanding what their lives were like help give us a greater appreciation of the heritage we follow. Guided by the examples of those historic figures, we gain a sense of thankfulness and encouragement. Studying the Scriptures helps us understand the way that God works not only in the world but also in our lives. As we increase in our biblical and doctrinal knowledge, our love and understanding for what we believe also will increase, so that we may be faithful people called by God.

May we always want to hear the "old, old story" over and over again, and may its retelling help us live both faithfully and fully.

Prayer Focus: *What are some of the great stories of your faith? Reflect on the importance of these stories to your life. How do they help you live faithfully?*

July

CHRISTLIKE RELATIONSHIPS

Christopher Cropsey

July 1 ~ Following a Basic Blueprint

"So in everything, do to others what you would have them do to you, for this sums up the Law and the Prophets."

—Matthew 7:12 (NIV)

*I*t's so easy for us as Christians to focus on all the little details of our faith and forget the big picture. In other words, we often forget how simple living the Christian life can be. As a matter of fact, the perfect guideline for all our interactions with other people can be summed up in one short verse: the Golden Rule.

Some might think that the Golden Rule is something for little kids to memorize in Sunday school, that it's a bit childish for the complexities of adulthood. What a fallacy! After all, it's one of the two commandments that Jesus said summed up the whole law of God. How can we gloss over that?

Often in our relationships with others, we focus on the situations we find ourselves in rather than the way we should treat those involved. Although the situations themselves are important, even more important is this timeless principle: We are to love others as ourselves. Interestingly enough, at times when we aren't sure exactly how to deal with someone, simply remembering this principle seems to clear up most of the confusion.

You might say that the Golden Rule is a basic blueprint for Christlike relationships. This month we'll take a closer look at what it means to build relationships with others in a Christlike manner. It's an essential part of our Christian walk, for virtually every aspect of our lives involves relating to others in some way. If we are to be followers of Christ, then we must learn how to relate to others as he did.

Prayer Focus: How often do I love others as I love myself? How might following the Golden Rule affect my relationships with others—particularly relationships with difficult people?

July 2 ~ Extending Christian Love

Dear children, let us not love with words or tongue but with actions and in truth.
—1 John 3:18 (NIV)

When we think of Christian love, we often think of 1 Corinthians 13, the "love chapter" of the Bible. Certainly this passage is one of the most beautiful in the Bible—and a favorite of many people. However, it is one thing to read the passage and another thing to truly apply its principles in our lives.

As Christians, we are supposed to extend these qualities of love to every person in the world. This concept confuses some people, because they think they are supposed to *like* everyone. But as C. S. Lewis points out in his classic *Mere Christianity*, it is possible to love yourself and, at the same time, not like yourself. Similarly, we don't have to like others in order to love them.

We are not called to enjoy being around everyone, but we are called to be patient, kind, and courteous to everyone. What a difference we could make if we actually lived out that ideal! "Dear friends, since God so loved us, we also ought to love one another" (1 John 4:11).

Prayer Focus: How can I extend Christian love to the people I know? How can I show Christian love to strangers?

July 3 ~ Encouraging Others

Therefore encourage one another and build each other up, just as in fact you are doing.

—1 Thessalonians 5:11 (NIV)

174

We all know the great feeling that comes when someone lifts us up on a bad day. Just when we think no one could care whether or not we existed, someone comes up to us and shows us that, yes, there actually is someone out there who truly cares about us. If it weren't for these people, we probably would despair and just give up. But as much as we appreciate it when others give us this kind of support, we too seldom look for opportunities to give it to others.

Think about it: when was the last time you took the effort to intentionally encourage someone? If it has been recent, congratulations. If not, the time is now! We are surrounded, unfortunately, by many people who are suffering. Some may show it clearly; others may keep it hidden or may wear "masks." Either way, a kind word can go a long way for someone who's hurting.

Send a card to someone you know who has been having a rough week. This only takes a second, but the potential for affecting a life is huge. Not only will this improve the person's outlook on life, but it also will strengthen the bond between you in a way that nothing else can. And if that isn't reason enough, then remember that it's a command from God. So keep your eyes open for hurting people; your encouragement will help make the world a better place.

Prayer Focus: Who around me is hurting and reaching out for love, either verbally or nonverbally? How can I encourage this person?

July 4 ~ Praying for Others

Therefore confess your sins to each other and pray for each other so that you may be healed. The prayer of a righteous man is powerful and effective.
—James 5:16 (NIV)

"I'll be praying for you." How many times have you either spoken or heard these words? Probably more than you can count. This is perhaps one of the most used and, consequently, least appreciated phrases of Christian expression. That is a strong statement, and one that is sad to admit; but nonetheless, there is some truth in it.

Why has such a powerful expression been relegated to such an unappreciated level? Two reasons come to mind. First, how often do we forget to pray for people after we have told them we will? This, needless to say, is a big problem. The second reason goes a bit deeper: We often forget the true power of prayer. If someone is having a bad day and we offer to pray for the person, do we not believe that in doing so we can actually have an impact on that person's life? If we do, then there is no excuse not to do so.

Simply put, we have forgotten that prayer really does work. So the next time you tell someone you will pray for him or her, get on your knees and do it. Remember, prayer is "powerful and effective"!

Prayer Focus: Who needs my prayers today? How can I be more effective in my prayers on behalf of others?

July 5 ~ Forgiving Others

Be kind and compassionate to one another, forgiving each other, just as in Christ God forgave you.

—Ephesians 4:32 (NIV)

Sadly enough, being hurt is a fact of life; there can be no candy coating over it. People make rude comments, let us down, abuse our trust, and otherwise injure us both physically and emotionally. Since there is no question of whether or not we get hurt, the question becomes, how do we respond to it and learn to forgive?

There are few times when forgiveness comes easily. As a matter of fact, it is probably the hardest response for many of us to make. And why shouldn't it be? The person did wound us, after all. Is this the kind of person who really deserves our forgiveness anyway? Well, we know that Jesus' answer to that question was an emphatic yes. And just to show us how serious he was about it, he gave us the ultimate example: After we spurned him, he forgave us. He even forgave us for everything we were yet to do! How incredible that is!

In light of this truth, we have no other choice but to forgive others when they hurt us. And as always, God is there to help us. Often, it is only through God's strength that we are able to forgive others for the deep pain they have caused us. Last, our forgiveness must be unconditional; we aren't allowed to give up on someone simply because we're sick of broken promises and empty apologies. Our forgiveness must be complete, genuine, and God-centered.

Prayer Focus: Is there anyone I am harboring a grudge against? How can I draw upon God's love to forgive this person?

July 6 ~ Judging Others

You, then, why do you judge your brother? Or why do you look down on your brother? For we will all stand before God's judgment seat.
—Romans 14:10 (NIV)

"People in glass houses don't throw stones." I don't know about you, but when I was growing up, I heard my parents, teachers, and relatives tell me this so many times I thought I would go crazy. I suppose I need to keep hearing it, because judging others is still a struggle.

Judging others might be considered the evil cousin of accountability. Often, instead of holding one another accountable in Christian love and nurturing one another in the right way of living, we condemn one another through our words and actions. Why is it that we forget to pull the plank out of our own eye before we try to get the splinter out of someone else's eye? What is it that makes us so prone to judge others? Perhaps we inherently think that we are always right. After all, we probably wouldn't criticize someone else's habits if we didn't think ours were correct. So the question becomes, how can we avoid this bad habit?

A good first step is to realize that we may not be absolutely correct in our opinion of the other person. Obviously, there are going to be times when our judgment *is* correct, but there also will be many times when we make hasty generalizations. Second, we must be careful never to personally vilify someone. Simply changing our attitude toward the other person can help. Remember, the more often we throw stones, or judge others, the more often our glass houses are going to get broken.

Prayer Focus: Is there anyone I am directly or indirectly judging? What would God have me to do? How can I stop this pattern?

July 7 ~ Gossiping

A perverse man stirs up dissension, and a gossip separates close friends.
—Proverbs 16:28 (NIV)

Gossip is fun; there's no sense denying it. If it weren't, we wouldn't indulge in it so freely! And who hasn't ever felt a strange kind of excitement when hearing an especially juicy tidbit? Of course, we all love to gloss over the ugly side of gossip: the damage to the person who is being talked about. We hope this person will never know what has been said—and besides, he or she should have thought about that possibility before doing whatever he or she did, right?

It's so easy to gloss over the ugliness of gossip. Compassion flies out the window in a heartbeat to be replaced with our own selfish desires. Sure, we come up with some clever ways to justify it. How many times have you said, "Let me tell you about what so-and-so did so that you can pray for him or her"? Yet that's nothing but spiritualized gossip. With it come the same problems that accompany all gossip: (1) It tends to lose its truthfulness; and (2) It's as impossible to take back as it is to put toothpaste back in the tube. In reality, gossip is one of those things in life that harms all involved, not just the person(s) being talked about.

So, as tempting as it may be to share some wonderful secret we just discovered, we must remember to bite our tongues. God, the others involved, and even we ourselves will be glad we did!

Prayer Focus: Am I helping to spread rumors? How might these rumors be causing harm, whether or not the persons involved know about the rumors? What steps can I take to stop the rumors?

July 8 ~ Combating Peer Pressure

Do not conform any longer to the pattern of this world, but be transformed by the renewing of your mind. Then you will be able to test and approve what God's will is—his good, pleasing and perfect will.
—Romans 12:2 (NIV)

One of the things we often think we've outgrown is peer pressure. Sure, we had peer pressure as teenagers, but it's a thing of the past—the same as "puppy love" and all those other childish issues, right? What a misperception! Peer pressure is alive and well in adulthood; it simply has become more passive. Don't we feel we must work hard to earn money in order to compare with those around us? Although no one may directly say anything to us about it, we still feel the silent pressure to achieve, perform, and excel.

There are several things we can do to combat this pressure. First, we shouldn't compare ourselves to others. Not only can making comparisons lead to feelings of inferiority, but it also can lead to bad decisions. If we're not careful, the unspoken pressures placed on us by society can subtly lead us into behaviors that contradict our values and beliefs. Instead, we should focus on what God calls us to do—on what God wants for our lives. We must let God be our measuring stick, allowing his influence, rather than the influence of others, to be our guide.

Prayer Focus: What areas of my life are being dictated by what other people think or say? How can I give these areas over to God's plan for me?

July 9 ~ Comparing Yourself with Others

To this you were called, because Christ suffered for you, leaving you an example, that you should follow in his steps.
—1 Peter 2:21 (NIV)

A destructive habit that is dangerously deceptive is comparing ourselves to others. Think of it as self-imposed peer pressure. Instead of being convinced by our friends to act a certain way, we convince ourselves that we need to be like them. Often we view ourselves as "below" them somehow—as inferior because we aren't as smart, good-looking, or rich as they are. And, we reason, this makes us less worthy in some way. In Dr. James Dobson's book *Life on the Edge*, he says that comparing ourselves to others causes us to feel inferior. It's a serious problem.

While this kind of comparison is decidedly negative, there is a positive kind of comparison. Instead of trying to meet the supposed standards of others, we should be trying to attain the example set by Christ. Who better is there to compare ourselves to, and to work toward emulating? Jesus was sinless and righteous; and, as Christians, our ultimate goal always should be to act as much like him as possible. After all, the word *Christian* literally means "little Christ."

179

The next time we are tempted to compare ourselves to those around us, let us instead shift our focus to Jesus. Although his standard is higher than any we could set for ourselves, he is always there to give us guidance and help. And that's a promise others can't fulfill.

Prayer Focus: Am I comparing myself to the people around me or to Christ's example? Am I allowing comparisons with others to push my self-image down? How can I use comparison to conform myself to Christ's standards?

July 10 ~ Getting Along with Others

Show proper respect to everyone.

—1 Peter 2:17a (NIV)

One of the biggest adjustments I faced after leaving home for college was living with a roommate. Even though I had lived with a brother at home, at least I could go to my own room, shut the door, and be alone for a while. Those days are gone! With dorm living, privacy flies out the window. It's kind of like taking a crash course in how to get along with people.

How do we get along with others—particularly those we interact with on a daily basis? A good guideline is to show proper respect at all times. First of all, it smoothes over many of the wrinkles that are bound to come up when living or working in close quarters with someone. Second, it is what God requires of us. Simply put, we are to put our desires second and look out for the other person first. If we are able to do this, or at least are willing to try, then our relationships will be much more pleasant—and, more important, more pleasing to God.

Prayer Focus: Do I show proper respect to everyone I encounter—particularly those I interact with on a daily basis? What can I do to show respect in each of these relationships?

July 11 ~ Arguing with Other Christians About Beliefs

Don't have anything to do with foolish and stupid arguments, because you know they produce quarrels.

—2 Timothy 2:23 (NIV)

180

Disagreements, as we all know from experience, are as inevitable as death and taxes. This is especially true when discussing doctrine, or beliefs, with other Christians. We all know people who are so headstrong that they will attack anything they find remotely different from their own beliefs. You probably have had at least one conversation in which you felt you were criticized by a fellow Christian for holding a particular view. Interestingly enough, it seems that the most trivial tenets raise the most dander in such discussions.

So is there a proper way to argue about doctrine as a Christian? Absolutely! Most important to remember is that the person you are talking to is a fellow brother or sister in Christ. This means that you aren't allowed to take personal potshots at the other person. After all, he or she probably thinks your position has as many shortcomings as you see in his or hers. Instead, try to understand before making yourself understood. Many times a conflict can be cleared up if one person will stop pushing his or her own doctrine and really listen to the different viewpoint.

Above all, we should remember that it's all right to differ. After all, we cannot agree with everyone on everything. There are going to be times when we just have to accept our differences; let us do so in a Christlike manner.

Prayer Focus: Whom do I disagree with? Whom do I disagree with frequently? How can I discuss our opposing views in a more Christian manner?

July 12 ~ Being Accountable

As iron sharpens iron, so one man sharpens another.
—Proverbs 27:17 (NIV)

I find the whole idea of accountability to be difficult to implement. By accountability, I mean looking out for another Christian—helping to keep him or her in step with Christ and away from sin. There are so many ways to go awry with this process. Many times pointing out problems in a friend's life often stems from—or leads to—self-righteousness in our own. And sometimes the other person does not receive this advice in a positive manner and is offended. Yet regardless of the possible ill effects, accountability is a critical part of any Christian relationship.

Who can help us in our spiritual walk besides others who are on the path with us? In fact, it is precisely because we are en route to the same destination that we are charged with the duty of helping our brothers and sisters in Christ. The important thing to keep in mind with accountability is that we are trying to help, not judge, another. With prayer and love and good intentions, accountability can be one of the greatest relationship-builders between Christians.

Prayer Focus: Do I know anyone I should be helping in his or her spiritual journey? How can God help me to do this lovingly, sincerely, and humbly? Do I have someone in my life who can encourage me and help hold me accountable? If not, how can I go about finding such a person?

July 13 ~ Worshiping Together

"God is spirit, and his worshipers must worship in spirit and in truth."
—John 4:24 (NIV)

One of the most powerful interactions we can have with our brothers and sisters in Christ is in the context of worship. In many situations, the only thing we have in common with other believers is our faith in God; how awesome it is to worship together and celebrate our faith! Not only do we grow closer to God through worship, but we also grow closer as a community of faith. Obviously, this is an extremely important part of our Christian interaction.

All too often, however, we go into the worship setting with the wrong attitude. I can personally confess to going to church at times to see my "romantic interests." Looking back, I don't think I could have found a much shallower reason for going. I not only had the wrong attitude, I missed the entire point of worship.

Jesus himself tells us that we are to worship "in spirit and in truth." How do we do this? By forgetting those around us—and even forgetting ourselves—and focusing on God completely. It is not wrong to go to church hoping for some positive Christian interaction; but if this is our only purpose in going, then we are sorely missing the mark. We must set our eyes on God and give all our mind, body, and soul over to him. Only in this way will we fully appreciate the wonder and joy of true worship.

Prayer Focus: What kind of attitude am I bringing to worship? Do I see worship as a fun time with friends, or as a chance to focus on God?

July 14 ~ Being Your Brother's (or Sister's) Keeper

How good and pleasant it is when brothers live together in unity!
—Psalm 133:1 (NIV)

When we're growing up, having a sibling can be tricky business. But as we get older, most of us begin to understand how important the bond that exists between us really is. Perhaps for the first time in our lives, we're ready to work on improving or deepening our relationships with brothers and sisters. This may come easier for some of us than others, depending on the kinds of relationships we have had with our siblings. But regardless of the past, it *is* possible to have a strong, Christ-centered relationship with every brother or sister. How?

One of the best ways is to be in constant prayer for each other. It is amazing to see the level of emotional closeness we can achieve through something as simple as prayer. Many times, frequent communication with siblings is difficult or impossible, yet we can still pray for the general well-being of our siblings.

Even if we don't have biological brothers or sisters, all of us have brothers and sisters in Christ, who deserve the same respect and love that we give to our "true" siblings. If you are an only child, you have a unique perspective and the opportunity to appreciate Christian fellowship in a way that people with brothers and sisters cannot. Above all, whatever your particular situation may be, always give thanks for the brothers and sisters God has provided for you.

Prayer Focus: *How am I treating my brothers and sisters, be they biological or spiritual? How can I allow God to help me strengthen the bond that exists between us?*

July 15 ~ Dealing with Parents

"Each of you must respect his mother and father, and you must observe my Sabbaths. I am the LORD your God.'"
—Leviticus 19:3 (NIV)

When we enter the young adult years, we begin to assert ourselves in ways that we have never done before. We begin to make our own life choices, which can be frustrating both for us and for our parents or guardians. Sometimes parents just can't—or won't—seem to accept the fact that we are becoming independent. Even those young adults who have been on their own for years sometimes struggle with "meddling"—though well-intentioned—parents.

Yet no matter how old we get, we never outgrow the need to respect our parents. In other words, we are to show them patience, compassion, and kindness. This is certainly what the Bible demands on our part.

Occasional disagreements or confrontations with our parents are an inevitable part of life, but they don't have to be hurtful experiences! A little bit of respect will go a long way toward keeping the peace.

Prayer Focus: Are my words and actions toward my parents Christlike? What areas of our relationship lack respect? What changes do I need to make?

July 16 ~ Having Friendships with the Opposite Sex

Be devoted to one another in brotherly love. Honor one another above yourselves.
—*Romans 12:10 (NIV)*

I have found that friendships with the opposite sex can be about as tricky as . . . well, there's no need for a metaphor; we all know exactly how sticky things can get! Still, for those of us who are single, having friends of the opposite sex can be immensely satisfying and beneficial. Not only does it give us insight into the differences that are inherent between males and females, but it also helps us learn how to "bridge the gap." (For those who are married, friendship with the opposite sex is another matter altogether; and since I'm not married, I won't attempt to speak about that!)

The question is, how do we keep things platonic—away from the romantic side? Actually, many problems come not from one person thinking about the other in a romantic way, but from one person questioning the other's feelings or motives. Here's an important ground rule: Trust each other. Without trust, any relationship is destined for trouble. If you are unable to trust each other, then perhaps a friendship between you just isn't possible.

Also crucial is openness tempered with discernment. If one person develops a romantic interest in the other, being up-front in a considerate and appropriate manner can be a friendship-saving step. Of course, sometimes a friendship naturally develops into a romantic relationship; but, obviously, this should be a mutually desirable progression, rather than an expectation or hope of only one person.

Above all, think of the other person as a brother or sister in Christ—as someone to be respected and loved in the same way as a same-sex friend. After all, shouldn't all our friendships be based on this principle?

Prayer Focus: Am I relating to my friends of the opposite sex in a Christlike manner? On what specific areas of these relationships do I need to focus my attention?

July 17 ~ Dating

Jesus replied: "'Love the Lord your God with all your heart and with all your soul and with all your mind.' This is the first and greatest commandment."
—Matthew 22:37-38 (NIV)

Dating. Now there's a subject that raises incredibly diverse reactions. When we think of dating, we may think of joy, excitement, pain, bitterness, or even terror! Whatever emotions dating elicits from us, it is undeniably an important part of life for many of us. Unfortunately, most young people today rarely look at dating from a spiritual standpoint. In fact, many just bend to their hormones and let things go where they may. This may be fun for a while, as long as the wonderful rush lasts, but the consequences—emotional, physical, and spiritual—are high; and this kind of carefree attitude usually leads to some sort of bad ending.

Instead, as Christians, we ought to consider dating not to be a two-person relationship, but a three-person relationship. God should have a prominent place. This is not easy at times, because often our desires in the relationship don't mesh with what God wants for us. But isn't God's plan always better? If both people are growing together in Christ, then there's a much better chance that things will go smoothly—and certainly the relationship will be much more glorifying to God.

Often we just want to put our spiritual side "on hold" for a while in order to focus on the fun of dating—or even worse, to hide our spirituality from the other person until it's "safe" to reveal more of ourselves. But

185

being a Christian isn't an on-again, off-again thing (as opposed to some dating relationships, ironically). In fact, it is through a steady relationship with God that we can experience true fulfillment with our dating partner.

Prayer Focus: Am I in a dating relationship that is pleasing to God? If not, what would God have me to do? If so, how can our relationship bring even more glory to God?

July 18 ~ Becoming a Generation of Sexual Purity

Since we have these promises, dear friends, let us purify ourselves from everything that contaminates body and spirit, perfecting holiness out of reverence for God.

—2 Corinthians 7:1 (NIV)

If there's one topic we get bombarded with today, it's sex. Television, news, movies, music—there's no escaping it. By the time we reach adulthood, many of us have heard numerous "sermons" on sex—from parents, pastors, youth leaders, teachers, and other caring authority figures. With so much information and guidance available to us—much of which is contradictory—it can be a bit confusing and sometimes misleading. In fact, many of us think we know exactly what God wants from us: sexual abstinence outside of marriage. But the truth is, God doesn't want chastity; he wants *purity*.

We singles have a tendency to think that just because we aren't sexually active, we are behaving exactly as God wants us to in this aspect of our lives. But this simply isn't the case. Of course God wants us to save sex for marriage, but he also wants us to be pure in our thoughts, desires, and motives. Abstaining from sex outside of marriage is a good thing; but if we believe that's the only limit required of us, we need to reevaluate God's desire for sincere purity as opposed to legalistic virtue. And God's desire for sincere purity applies to those who are married as well. We are to keep our thoughts, desires, and motives pure not only outside of marriage, but also within the holy covenant of marriage.

Some of us have made mistakes in the past, and some of us will make mistakes in the future. But we need to remember that God is ready to forgive us as soon as we turn our hearts to him and honestly repent. We need to be a generation of sexual purity and set an example for those around us.

186

Prayer Focus: Am I living inside God's will for my sexuality? Am I trying to attain true purity?

July 19 ~ Choosing a Mate

For this reason a man will leave his father and mother and be united to his wife, and they will become one flesh.
—Genesis 2:24 (NIV)

Choosing the right mate is one of the most daunting decisions we face. When we think about the subject, it often seems we have more questions than answers. Even if marriage seems far away, we can begin preparing ourselves to make a wise choice. And even if marriage isn't in *your* plans, you never know what surprise God may have for you in the future. So, how can we prepare ourselves for the possibility of choosing a mate?

First of all, we can prepare our hearts and minds. Are we keeping them pure? Are we establishing healthy friendships with the opposite sex? These things make us spiritually ready for marriage.

Second, prayer is crucial. There is no way we can expect to make a sound decision on a matter so crucial without the help of God's discernment. God can and will help us choose the right spouse, but first we must ask him.

Should you get married? Whom should you marry? Those are questions God will answer, if you let him. In the meantime, while you wait for God to reveal his plan for your life, pray about it and strive to live a pure life. Then you'll be ready for whatever God has in store for you!

Prayer Focus: Am I actively preparing my heart and mind for the possibility of marriage? If not, what changes should I make? Am I seeking God's will for my life concerning a potential mate?

July 20 ~ Having Non-Christian Friends

"When I say to a wicked man, 'You will surely die,' and you do not warn him or speak out to dissuade him from his evil ways in order to save his life, that wicked man will die for his sin, and I will hold you accountable for his blood."
—Ezekiel 3:18 (NIV)

Friendship between Christians and non-Christians is a touchy subject. Some people warn against it. Others go the opposite extreme and say it doesn't matter whether your friends are Christian or not. Things can get pretty tense between the opposing camps.

As with many issues, the best path lies somewhere in between. Yes, we should have non-Christian friends. One of the most effective ways of witnessing is through friendship. Jesus modeled this for us in his own life. When questioned about his association with tax collectors and "sinners," he said, "Those who are well have no need of a physician, but those who are sick. . . . For I have come to call not the righteous but sinners" (Matthew 9:12-13 NRSV). What good are we as Christians, then, if we completely isolate ourselves from those who are not Christians?

On the other hand, we must use some caution. Though we should encourage our non-Christian friends to turn away from sinful behavior, we must remember that their standards are not the same as ours because they have not embraced the Christian lifestyle. We also must be careful that they do not cause a hindrance in our own relationship with Christ. Picture yourself standing on a chair and your friend standing on the ground. It is much easier for him or her to pull you down than it is for you to pull your friend up. This is why it is important for us to spend the majority of our time with Christian friends who encourage us and hold us accountable.

In spite of the challenges and risks, we have a responsibility to God to have non-Christian friends. After all, we can make an eternal impact on their lives.

Prayer Focus: How can I improve my relationship with a non-Christian friend? How can I better show Christ to this person? What hindrances or temptations does this relationship pose in my Christian walk?

July 21 ~ Taking a Stand

Therefore, my dear brothers, stand firm. Let nothing move you. Always give yourselves fully to the work of the Lord, because you know that your labor in the Lord is not in vain.

—1 Corinthians 15:58 (NIV)

One of the things that God calls us to do—and that I often find hard to do—is stand up for what I believe in. It's not easy to say, "I believe that

188

Jesus Christ is the only way to everlasting life" when people all around are saying that I'm wrong, or that there are many equally valid paths to God, or that it doesn't even matter anyway. How can we Christians share our beliefs without being labeled as fanatics—or even worse?

I believe the answer lies in consistency. Sure, we all screw up and fall short of being the persons God wants us to be—probably more frequently than most of us would like to admit. But are we constantly *striving* to show others a steady representation of what Christianity is all about? Do we do our best to try to imitate the kind of life that Christ lived? And do we admit when we have made bad choices and mistakes?

Don't be afraid to take a stand. We never "stand firm" in vain.

Prayer Focus: *In what ways is God calling me to take a stand? How can I be aware of situations that will enable me to show or tell others what I believe?*

July 22 ~ Being Tolerant

Is God the God of Jews only? Is he not the God of Gentiles too? Yes, of Gentiles too.
—Romans 3:29 (NIV)

Yesterday we considered the need to take a stand, but what about the need to be tolerant? Tolerance is one of the biggest catchwords in our society today. No one wants to be seen as a religious fanatic or a bigot. As a result, we all clamor to prove that we are the most accepting. At times, this can lead us to say that all religions are equally valid, or that right and wrong are relative. Now, don't get me wrong, there is goodness and truth to be found in other faiths. However, as Christians, there is a central Truth that distinguishes us from other religions—namely, the living Christ—and we must believe wholeheartedly in this Truth.

It can be very difficult to stand firm in our faith without seeming judgmental or intolerant. In fact, many Christians just write off other religions as completely wrong; but this is just as bad as saying that all religions are equivalent. Christianity has had a sorrowful history of interaction with other faiths, and as the emerging leaders in our faith, we are called by God to mend this bridge and to give all religions respect. However, this does not mean that we should go as far as to accept their doctrines. We must be compassionate toward the followers of other faiths and respectful of their

189

beliefs while standing firm in our own. By doing this, we will provide a wonderful witness to the world of Christ's love for all.

Prayer Focus: Am I intolerant of the beliefs of others? Am I too accepting of beliefs of other religions? How can I use God's wisdom to help navigate these tricky situations?

July 23 ~ Guarding Against Discrimination

There is neither Jew nor Greek, slave nor free, male nor female, for you are all one in Christ Jesus.

—Galatians 3:28 (NIV)

Do you have prejudices against certain types of people? If asked this question, most of us would automatically answer with an emphatic no. No one wants to be seen as racist, sexist, or homophobic. The problem is that often we examine these attitudes only in their extreme contexts. We think of a racist, for example, as someone who hates people of a different ethnicity. But this isn't the case; racism exists any time we think less of a person because of her or his ethnic background. The same is true for sexism and for discrimination against homosexuals.

Even if we are completely unbiased and nondiscriminatory toward those who are different from us, we still have a responsibility to reach out to them and to help eradicate the malevolent beliefs of others. Are we actually doing something to stop discrimination, or are we idly condemning it from our living rooms?

There is much to be done, and as Christians, we are called to love everyone, including those who don't look, act, or talk like us. One of the best illustrations of this is the parable of the good Samaritan (Luke 10:25-37). In the time of Jesus, the Samaritans were despised by the Jewish community for being a mixed race. However, the parable clearly shows that we are to reach out to those who are different from us. The time for hatred is gone; the time for love is now.

Prayer Focus: Am I harboring dislike or hatred for people of different races, backgrounds, or gender from my own? Am I doing something to help stop this discrimination by others?

July 24 ~ Being a Role Model for the Younger Generation

In everything set them an example by doing what is good. In your teaching show integrity, [and] seriousness.

—Titus 2:7 (NIV)

I don't think many of us truly realize how often we serve as role models. It happens almost every time we interact with children and youth, who look to us for guidance and leadership. It has been said that there are fewer heroes today than in times past, but this is untrue. The heroes of today include people like us who interact with the younger generation. Ask children to name some of their heroes, and they are virtually guaranteed to choose someone who is close to them and active in their life. The truth is, today's youth are hungry for heroes and role models, and they're looking to us!

This is why it is so important for us to examine the kind of model we are providing. By living out Christian principles, we have the opportunity to show the next generation a godly way to live. Or, by leading hypocritical lives, we have the potential to lead them astray. When we let children and youth see us curse, be cruel, and otherwise live amoral lifestyles, we are essentially saying that these values are the ones they should embrace. We must stay on our toes to provide Christlike examples.

Prayer Focus: *What kind of example am I setting for the young people watching me?*

July 25 ~ Being a Christian on the Job

Whatever you do, work at it with all your heart, as working for the Lord, not for men.

—Colossians 3:23 (NIV)

Finding a job that matches our skills and abilities, that we enjoy doing, and that pays adequately isn't easy. Often we take a temporary or in-between job while finishing school or waiting for the right job to come along; and, consequently, we're often tempted to cut corners or do less than we should.

Being a Christian in the workplace involves so much more than verbally witnessing to our coworkers. In fact, our actions speak more loudly than our words. Have you ever seen someone witness to a coworker with words while trying to do the least amount of work possible? Perhaps this person doesn't see the irony and hypocrisy in the situation, but you can be sure that others do! The Bible is very clear about our proper work ethic in relation to our supervisor—we are to do exactly what we are told, and do it to the best of our ability. We are not to look for loopholes in our assigned tasks that we can exploit.

We can provide a powerful witness to our coworkers and our supervisor through our example. If we think people won't notice our hard work and obedience, we are mistaken. This is one of the most visible ways that we can show our Christian values and beliefs, even though we are not openly proclaiming the gospel. If we want to lead coworkers to Christ, a strong work ethic and upstanding character must accompany our words.

Prayer Focus: What kind of example am I giving in the workplace? Are there aspects of my work life that need to be brought into line with God's will?

July 26 ~ Being a Servant Leader

Jesus called them together and said, "You know that the rulers of the Gentiles lord it over them, and their high officials exercise authority over them. Not so with you. Instead, whoever wants to become great among you must be your servant.
—Matthew 20:25-26 (NIV)

Do you think of yourself as someone having authority? Are you a leader? Perhaps you hold a leadership or supervisory position in a particular group, organization, or company. Or perhaps, whether you realize it or not, you are an unofficial leader among your peers or coworkers.

At one time or another, all of us have been or will be leaders; and as leaders, we have certain responsibilities and duties to those who follow us. We also have the opportunity to make changes that will have far-reaching implications. What principles should govern our decisions and actions? What kind of leaders should we be?

As Christians, we are called to be servant leaders. We are called not to "lord it over" our followers, but to set an example for them. We are called not to be monarchs, but to be the first among equals. As such, we should never ask someone to do something that we would refuse to do ourselves. We are to have respect and concern for those under our authority; as leaders, we are responsible for their well-being.

God is looking for a generation of leaders who will follow his standards, and we are that generation. Will we use our influence in a way that advances God's kingdom here on earth?

Prayer Focus: What leadership roles do I have now or would I like to have in the future? Am I leading by God's example, or how can I prepare to lead by God's example? How can I use my influence for God's good?

July 27 ‧ Being Humble

Do nothing out of selfish ambition or vain conceit, but in humility consider others better than yourselves.
—Philippians 2:3 (NIV)

One of the most important attitudes we need in our relationships with others is humility. Humility is a concept that is often misunderstood, partly because we usually see it as the opposite of self-centeredness. However, humility is more than simply refusing to put yourself first. It is an attitude— even a way of living—that reflects our profound respect for those around us.

Let's say that I am going out to eat with a friend. I really want to go to one place, but my friend opts for another. Now, assuming that I go along with my friend's desires instead of mine, I have one of two options. The first reaction I can have is a kind of miserable resignation, which often is accompanied by a feeling of pride because I didn't override my friend's desires. This reaction is what I call "negative self-sacrifice," and it is not to be equated with humility. The humble response would be sincere appreciation for our difference of opinion and a willingness (if not downright happiness) to go to wherever my friend wants to go.

True, humility is much harder to achieve than simple self-denial, but it's essential for strong, godly friendships. And if we practice it regularly, humility has the potential to positively affect all our interactions with others.

Prayer Focus: Do I display humility in my relationships—or merely self-sacrifice? How can I change my attitude from one of pride to one of humility?

July 28 ~ Overcoming Loneliness

As the mountains surround Jerusalem, so the LORD surrounds his people both now and forevermore.
—Psalm 125:2 (NIV)

Loneliness is something we all experience at one time or another. You might say that loneliness is a lack of meaningful interaction with others. I say *meaningful* interaction because it is definitely possible to feel lonely and still be surrounded by people. This was my experience when I first arrived at college: In spite of constantly being around other people, I felt very alone. I was craving some sort of real communication with others. Loneliness can come even when we are not physically isolated from others.

Feelings of loneliness are inevitable as we undergo the many changes in our lives. Yet there are things we can do to assuage the effects. Most important is to remember whose we are. God is always available to listen and to comfort us. Despite this very reassuring fact, often what we really desire is a physical body to listen to us, to hold us, and to be part of our lives. At these times we sometimes must make the first move and reach out to others. It is quite probable that some of the people around you are experiencing similar emotions and simply are waiting for someone to take the first step. We can rest assured that God will put people into our lives to help meet our needs; even more assuring is knowing that God is with us even when others are not.

Prayer Focus: When do I experience loneliness and isolation? What steps can I take to utilize God's provision for these times?

July 29 ~ Dealing with Change

Jesus Christ is the same yesterday and today and forever.
—Hebrews 13:8 (NIV)

One of the most definitive and inclusive aspects of our lives as young adults is that of change. These years bring numerous, and often painful, changes. Although they have the potential to be some of the richest years of our lives, they also can be extremely trying. It sometimes seems that we simply have nothing to cling to—nothing that remains steady in our lives.

194

When I left for college, I thought, rather naively, that I would remain just as close to my high school friends as ever. At the same time, I was being thrown in with a whole new set of friends. My world was changing.

Others of us are experiencing the uncertainties of moving to a new city, beginning a new job, getting married, or starting a family. Even in more subtle ways, our worlds are changing every day.

Of course, it is during times of change that we need to remember the One who is with us constantly—and has been with us throughout our entire lives: God. God has never left us, never forsaken us, and never stopped loving us. At times I know that God has been the only thing that has been unchanging in my crazy world. As we go through times of struggle and transformation, we must remember that our foundation is in God, who is with us permanently.

Prayer Focus: *Am I building my foundation on the constancy of God, or am I letting myself be blown around? How can I rely more on God for stability?*

July 30 ~ Finding Your Call

And you will be called priests of the LORD, you will be named ministers of our God.

—Isaiah 61:6 (NIV)

One of the most important things I've ever been told is that every Christian is a minister. We often confuse the terms *minister* and *pastor*. A pastor is a leader of a church, whereas a minister is anyone who serves the needs of others. Of course, not all of us will be pastors, but all of us are called to be ministers for Christ.

So the question remains: Where is God calling us to minister? Obviously, that answer will be different for each of us. God requires that we use whatever position we hold in life to serve others. If you are a teacher, you have the ability to help mold future generations for Christ. If you are a doctor, you can show God's compassion to all your patients. Full-time ministry is not the only type of ministry; it is just one among many.

Discovering exactly where and how God wants us to minister is not always easy. I have never physically heard God's voice, and God has never sent me a letter telling me what to do. However, God will lead us to the people or places needing our ministry. A pastor of mine once told me that your call to ministry exists where the world's deepest need meets with your deepest desire to give. We should each be praying daily that God will show us where this juncture is, and will give us the strength to serve.

Prayer Focus: Where does the world's deepest need meet my deepest desire to give? In what ways is God calling me to minister? What people or places are in need of my service? How can I listen for God's call?

July 31 ~ Depending on God Rather Than on Others

My salvation and my honor depend on God; he is my mighty rock, my refuge. Trust in him at all times, O people; pour out your hearts to him, for God is our refuge.
—Psalm 62:7-8 (NIV)

How often have you been disappointed by someone close to you? Why is it that at the times we most need others, we're often let down? The answer to this question, at least in part, can be found in the question itself. Often we think that other people are what we need—that they will meet all our needs. But this is a twisted understanding. In truth, all we need is God. Of course, having a physical presence to hold you when you are hurting is a very welcome thing, just as having a voice you can audibly hear when you need encouragement is very comforting. But when you get to the very heart of the matter, it's God we are totally dependent upon. Sometimes we forget that it's God who brings the people we care about into our lives in the first place. If it weren't for God, we wouldn't even have others to depend on.

It's easy to get wrapped up in another person and start turning to her or him for things that should be left to God. Sometimes it takes a major letdown for us to realize how much we've been trusting in someone instead of trusting in God, and as painful as it may be, such an experience provides the ideal time for us to shift our focus from temporal, human relationships to God. Eventually every person will let us down, whether intentionally or not. God will never fail us.

Prayer Focus: What relationships, if any, have I been giving more prominence than God? What needs am I expecting others to meet instead of turning to God?

196

August

LIVING WITH INTEGRITY

Kwasi Kena

August 1 ~ Integrity

"But what about you?" he asked. "Who do you say I am?"
—Matthew 16:15 (NIV)

*I*ntegrity is a godly virtue. This month we will consider the various nuances of living a Christian life of integrity; but, first, let us spend time with a question of eternal significance. Jesus asked his disciples, "Who do you say I am?" The people in Jesus' time circulated many rumors about who *they* thought he was. Some said he was John the Baptist. Others claimed he was Elijah or Jeremiah or one of the prophets. Likewise, there is no shortage of rumors about Jesus today. Some say Jesus was merely a historic figure. Others say he was a "good man," a teacher, or a prophet. But, who do *you* say Jesus is?

When Jesus asked his disciples to answer the question, he was addressing people who had made a commitment to follow him. They had experienced life with Christ "up close and personal." Even among the twelve, however, only Peter recognized Jesus as "the Christ, the Son of the living God" (Matthew 16:16 NIV).

Peter's answer did not come from the rumors of the people; it came directly from heaven. As Christians, we can live with integrity by listening to God—especially in difficult situations. God's standards of morality and ethics are higher than the world's standards. It is hard to imagine living a life of integrity without God's guidance.

Who do you say Jesus is: God, Savior, Lord, Friend? The test of your integrity begins with the acknowledgment of your honest beliefs about who Jesus is to you.

Prayer Focus: Reflect on Jesus' question, "Who do you say I am?" Express your honest beliefs about Jesus Christ in prayer to God.

August 2 ~ Lost and Found

But whatever was to my profit I now consider loss for the sake of Christ. What is more, I consider everything a loss compared to the surpassing greatness of knowing Christ Jesus my Lord, for whose sake I have lost all things.
—Philippians 3:7-8 (NIV)

Diana couldn't stop the tears from flowing. It seemed so ironic. All her life she had enjoyed being "everyone's favorite." She was her doting father's only daughter. She always got the best. Without realizing it, however, Diana began to assume that she was entitled to the best—even if it meant manipulating others to get it. With the intent of becoming an executive by age thirty, she dressed for success, associated with "winners," and used only the latest industry buzzwords. Diana carried the persona of one who wins through intimidation. Everyone said, "She's got success written all over her." So why was she crying now?

Recently Gill, Diana's best friend, had shared an intriguing conversation with her. "I've never felt like this before," Gill had said repeatedly. "I don't know how, but I had an overwhelming experience with God. One minute I was saying, 'Jesus, help me; my life is all messed up.' The next thing you know, I felt this overwhelming sense of love inside."

For the next few weeks, the only thing Gill had seemed to talk about was her relationship with God. That had been strange to Diana, because previously she and Gill had talked only about whatever their latest "conquest" was in life. Gill was different now. She had *lost* her compulsion for recognition, but she had *found* Christ.

Diana's vision remained blurry as she peered through her tears. For the first time in her life, Diana questioned whether or not she was pursuing the right things in life.

198

Prayer Focus: Meditate on this question today: What are you willing to lose in order to gain Jesus Christ?

August 3 ~ Distraction

See to it that no one takes you captive through hollow and deceptive philosophy, which depends on human tradition and the basic principles of this world rather than on Christ.

—Colossians 2:8 (NIV)

Do you ever watch late night television *just* to see the commercials? I am amazed at the offers to help us make more money, sculpt our bodies, or peer into the future—all for only three easy payments of. . . . Do these ads continue to air because they are entertaining or because we need to believe them? Are we distracted into hoping that if we try one more product, we will become better than we are now? The kind of promises offered in some TV ads says something about our level of dissatisfaction with life.

Too many voices offer enticing remedies to life's challenges. It seems as if a new strategy or philosophy is born every day. The question is, are they pathways that Christ would have us choose, or are they merely distractions?

The lyrics to a gospel song speak of a traveler who meets a man while walking on "the road of good intentions." The man insists that he can show the traveler a better way to reach his destination. The traveler seems genuinely interested and is nearly ready to follow when he asks, "What is your name?" With a mischievous grin, the man answers, *distraction*. Be careful of who you follow.

Prayer Focus: Today, keep track of what grabs your attention. Reflect on your observations and ask yourself the following question. Am I preoccupied mainly with useless distractions or with activities that will please Christ?

August 4 ~ Life Beyond the Cocoon

By faith Moses, when he had grown up, refused to be known as the son of

Pharaoh's daughter. He chose to be mistreated along with the people of God rather than to enjoy the pleasures of sin for a short time.
—*Hebrews 11:24-25 (NIV)*

Privilege is an enticing temptation. Who wouldn't like to enjoy special benefits because you "know the right people." Today's scripture reveals that Moses not only knew the right people, but he also lived in their house! As an accepted member of Pharaoh's household, Moses could have had anything he wanted. Surprisingly, he turned away from a life of pleasure. Imagine what Moses must have been thinking as he made that life-changing decision.

Choosing the privileges of luxury, power, and pampering would have required Moses to turn his back on his *true* identity. He would have struggled with whether or not he could have enjoyed a sheltered life when his real family members were being oppressed by Pharaoh. Could Moses have denied who he was spiritually and ethnically in order to live in isolated comfort? Evidently, the cost of privilege was too great a price for Moses to pay.

What Moses apparently lost in material privilege, he gained in spiritual integrity. God used him to deliver a nation from oppression. Like Moses, we too will face difficult choices in life. The decision to live a life of Christian integrity often throws us into tension and inner struggle. As Christians, we are called to offer relief to the hurting and to enter into solidarity with the oppressed. The more we "cocoon" ourselves inside of privilege, however, the more difficult it becomes to "suffer with God's people." Perhaps this is the day to embrace the transforming lifestyle of Christian integrity and discover life beyond the cocoon.

Prayer Focus: *Ask God to give you the courage to live beyond the cocoon of privilege and make choices that will build Christian integrity within you.*

August 5 ~ A Two-Way Street

"If your brother sins, rebuke him, and if he repents, forgive him."
—*Luke 17:3b (NIV)*

Have you discovered that Jesus expects more of us than we do of ourselves? The people in Jesus' day had always observed the old law of "an eye for an eye" whenever someone committed an offense against someone else. With that in mind, it must have seemed strange for people to hear Jesus saying, "If your brother sins, rebuke him. . . ." Rebuking was a far cry from physical retaliation. Rebuking involved face-to-face *nonviolent* confrontation.

In contemporary language, to rebuke means to confront someone who has committed a sinful offense. Confrontation is a process that is not easy for many of us. Christlike confrontation is even more demanding because the goal is reconciliation, not revenge. Christlike confrontation involves telling a person what he or she did wrong. It seeks an explanation. This type of confrontation also involves some risk.

In order for people to understand the magnitude of their offense, you may need to share your feelings about how their act offended you. Many of us would rather avoid actions that require vulnerability, honesty, and courage. When we take the risk to confront people "in love," however, we create an opportunity for healing damaged relationships.

Though Jesus expects us to initiate the confrontation, he also expects action from the other person—repentance. The other person must admit that he or she was wrong and vow not to repeat the offense. Clearly, the road to forgiveness and reconciliation is a process that involves rebuking and repenting. People of integrity cannot avoid this two-way street.

Prayer Focus: *Ask God to give you the courage to confront in love, repent in humility, and forgive with grace.*

August 6 ~ The Gift of Ten Feet

Do not conform any longer to the pattern of this world, but be transformed by the renewing of your mind. Then you will be able to test and approve what God's will is—his good, pleasing and perfect will.

—Romans 12:2 (NIV)

"Get outta my way!" Larry shouted, as if anyone in the car ahead could hear him. As usual, the frantic morning traffic had transformed the normally mild-mannered Larry into a menacing road warrior. Larry didn't drive; he conquered. With reckless abandon, Larry used his car to slash through traffic. Shirley, his wife, often suggested that he slow down, but that only infuriated him more. "Everybody's in a hurry out here. You've got to drive aggressively or you'll never get anywhere," he insisted.

One day, Larry joined a carpool and rode to work with Mark, his co-worker. It didn't take long for Larry to discover how different the commute to work was from the passenger seat of the car. Before long, Mark's careful driving completely unnerved Larry. Unconsciously, Larry found himself wanting to be in control. Silently he thought, *There's an opening, Mark, hit the gas; let's go, man!* Instead, Mark seemed more interested in carrying on a relaxed conversation with Larry.

In traffic jams, Mark looked into the eyes of the other drivers and often invited them to turn in front of him. When a frantic driver swerved in front of him, Mark shook his head and said, "All of that for ten lousy feet. When I see impatient drivers like that, I smile and give them the gift of ten feet. I'd rather stay calm and prevent accidents out here, wouldn't you?" Larry muttered an unconvincing "yeah" and began to realize the need to change his driving habits.

Prayer Focus: Ask God to help you not to rush through life, imposing your personal needs or desires on others. Ask God continually to renew your mind and enable you to give others the gift of ten feet.

August 7 ~ "Just an Imitation"

Be imitators of God, therefore, as dearly loved children and live a life of love, just as Christ loved us and gave himself up for us as a fragrant offering and sacrifice to God.

—Ephesians 5:1-2 (NIV)

How many times have you heard someone say, "Accept no imitations"? When we get our cars repaired, we want "genuine" parts. If we study art, we want to see the original paintings. We want to be treated as unique individuals—not as ID numbers. We want to be recognized as someone special with particular needs and interests. Given our quest for originality and uniqueness, what I am about to suggest may sound strange.

If we really want to be regarded as original and unique, we should be imitators of God. There is no one like God. God is amazingly creative and resourceful. God appreciates the vast diversity of people across the globe. God is bold and courageous—and even knows how to deal with babies and in-laws!

A few years ago, advertisers exploited the "Jordan" effect by encouraging people to "be like Mike." As I write, another media craze is "Tiger mania" because of the phenomenal success of Tiger Woods. There is no denying the inspiration that comes from aspiring to attain the excellence displayed in a star athlete. But, if we really want to turn heads and cause people to stand up and take notice, we should decide to be more like Christ every day. If we choose to love as Christ loved and sacrifice for others as Christ sacrificed for us, our lives will be nothing short of miraculous. In this instance, it's fine to be "just an imitation."

Prayer Focus: *As a spiritual exercise, identify one characteristic of Jesus Christ that you will imitate today.*

August 8 ~ So That the Grass Can Grow . . .

Fools mock at making amends for sin, but good will is found among the upright.
—Proverbs 14:9 (NIV)

"So you think *I* should apologize? That's crazy! *You* should be apologizing to *me*!" Marvin's words shot through the telephone with caustic power. He and his best friend, Sheldon, had had a terrible misunderstanding. The cause of yesterday's argument was soon lost in today's war of insults. Neither Marvin nor Sheldon would back down. Each one fought for his individual rights with such fervor that their friendship seemed destined to ruin.

There is an African proverb that says, "When the elephants fight, it is the grass that suffers." Relationships, like grass, can get stepped on, bruised, and uprooted through abuse. When left unchecked, our egos, like elephants, can run roughshod over anything that gets in their way. The pain caused by broken relationships leads some people to lash out with offensive words or physical abuse. Others refuse to speak out when there has been a breach in the relationship, and they suffer in silence. If relationships are valuable to us, however, we can choose a third option—reconciliation.

To live with integrity means finding ways to *mend* relationships rather than *rend* relationships. The strength of our friendships, dating relationships, and marriages depends on our ability to apologize humbly and make amends graciously. Saving a relationship is hard work, but it is worthwhile. Find ways to reconcile when your relationships are suffering. Corral elephant-like problems so that your relationships, like the grass, can grow.

Prayer Focus: Ask God to teach you new instincts that seek reconciliation rather than retaliation.

August 9 ~ A Lifesaver

A truthful witness saves lives, but a false witness is deceitful.
—Proverbs 14:25 (NIV)

As I write, there is a highly successful set of "Truth" television commercials aimed at discovering the truth about the practices of the tobacco industry and its products. Each thought-provoking commercial displays the groups' relentless pursuit of truth and their unwillingness to settle for anything less. Uncovering the truth about an unscrupulous people is the thing that heroic champions do. Such pursuits make for great novels and entertaining television, but what happens when our lives collide with the truth?

I asked the students in a college Christian ethics class if they *always* want people to tell them the truth. The automatic response was, "Yeah, of course." I pressed them to consider what they were saying by asking them a few questions. What if the truth hurts your feelings? What if people tell you that they honestly don't think you are attractive? After a few more questions, most of the class reconsidered their answer. They admitted that they would rather "stretch the truth" at times than hurt someone's feelings or be hurt themselves. The clear goal was to "save" themselves from painful realities.

Telling the truth is a costly venture. People battle between telling the truth and not reporting an abusive relative. We find it difficult to decide whether or not to reveal the truth about the addiction of a loved one. Still, in the midst of difficult situations, scripture reminds us that "a truthful witness saves lives." Perhaps the real decision is whether we are interested in being "a lifesaver."

August 10 ~ Who Sent You?

God said to Moses, "I AM WHO I AM. This is what you are to say to the Israelites: 'I AM has sent me to you.'"

—*Exodus 3:14 (NIV)*

Most of us are familiar with the saying, "It's not *what* you know; it's *who* you know." That statement reveals the value that we place on knowing the right people. Job applications ask for references—people who will vouch for your character and recommend you for the position. When Moses learned that he was to lead the Israelites out of Egypt, he knew that his people would ask, "Who sent you and what is his name?"

The Israelites were no different than we are today. People ask for our credentials and look into our family backgrounds. They look at our resumes to determine our work experience. More than that, however, they want to know *who* knows us. Who verifies your qualifications? Who agrees that you are suitable to marry anyone's daughter or son? Whose endorsement elicits your acceptance by others?

God knew that Moses had misgivings about assuming the role of "deliverer of Israel." You may have second thoughts about accepting a challenging position in life. Regardless of whether you come from "the right family" or have an impeccable scholastic record or an outstanding work record, God has something for you to do in life. Moses was a murderer and a fugitive, but God chose him to assume a great leadership role. Job readiness is shaped by who you know. If you know God, you too can do great things—as long as God sends you.

Prayer Focus: Does your confidence in meeting challenges come from your relationship with God?

August 11 ~ Family Priorities

"Who is my mother, and who are my brothers?" Pointing to his disciples, he said,

"Here are my mother and my brothers. For whoever does the will of my Father in heaven is my brother and sister and mother."

—Matthew 12:48-50 (NIV)

Family first! Those are noble words to profess and carry out these days—especially if you are constantly choosing between other responsibilities and your family's needs. The demands of family life don't just involve our spouses and children. Even as adults, our parents and siblings may want our unquestioned loyalty. They may expect to influence major decisions in our lives.

There is no question that the strongest relationships we have exist within the context of our families. That's why it may seem strange to hear Jesus asking, "Who is my mother, and who are my brothers?" *while his mother and brothers are standing nearby.* At first, it sounds like Jesus is disregarding his family.

In Jewish culture, rabbis often taught spiritual principles by asking questions. What does Jesus' question teach us? In God's family, integrity is honed and perfected—what else would we expect with Jesus as our relative? Jesus' question compels us to think about how God desires us to relate to our earthly family and our extended Christian family. If we are to live with integrity, we cannot be afraid to discern and carry out God's will—even if it challenges some of our strongest family ties and loyalties. Jesus never abandoned his earthly family, but he also kept his "family priorities" with God straight.

Whoever does the will of God is Jesus' family. As Christians and members of God's "extended family," we must carefully consider what our family priorities will be.

Prayer Focus: *Consider your "extended Christian family" and ask God to show you what your family priorities should be today.*

August 12 ~ Christian Perfection

"All these I have kept," the young man said. "What do I still lack?" Jesus answered, "If you want to be perfect, go, sell your possessions and give to the poor, and you will have treasure in heaven. Then come, follow me."

—Matthew 19:20-21 (NIV)

Can we really reach perfection? Many of us seem to think so. We want perfectly smooth skin. We want perfectly bright teeth. We exercise and take diet supplements to get the perfect body. If our hair falls out, we apply chemicals or pay someone to plant more hair lest we appear less than perfect. We search for the perfect mate. We look for the perfect job. We want the perfect vacation experience. Apparently, striving for perfection is a natural human trait.

The rich young ruler to whom Jesus spoke was striving for perfection. He had followed the religious rules since the time that he was a child. He also had managed to acquire so much wealth that people referred to him as "rich."

Being rich is more than the accumulation of wealth; it is a mind-set. After you get used to driving a luxury car, it is difficult to ride in an old clunker. After living in a nice condo, it's difficult to imagine living in over-crowded public housing. If you are not careful, you can become out of touch with the realities of the poor and oppressed. What if Jesus asked you to get rid of your most prized possessions and spend time giving to the poor? How might that affect you?

People of integrity learn to follow Christ even if it requires tremendous personal sacrifice. Are you willing to strive for Christian perfection? Follow Christ wherever he leads you.

Prayer Focus: *Ask God to lead you away from a mind-set that isolates you from the poor and oppressed. Commit yourself to Christian perfection and pray for the strength to follow Christ anywhere.*

August 13 ~ Get Out of the Boat!

"Lord, if it's you," Peter replied, "tell me to come to you on the water." "Come,"
he said. Then Peter got down out of the boat, walked on the water and came
toward Jesus.

—Matthew 14:28-29 (NIV)

Maria sat completely enthralled by the workshop leader, Dr. Sorenson. "Writing comes from the heart and soul of your being. The genius of inspiration comes from the depths of who you are," he spoke as if returning from paradise. Maria was an aspiring writer attending her first writer's workshop.

Dr. Sorenson continued, "Writing is an extension of yourself, splashed onto pages. Writing provides the reader with a transparent glimpse of who *you* really are." Maria wasn't sure if she was ready to expose her soul to the world yet. She still relished the security of being an "aspiring writer," concealed from the full scrutiny of editors and critics. As long as she remained an "aspiring writer," she avoided the full responsibilities of the writing profession. Still, Maria wondered what it would be like to live the life of a professional writer.

Jesus urges us to move beyond our estimation of what is safe or secure. To walk with Christ involves "getting out of the boat" and trusting God to support us. The demands of integrity may push you out of the security of avoiding responsibilities. You may not think that you are capable of doing better, but God knows what the "real you" is capable of doing. When God calls you to act, you will be stretched until the very thing you have been called to do seems as challenging as walking on water. Thankfully, the same God who calls you will support you; so don't be afraid to "get out of the boat."

Prayer Focus: Remember that God created you and knows you. Are you willing to answer your call to get out of the boat and discover what the real you is capable of doing?

August 14 ~ From the Heart

"Don't you see that whatever enters the mouth goes into the stomach and then out of the body? But the things that come out of the mouth come from the heart."
—*Matthew 15:17-18a (NIV)*

Marcus nodded his head slowly in agreement with his supervisor's comment. Marcus was beginning a counseling practicum. His supervisor, Dr. Klein, had just shared a bit of advice that he had learned after years of practice. "The best counselors are deaf," Dr. Klein had said with all seriousness. "People will *say* anything to you during a counseling session. My advice to you is to look beyond their words and determine what they actually mean and what they actually do." Dr. Klein was right: the key to discovering a person's true identity is locating the place where he or she translates thoughts and desires into actions. Jesus identified that place as the heart.

208

Jesus reminds us that paying attention to matters of the heart should be a top priority. He is not impressed by "outward religious practices." He confronted the Pharisees because they had become so preoccupied with *outward* compliance to the prescribed food laws that they had failed to develop *inner* spirituality. He showed his displeasure with their hypocritical practices by quoting from Isaiah: "'These people . . . honor me with their lips, but their hearts are far from me. Their worship of me is made up only of rules taught by men'" (Isaiah 29:13 NIV).

We cannot fake integrity. Our hearts will always betray our true spiritual identities. Jesus' message is clear: Christian integrity develops in a place that is beyond words. Integrity develops *from the heart.*

Prayer Focus: As a spiritual exercise, monitor the words that come from your mouth and originate from your heart today. Offer your heart to the Lord now and receive God's nurture, care, and cleansing.

August 15 ~ Completion

Perseverance must finish its work so that you may be mature and complete, not lacking anything.
—James 1:4 (NIV)

One definition of integrity is completeness. An aspiring composer left his teacher's studio mulling over the words he just heard. "Your compositions start well, but you never finish them." How many times have we started things in life without completing them? How many writers start books they never finish? How many careers end soon after their beginning? How many relationships end before they have a chance to mature? The act of completion is a characteristic of integrity. It takes character to complete a difficult task.

In today's scripture, James indicates that completion occurs when we learn to persevere. Great athletes persevere despite fatigue and physical ailments. Great leaders persevere despite insurmountable odds and tremendous pressures. Your character is judged by your ability to carry out your word and fulfill your promises. That can only happen when you learn to persevere to the end. Completion follows perseverance. The good news is that the process of completing your character is not a solo act. It occurs through partnership with Christ. Remember, "He who began a good work in you will carry it on to completion until the day of Christ Jesus" (Philippians 1:6*b* NIV).

Allow perseverance to work in you so that your integrity may reach completion.

Prayer Focus: Give thanks that the good work God started is being completed in you. Ask for the perseverance necessary to complete what is before you today.

August 16 ~ First Become *One*

"I and the Father are one."

—*John 10:30 (NIV)*

Single-minded. Focused. Unwavering. Each of these terms could be used to describe Jesus Christ during his earthly ministry. How was he able to escape the deadly lure of temptation? How was he able to complete his mission on earth? Clearly, Jesus never forgot that he and God were *one*. Jesus' goals were God's goals. Jesus' purpose was God's purpose.

As I write, there is a popular television program in which two master chefs compete against each other. The competition begins when the ingredient of the day is revealed. Then, the competitors are given one hour to prepare four or five original dishes using this ingredient. How can they handle such a challenge? Often these culinary giants served for years as apprentices under the demanding scrutiny of master chefs. Over time, the highest standards of the master chef became *their* cooking standards. Through constant demonstration, correction, and observation these apprentices learned the cooking philosophy of the master chef. By the end of such grueling apprenticeships, the students can produce outstanding culinary delights just like the master chefs. You could say that at the conclusion of the apprenticeship, the students have become *one* with their teachers.

Consider the benefits of becoming *one* with the Lord. As you spend time with God, you learn to adopt God's standards as your own. You then develop spiritual instincts and a godly "sixth sense." If you are serious about being a person of integrity, make this your priority: first become *one*.

Prayer Focus: Will you choose to serve as God's apprentice? Ask to be taught God's ways until you become one.

210

August 17 ~ Hi-Fi Christians

And whatever you do, whether in word or deed, do it all in the name of the Lord Jesus, giving thanks to God the Father through him.

—Colossians 3:17 (NIV)

Before the advent of MP3, CD, and cassette players, people listened to the Hi-Fi. Hi-Fi was short for high fidelity. Fidelity means accuracy. In music, high fidelity refers to the ability to reproduce sound accurately. The goal of Hi-Fi was to reproduce sound as closely as possible. As a child, I would sit in front of the Hi-Fi, close my eyes, and imagine that I was seated in front of musicians playing a live performance. I rarely made it to a live concert, so the Hi-Fi was the next best thing to being there.

Many people rarely make it to the organized church today. Far too many find it outdated and irrelevant. Church members lament that "we can't get people to *come* to church." Jesus never expected that people would wake up one day with a sudden urge to go to church. Instead, Jesus instructed Christians to *go* into the world and make disciples. Our role as Christians is to reflect Christ in word and deed *wherever* we are in the world. If we remember to do everything in the name of the Lord Jesus, we will reveal Christ to others. We can be "Hi-Fi Christians."

Everyone may not venture inside a church building, but everyone can have the opportunity to see Christ—through your life. As you go about your daily affairs today, consider the impact that you can make on others as a "Hi-Fi Christian."

Prayer Focus: Think of yourself as a "Hi-Fi Christian" today. Remember that every word you speak and every deed you perform should be done in the name of the Lord Jesus Christ.

August 18 ~ "Weight Loss"

Therefore, since we are surrounded by such a great cloud of witnesses, let us throw off everything that hinders and the sin that so easily entangles, and let us run with perseverance the race marked out for us.

—Hebrews 12:1 (NIV)

Do I really need more, or can I live with less? Integrity invites you to answer that question. If you lived in a developing country and had to relocate from one place to another, the answer would become apparent quickly. As missionaries, my wife and I shared the dubious distinction of moving six times in eighteen months. After constant packing and unpacking, we soon discovered that *moving* was not our main problem—things were. We were embarrassed when the movers strained to lower our furniture from the balcony and groaned under the weight of our household goods. It didn't take long to realize that we had too many *things*. Still, we played a never-ending tug of war. After painfully parting with some "necessity," we would find some other *thing* that we thought we needed. In the end, however, there was no denying the fact that we had too many "weighty" things—things that were hindering us.

The writer of Hebrews 12:1 makes reference to a similar reality. Ancient runners quickly learned that they could run more effectively if they were not dragging around so much excess weight. We could easily extend this thought to the excess baggage in our daily lives. How often do we purchase or hold on to items we don't really need? How much time do we waste daily doing unnecessary activities or worrying about improbable woes? Even more painfully, how much energy do we spend pursuing things that lead nowhere? Take inventory of your things and decide whether it's time for a little "weight loss."

Prayer Focus: Prayerfully consider what kind of "weight loss" you might need in your life. Ask God to accompany you to your closet, your storage room, and your basement or attic and show you what dead weight to get rid of.

August 19 ~ Exit Policy

So in everything, do to others what you would have them do to you, for this sums up the Law and the Prophets.
—Matthew 7:12 (NIV)

For the first few days, Jeremy was excited to have a new job. His supervisor boasted that this newly created job was extremely important. "This position has the potential to turn the entire department around," he told Jeremy. What he failed to tell Jeremy was that two "beloved" employees had been fired in order to create this new job because the company needed to show a profit. When the other workers in the department learned that these two employees were losing their jobs, they were all outraged.

Without knowing why, Jeremy had walked into a minefield. Those beloved employees who were being fired decided to make the company pay for letting them go. Methodically, they sabotaged the office files so that any replacement person would have to start from scratch. In solidarity, their coworkers silently decided not to lend assistance to anyone the company hired in the new position. Jeremy had no idea that he was entering such a volatile situation.

If you had been one of the two who were fired, or even one of the remaining employees, how would you have responded? Perhaps this is a good time to develop a godly exit policy.

Prayer Focus: Pray a simple prayer today, asking God to enable you to do to others what you would have them do to you.

August 20 ~ What If . . . ?

"But I tell you who hear me: Love your enemies, do good to those who hate you, bless those who curse you, pray for those who mistreat you."
—*Luke 6:27-28 (NIV)*

If you were to ask a question beginning, "What if . . . ," how would you complete it? Would you ask, "What if I were rich?" Would you ask, "What if I could have a chance to right some wrong?" Perhaps your question would be as practical as asking, "What if I had a car that wouldn't break down all the time," or "What if I had a peaceful moment to myself?"

You could spend the day chasing the possibilities raised by those two little words, but let's put a different spin on this. Imagine that you were deceived or betrayed by someone recently. Imagine that the lingering effect of anger still churns in your soul. Then, in the midst of those feelings, imagine hearing Jesus say, "Love your enemies, do good to those who hate you, bless those who curse you, pray for those who mistreat you" (Luke 6:27-28 NIV). Those words are never easy to hear, but what if Jesus asks you to do that today?

What if . . . ?

213

August 21 ~ Speak with a Samaritan

The Samaritan woman said to him, "You are a Jew and I am a Samaritan woman. How can you ask me for a drink?" (For Jews do not associate with Samaritans.)

—John 4:9 (NIV)

Marty listened to the newscaster describe a growing phenomenon in his city. A local meat packing plant had attracted a large number of immigrant workers to the area. Despite the company's announcement that it was no longer hiring, each day a greater number of people clogged the sidewalks looking for work. Some of the neighbors complained that they didn't appreciate having *those people* hanging around all day. A plan was proposed to build a work center to accommodate the transient workers in the daytime, but it was soundly defeated because of opposition by area residents.

One part of Marty wanted to turn away and ignore the situation. After all, he had his own problems. "Nobody told *them* to come to America anyway," he thought. As soon as that idea crossed Marty's mind, he felt uncomfortable. He was saying the very things about this immigrant population that people had said about his grandparents when they had come to this country. As Marty remembered the painful stories of his grandparents' rejection and isolation, he began to wonder what these immigrants were feeling. *Is there anything I can do?* he thought.

Jesus crossed a major barrier when he spoke to the Samaritan woman. In those days, Jews did not associate with Samaritans, but Jesus *chose* to speak to the Samaritan woman. Through that single visit, Jesus "humanized" someone society despised. Is there a modern-day "Samaritan" who needs to hear from you today?

Prayer Focus: *Ask God to help you remove the barriers of ignorance that separate you and other people by enabling you to speak to someone you would normally avoid.*

August 22 ~ Thank God You're Human!

The devil led him to Jerusalem and had him stand on the highest point of the temple. "If you are the Son of God," he said, "throw yourself down from here."
—Luke 4:9 (NIV)

Those who truly *know* their worth must avoid the temptation to *prove* their worth. Living a life of integrity often calls for something as simple as remembering that you are human. On the surface, that may sound like a no-brainer, but if we were to take a serious look at some of our lifestyle choices, it would appear to an outsider that many of us think we are invincible.

In the day-to-day quest for success, we are often caught between the temptation to impress onlookers with "fancy footwork" or to pout when exceptional gifts and sacrifices go unnoticed. Far too often, the need to be liked, loved, or simply appreciated tempts us either to attempt superhuman feats or to push our bodies beyond the threshold of human endurance.

Even for Jesus, the temptation to prove his worth was very real because he was both divine and human. Jesus was able to resist this powerful temptation by remembering his purpose—to redeem fallen humanity.

What about you? Have you determined what God's purpose is for your life? Whatever you discover, remember that you are human. God does not expect you to abuse your body through overwork, neglect, or chemical dependence. You don't have to prove your worth to God by attempting superhuman feats. You have worth because God made you and Christ died to redeem you. Today, thank God you're human, a person of sacred worth, loved by God.

Prayer Focus: Give thanks that you do not have to prove your worth to God because God made you a person of sacred worth.

August 23 ~ Let's Be Honest

He told her, "Go, call your husband and come back." "I have no husband," she replied. Jesus said to her, "You are right when you say you have no husband. . . . What you have just said is quite true."
—John 4:16-17, 18b (NIV)

215

Have you ever needed to tell someone something, yet didn't because it involved more than you were ready for? Imagine yourself speaking to the police. You have seen something that they need to know about, but if you talk to them, you will be more involved than you intend to be. So you stand, hoping that they won't ask you anything about it. Or maybe you start a conversation about something else, silently hoping that they will never get around to this thing. Because you feel that it is not time—not today, not yet, maybe never.

Or, have you ever needed to confess a wrongdoing, but you couldn't figure out where to begin? You begin to wonder, *What will people think of me if they learn what I have done? Will they make a mistake and think that I am like "bad people" who do such things? Will they still be my friends? Will they still love me? Will my children be ashamed of me?*

Sometimes we spend too much time hiding the painful truth from others. We smile and pretend that sin never happened. We pretend that we have not offended our neighbor. We even pretend that we are all right with God. We get so good at the game of pretending that we even fool ourselves.

But in the prayer room with God, there are no secrets. Today, in prayer, let's be honest. God already knows.

Prayer Focus: Complete the following sentence: Dear Lord, I need to be honest with you about . . . .

August 24 ~ Exhibit Unusual Behavior

As he was going into a village, ten men who had leprosy met him. They stood at a distance and called out in a loud voice, "Jesus, Master, have pity on us!" When he saw them, he said, "Go, show yourselves to the priests." And as they went, they were cleansed. One of them, when he saw he was healed, came back, praising God in a loud voice. He threw himself at Jesus' feet and thanked him— and he was a Samaritan.

—Luke 17:12-16 (NIV)

It should be a natural response. No one should have to remind us. But, nine times out of ten, we forget to say thank you. Your spouse prepares a tasty meal as usual—silence. You work overtime again to get the report in on time—silence. You regularly send money to help a family member—no response. Doing something repeatedly—say, nine times out of ten—indicates usual behavior.

Problems erupt in marriages, jobs, and families when our efforts are usually unnoticed and unappreciated. There are books on the market with entire chapters devoted to teaching business managers how to show appreciation for their workers. The same advice is found in books on marriage and family relationships.

We know we ought to say "thank you," but somehow we let the opportunity slip by too often. The nine lepers who went on their way are a commentary on the ungrateful nature of human beings. Consider the implications of this. Nine out of ten miracles of God were not mentioned. Nine out of ten blessings went unreported. Nine out of ten times, God was ignored and taken for granted. Instead of saying thank you, 90 percent of the time we are usually off doing something else.

Perhaps, like the lepers, we're so preoccupied with our own condition that we fail to acknowledge others properly. Like the lepers, we often fail to realize when someone has blessed us and deserves thanks. Whatever the reasons, today you have an opportunity to exhibit unusual behavior by saying thank you.

Prayer Focus: *As a spiritual exercise, begin your prayer with a word of thanks to God for the blessings you have received.*

August 25 ~ What Are You Thinking About?

Whatever is true, whatever is noble, whatever is right, whatever is pure, whatever is lovely, whatever is admirable—if anything is excellent or praiseworthy—think about such things.

—Philippians 4:8 (NIV)

"Why do my projects have to pass through so many checkpoints? By the time they get approved, the information will be obsolete."

Justin was new in the department and struggled with company policies. When he learned that his latest project was still in review, he nearly exploded.

Justin stormed into his supervisor's office. "What does it take to get a project off the ground?" he blurted out. Justin's supervisor looked up and signaled "time out." In firm, deliberate tones, the supervisor explained that this company prided itself in maintaining a 95 percent customer satisfaction rate.

"We learned the hard way that rushing a project along without proper consideration is senseless," the supervisor continued. "We had to broaden our thinking to provide a larger perspective. Do you know what we do with proposals like yours?"

Justin shook his head sheepishly.

"Our best people evaluate them, and if we think they have merit, we test them on the public to get their reactions. Then, we pay careful attention to every concern. Your project is good, but we want it to be excellent. Excellence cannot be rushed. It's a process."

Integrity is also a process that cannot be rushed. An essential portion of that process involves thinking. Without considering God's perspective, our thinking can become shortsighted and self-serving. Today's scripture focuses our mental gaze on admirable thoughts. If we are what we think all day, why not think about noble things? So, what will you be thinking about today?

Prayer Focus: *Offer God your sacred thoughts today as an act of worship.*

August 26 ~ R-E-S-P-E-C-T

Make it your ambition to lead a quiet life, to mind your own business and to work with your hands, just as we told you, so that your daily life may win the respect of outsiders and so that you will not be dependent on anybody.
—1 Thessalonians 4:11-12 (NIV)

R-E-S-P-E-C-T. Radio stations that play music from the 1960s and 1970s sometimes play the hit "Respect," made famous by Aretha Franklin. It seems that everyone *wants* respect, but few people talk about how to *earn* the respect of others. Don't struggle too hard to find the answer. The process is simple according to today's scripture. Lead a quiet life and mind your own business. In other words, steer clear of spreading ill will. Work with your hands; that is, put in an honest day's work whether you're being watched or not.

Paul's words may seem a little blunt, but he makes a valid point. He was

218

a self-employed missionary. Paul supported his ministry by making tents early in the day, and then he shared Christ from the hottest part of the day into the evening. Because he was a frequent "outsider," people watched him closely before they would listen to him. By observing his diligent, unassuming work ethic, people learned something valuable about Paul's character, which probably earned their respect. Because of that respect, people listened to Paul.

What do people learn by watching you? Setting a good example through your daily living may be the greatest *living sermon* that you can ever preach to another person. Earning the respect of others may allow you the privilege of developing meaningful relationships. Ultimately, you may be able to share the joy of being in relationship with Jesus Christ. Why not earn more than a paycheck? Earn a little R-E-S-P-E-C-T through your daily living.

Prayer Focus: Let your ambition for today be to live in a manner that earns God's respect as well as the respect of others.

August 27 ~ Fly Like an Eagle

But those who hope in the LORD will renew their strength. They will soar on wings like eagles; they will run and not grow weary, they will walk and not be faint.

—Isaiah 40:31 (NIV)

Perhaps you have heard how eagles respond to approaching storms. Instead of fleeing from an impending storm, the eagle turns toward it, spreads its wings, and allows the up-draft from the winds to lift it above danger. The eagle's ability to soar above the storm hinges around two vital actions. First, it instinctively turns toward the approaching storm. Second, it realizes that it has been equipped to rise above the storm with its mighty wings. These actions are clear examples of transcendence.

The writer of Isaiah points out that we too can transcend life's challenges by learning to hope in the Lord. As we develop our spiritual instincts, we too will learn to face problems rather than try to outrun them. The more we learn to trust God, the more we will realize that God has equipped us with the ability to overcome the forceful energy

219

of conflict and confrontation. Hope in the Lord provides the inner motivation to press on despite formidable obstacles. Hope in the Lord builds the belief that we can overcome bad situations.

Storms in life are inevitable. All of us experience them. But people of integrity learn to transcend them. Like the eagle, we too can face the storms of life instead of turn away from them. Place your hope in God today. Face your problems, spread your wings, and expect to fly like an eagle.

Prayer Focus: Place your hope in God today. Expect God to renew your strength so that you may walk.

August 28 ~ Restore the Original Beauty

Brothers, if someone is caught in a sin, you who are spiritual should restore him gently.

—Galatians 6:1a (NIV)

Larry parked his car in front of a run-down house for sale. Neighbors regularly remarked that it was shameful that this once-glorious dwelling had been allowed to deteriorate to such a deplorable state. When Larry saw the old house, however, indescribable joy consumed him. As the owner led him through the rooms, Larry imagined how beautiful the hardwood would look if he refinished the floors. Larry was a carpenter. Restoring historical buildings was his hobby. When Larry walked into a house, he was never discouraged by the actual condition of the structure; he saw only the original beauty of the place waiting to be coaxed to life again.

When we encounter someone whose life has deteriorated because of bad decisions, our first response may be to avoid the person. Without finding out about the person's situation, we may even try to find ways to make the person feel unwanted and unwelcome around us. It's easy to dismiss someone, but people of integrity should consider developing the means to restore people to wholeness.

"If someone is caught in a sin, you who are spiritual should restore him gently." Those are the words of a person interested in restoring lives. People in the restoration business look beyond the present condition. To restore something requires the ability to see the original inner beauty of something. Look beyond the exterior of people today. Imagine people as

220

God must see them, and pray about ways to coax the original beauty out of someone.

Prayer Focus: Accept the challenge to look for the original beauty that God has placed in all people. Ask God to lead you to one person whose original beauty needs a little coaxing today.

August 29 ~ Touchstone

Young men, in the same way be submissive to those who are older. All of you, clothe yourselves with humility toward one another, because, "God opposes the proud but gives grace to the humble."

—1 Peter 5:5 (NIV)

"You've got it made, man." Barry still remembered hearing his friends' congratulations after a leading "tech" company had hired him. Barry was a whiz kid. For him, success was common. By age twenty, Barry already had been in demand as a systems analyst consultant. Those were the "good old days" in Barry's career. His new job in Silicon Valley demanded a new set of skills that Barry was not prepared for. Despite his expertise with computers, Barry had failed to learn people skills.

Mr. Roberts, Barry's new boss, knew considerably less about computers than Barry did, but he was the head of the department. This irked Barry to no end. In many instances, Barry had discovered new and innovative ways of achieving results, but he failed to consider the rationale of Mr. Roberts, who still did things "the old way." After a year of heated confrontations with his boss, Barry found himself unemployed.

Having job skills does not negate the necessity of being humble and respectful toward others. A friend of mine considers humility to be a part of his everyday attire. He never feels completely dressed until he puts a small weathered rock into his pocket. That rock is his "touchstone." Each time he feels that rock in his pocket, he is reminded to pray and humble himself to God and others. Is there something that can become your "touchstone"? Find something to touch daily that reminds you to pray and be humble.

Prayer Focus: As a spiritual exercise, find a "touchstone" to carry throughout the day to remind you to be humble in your dealings with God and others.

August 30 ~ May I "See You"?

Whatever you have learned or received or heard from me, or seen in me—put it into practice.

—*Philippians 4:9a (NIV)*

"I seeee yooou," squealed three-year-old Marsha. With a broad smile on her face, she peeked around the edge of the sofa and clutched her mother's knees.

Marsha was a joy to have around. Her mother, Brenda, never thought that having children would be so fulfilling. Brenda wanted to be a good parent and often had concerns about her daughter. What type of school is best for Marsha? Will she find good friends to play with? One night, a question turned Brenda's thoughts inward: What kind of example should I set for Marsha?

Brenda was a single parent. She hadn't been to church since Marsha was baptized. Brenda dressed Marsha in her grandmother's baptismal dress. The pastor was gentle with Marsha and personable toward Brenda. At one point in the service, the pastor asked Brenda, "Will you nurture Marsha in Christ's holy church and be a godly example for her to follow?" Brenda said yes, but now she wondered, "Am I doing enough for you, Marsha? Maybe I should find out what time church starts Sunday."

Are you someone's example? Is there a child, a relative, or a friend who "sees you" and looks up to you? Paul made a conscious decision to be the kind of example that the people of Philippi should imitate. "Whatever you have learned or received or heard from me, *or seen in me*—put it into practice." Someone who needs a good example may need to "see you" today.

Prayer Focus: Choose today to be a godly example for others.

August 31 ~ Loaded with Potential

Then Jesus asked, "What is the kingdom of God like? What shall I compare it to? It is like a mustard seed, which a man took and planted in his garden. It grew and became a tree, and the birds of the air perched in its branches."

—*Luke 13:18-19 (NIV)*

222

People with integrity move with steadfast persistence in life. Perhaps it's because they realize their God-given potential. An example of potential can be observed in the lowly mustard seed. It is so tiny and seemingly insignificant that it could easily get lost. To the naked eye, it appears just slightly larger than a grain of sand or a speck of pepper from the pepper mill. If you are not careful, a mustard seed could slip through your fingers and be lost forever. On the other hand, if you placed that tiny seed in the right place, it could grow into a magnificent plant. Perhaps Jesus chose to use the mustard seed in this short parable about the kingdom of God because of its tremendous potential.

Jesus' parables celebrate the potential of things that seem to be small or insignificant. Mustard seeds grow into trees. Yeast influences an entire measure of flour. Can you see your own potential when you look at the mustard seed in the parable? Even if you think that what you have to offer to the Lord's service is no more useful than a handful of sand, today you are encouraged to allow even the smallest gift or talent to take root and be a blessing to God and others.

Are you facing a difficult situation? Are you overwhelmed at the enormousness of a task? Are you simply striving to become all that God wants you to become? Remember that, like the mustard seed, you are loaded with potential. And if you will live a Christian life of integrity, you *will* realize your God-given potential!

Prayer Focus: Acknowledge that God has loaded you with enough potential to do whatever is before you—today and every day. Ask God to help you be steadfast in integrity so that you may realize your full potential.

September

KEEPING COMPANY— WITH GOD, WITH OURSELVES, WITH OTHERS

Barbara Mittman

September 1 ~ Warm Welcome

"Be dressed for action and have your lamps lit; be like those who are waiting for their master to return from the wedding banquet, so that they may open the door for him as soon as he comes and knocks."

—*Luke 12:35-36 (NRSV)*

I belong to a clan that cherishes reunion times. These together times are both greeting card occasions and real-time family reunions. Whenever we meet, there always is a designated "home base," lots of food, great company, and a few strangers to welcome.

We recover some of the most ancient traditions of hospitality when we are together. I'm not talking about a professionally produced Martha Stewart–type of hospitality. Our home base is not usually a perfectly decorated and furnished place. Our food is not usually rated according to five-star restaurant standards. Our companionship is not contingent on events or entertainment. Our embracing welcome of new clan members

225

is different from the pleasant warmth of a hotel jacuzzi. Our hospitality welcomes the stranger, provides food, furnishes shelter, and supplies togetherness.

As soon as the home base doors begin to open, it's reunion time! Anticipation and frantic preparations give way to open embraces. Doorbells ring and knocks are answered. Reunion hospitality takes a real interest in whoever appears at the door. There is always plenty of room— room to give and receive a warm welcome.

These devotions for the month of September are just like the doors of our family's home base during reunion times. Here you will find plenty of room for giving and receiving, loving and being loved. Doorbells will invite heart, mind, and spirit. Knocks will be answered. Together, we will make room to keep company with God, our own spirit, and our neighbors. Together we will explore the richness of these relationships.

Get ready to answer the knock and be warmly welcomed!

Prayer Focus: Ask Christ to meet you at the door. Listen for a knock. Be ready to give and receive a warm embrace.

September 2 ~ An Openness to God's Spirit

Then Mary said, "Here am I, the servant of the Lord; let it be with me according to your word." Then the angel departed from her.
—Luke 1:38 (NRSV)

Imagine that you are standing near Mary when the angel of the Lord appears to her. You eavesdrop as the angel tells Mary that she is to carry and give birth to the Son of God. Now, as the angel departs, Mary turns and speaks to you:

I get it now! I have been chosen by God! God has found favor with me! This is God, the power Most High. God, for whom nothing is impossible. I will bear God's Son, the Holy One. My life is no longer mine—I am God's. I have nothing to fear. I have met God's angel and believe that it will happen just like he said.

Mary is so sure. No doubts or second thoughts. Mary says *yes* to God's possibilities. She is open and agreeable to the power of the Most High.

Mary is Mary, blessed among women. I am not Mary! But, like Mary, I am chosen by God to make a difference. You are chosen and have found favor with God, too! Mary was called to bear God's son. To what might God be calling you?

226

Knock on the door and check out God's possibilities for you. Open up to the power of God's Spirit. Make room to "get it" according to God's promises and love for you!

Prayer Focus: Open your heart and make room for God's Spirit. Offer your all so that God's possibilities can be.

September 3 ~ Holy Space

How lovely is your dwelling place, O Lord of hosts! My soul longs, indeed it faints for the courts of the Lord; my heart and my flesh sing for joy to the living God.
—Psalm 84:1-2 (NRSV)

"How lovely is your dwelling place, O Lord of hosts!"
Dwarfed by tall skyscrapers and high-rise condominiums; in the alley behind a homeless shelter; camouflaged by autumn-dulled brush alongside a still mountain lake;
"How lovely is your dwelling place, O Lord of hosts!"
In the home of a loved one, recently deceased; in a public school classroom;
"How lovely is your dwelling place, O Lord of hosts!"
In the candlelit warmth of a quiet sanctuary on Christmas Eve; across the room from one who had cause to hate;
"How lovely is your dwelling place, O Lord of hosts!"
On a crack-ridden, weed-jammed inner-city sidewalk; held tight in the crook of a loved one's arm;
"How lovely is your dwelling place, O Lord of hosts!"
In a medical clinic's examination room; down a mountain pass on a Greyhound bus;
"How lovely is your dwelling place, O Lord of hosts!"
On a beach where walls of water miraculously turn into waves of love;
"How lovely is your dwelling place, O Lord of hosts!"

These are some of my holy places. I am often lured back to the places where I have found room in the heart of God. You know about some of God's other glorious dwelling places—places where you have found God's Spirit and been received into the arms of our Loving Host.

September 4 ~ Cordial Silence

[The Lord] said [to Elijah], "Go out and stand on the mountain before the LORD, for the LORD is about to pass by." Now there was a great wind, so strong that it was splitting mountains and breaking rocks in pieces before the LORD, but the LORD was not in the wind; and after the wind an earthquake, but the LORD was not in the earthquake; and after the earthquake a fire, but the LORD was not in the fire; and after the fire a sound of sheer silence.
—1 Kings 19:11-12 (NRSV)

We picked up food and headed for the mountains. The car's resident deejay went to work. We got lost and then stuck in stop-and-go traffic. We'd been driving for more than two hours and had not even seen a mountain. All I wanted was a place to stop the car and a little bit of peace and quiet.

We finally spotted one of those picture-perfect mountain streams— wide, shallow, and clear. It had a current that moved right along and *big* rocks all over. We splashed and played in the water. We told jokes and started to shape the story that would explain our impromptu "flight" once we got back.

Later, without anyone saying so, we each crawled up onto our own big rock and quit talking. We basked in sun and silence for more than an hour. As water rushed through my toes, I found room to be with God. My silent prayers were interrupted by the prayers of another giving thanks to God for meeting him in the quiet. Our "Amens" to his prayer led to an outpouring of testimonies that continued until the late afternoon shadows began to fall on the water.

On the way back to the car, we walked over a bridge that stretched across the stream. We looked downstream to where we had been. We each grabbed a stick and dropped it into the water. As the sticks floated down- stream, we watched in awe as they aligned to form a cross.

Prayer Focus: *Try to make room to keep a time of silence. Offer a quiet heart, ready to welcome God's Spirit.*

September 5 ~ Freeing Sounds

About midnight Paul and Silas were praying and singing hymns to God, and the prisoners were listening to them. Suddenly there was an earthquake, so violent that the foundations of the prison were shaken; and immediately all the doors were opened and everyone's chains were unfastened.

—Acts 16:25-26 (NRSV)

It was some of *the* most exciting Christian worship we had ever experienced! Light and sound witnessed to the presence of God's Spirit. Thousands of voices sang praises. Clear and sure testimonies echoed throughout the arena. Fireworks celebrated lives turned around by Christ's love. Karla's life was one of them.

Karla is a young woman who would say that she has always known God. If you asked and really wanted to know, Karla would show you where she teethed on the pews of her local church. Karla loves the church. She grew up in the usual ways around those who really knew her, and she left her mark as a committed church leader.

Karla was playing the part of Paul and Silas during worship that night. She was singing aloud to a mighty and awesome God. She prayed together with the thousands who had gathered. Then she stopped to listen. God's Word found her heart to be chained by doubt, temptation, and fear. The music, testimonies, and prayers made room for the Spirit to break through and shake her faith clear to the core!

Karla claimed Jesus Christ as her Lord and Savior that night and celebrated at a party with thousands of guests. God rejoiced with her, a prisoner set free! Praise God with fireworks, confetti, singing, and dancing! Praise God for new life!

Prayer Focus: Turn up the sound! Pray that God might use the sounds of your day to make room for the earth-shaking power of the Spirit.

September 6 ~ Beckoning Christ's Love

Devote yourselves to prayer, keeping alert in it with thanksgiving.

—Colossians 4:2 (NRSV)

Come, Lord Jesus! is the next to last verse in the Bible. Boldly prayed, these words make room for me to meet the Holy. *Come, Lord Jesus!* signals my eagerness to be open to God's Spirit. It may be a desperate plea to the One who has the power to save me. *Come, Lord Jesus!* is my way of knocking.

Come, Lord Jesus! witnesses to the promises of God. *Come, Lord Jesus!* beckons God forward through history and back from the future that God desires for you. *Come, Lord Jesus!* meets you in a relationship that will make a difference. *Come, Lord Jesus!* gently reveals the treasures of God.

When we pray, *Come, Lord Jesus!* God breathes new life in us. Our hearts open and accept Christ's gracious mercy and love. We become the recipients of the generous gifts of the Spirit.

And so, I pray, *Come, Lord Jesus! Come, Lord Jesus!* Meet me, a woman whose heart longs for your love. *Come, Lord Jesus!* Open my eyes to my unbelief. *Come, Lord Jesus!* Welcome me into your house of love. *Come, Lord Jesus!* Swing wide the doors of my heart. *Come, Lord Jesus!* Help me seek the love that will give me life.

Prayer Focus: *Beckon Christ's loving power and Spirit into your life. Boldly pray, "Come, Lord Jesus!"*

September 7 ~ Willing to Ponder

We ponder your steadfast love, O God, in the midst of your temple.
—Psalm 48:9 (NRSV)

Recently, I spied on a four-year-old as he examined the workings of a clock. The interlocking gears and shafts held such fascination for Rangsey. His attention span allowed him to be quite deliberate. He would investigate the workings, go away, and return to check it out all over again. Rangsey seemed truly taken in by the questions posed by the workings of that clock.

The shepherds found Mary and Joseph and the child lying in the manger. As soon as they saw them, they told them what the angel had said. All who heard were amazed. Mary paid careful attention and held the details deep within her heart.

I can be easily overwhelmed by the unexpected. Surprises really require me to think twice. I need room to reflect. I just cannot appreciate the significance of what is unforeseen without having a chance to ponder. I need to stash the experience for awhile and wait to take it out when I have a chance to mull things over.

Like the psalmist, we make room to ponder God's steadfast love. Maybe we are fascinated with how God's unfailing love works in our world. We might be amazed by the details of God's love in action in the lives of our neighbors. It's possible that we are surprised by God's unexpected goodness in our own lives. Time for contemplation and meditation can open the door to God's Spirit.

Prayer Focus: Let God's love captivate your attention.

September 8 ~ Being Still

"Be still, and know that I am God!"'

—Psalm 46:10 (NRSV)

"Be still, and know that I am LOVE!"
—Psalm 46:10 (paraphrase: Nan C. Merrill, Psalms for Praying*)*

My mind is racing. I'm wondering what my daughter is doing. I've got a song stuck in my head. I keep re-playing a recent conversation over and over again. Obligations that are more than a week away are making me anxious. I am sitting still, but it's really forced—muscles tight, shoulders hunched, neck stiff, chin out. I take a breath and exhale a prayer. I can't quiet myself. Not even the flame of the candle by my side can sit without flickering.

I have a tendency to be a moving target. I am rarely still. I know that the power of God is like the wind. I know that Jesus walked and taught and healed. I know the Holy Spirit as Advocate, Counselor, and Friend. I can testify that I am hospitable to God's working in my life as a moving target. God can keep up! Playing "catch me if you can" works for me and God. Father, Son, and Holy Spirit are not static—the action of God is dynamic!

Still, my heart longs for the peace and knowledge of God's love. It feels like a dull ache—like something isn't quite right. It's like a bruise without a break—not truly debilitating, but somewhere deep and at the very center of my being. I get this all-over desire to be still.

I cannot be still on my own. To be still is to make room for a love that I do

231

not deserve. I know of this love but struggle to accept that God could love me. I need God in order to know God. God hears the cry of my heart. God calms the waves and stills the wind. God makes room for me to know love.

Prayer Focus: Call on God to still your turbulence and make room for love.

September 9 ~ Minding the Sabbath

Remember the sabbath day, and keep it holy.

—Exodus 20:8 (NRSV)

Pay attention to the rhythm! Rhythm is the throbbing and beating heart that gives life to music. The style of a particular tune is characterized by its rhythm. The rhythm gives the tune room to be rap or jazz. Without rhythm, a tune can lose its bearings.

When musicians read a musical score, they pay attention to both sound and silence. If a rest is marked, the sound stops. Rests in the music are revered and honored. When a rest is welcomed, it can activate the syncopation of classical jazz or set up the final cadence of a march. A marked rest makes room for the music to be!

Pay attention to your own rhythm. You chew your food and brush your teeth with a beat. You walk and talk in rhythm. You keep your own "work and rest" cadence, day in and day out.

Sometimes it's hard to get the work to stop so we can make room to rest. I know that if I can give in to a quick nap or surrender to blue sky and sunshine, the rest will get me going again. So, I mark my calendar with sabbath rests. I make sure I stop for vacations and keep set-apart days to meet God. I keep the rests and make room for me to be!

Prayer Focus: Find your pulse. Feel the throbbing as your heart works and rests. Ask God to bless your work and your rest.

September 10 ~ Trusting God

Steadfast love surrounds those who trust in the LORD.

—Psalm 32:10b (NRSV)

A Son's trust released a Parent's love. We hear of that love in the Gospels. It's the calm in the midst of a great storm and the grace of a good catch. It's being present to a woman you're not supposed to be seen with. It's the generosity of a little boy in a crowd. It's community gathered at a table, and anger in the temple. It's despair and desperation pleading in a garden. It's disappointment about promises broken, loyalties dashed, and the kiss of a betrayer. It's peace at a moment of temptation, and endurance under duress. It's mercy for a criminal and forgiveness for all humanity.

If we trusted God, we could make room for that same love. But I'm not Jesus—I don't measure up! I can't even "play" at trusting without wavering.

My daughter and I often play at being "blind." We walk around the corner or down the street with the sighted one leading the "blind one." Although neither of us has ever betrayed the trust of the blind one, I sometimes get this uncontrollable need to pull back and sit down on the spot. I end up pulling back just as hard as my daughter is pulling forward. I want to trust, but I can't seem to get over whatever makes me want to pull back.

I don't trust my own ability to trust, so I have to trust God. We can trust God's faithfulness even when we can't trust ourselves. God keeps the trust and loves us!

Prayer Focus: *Offer your life to the only One you can trust to love. Give thanks for God's faithfulness.*

September 11 ~ Keeping Company with the Faithful

Day by day, as they spent much time together in the temple, they broke bread at home and ate their food with glad and generous hearts, praising God and having the goodwill of all the people.

—Acts 2:46-47a (NRSV)

I am part of a small group of people who intentionally seek Christian community at our denomination's annual area conference. We are strangers when we move into our "home" for the long weekend. We fully participate in the worship, study, and decision making of the larger body as they gather and make room to enjoy one another's company.

233

We really do live together and take most meals together. We invite God to "host" our life together. We devote ourselves to scripture. The promises of God seem to unite us in a way that settles most differences. We find out that we all hear the same voice. We pick up the language of prayer. Our interest in one another's stories draws us out of ourselves.

But, this is not a perfect weekend! Doors open and slam shut. We are touched by God and, at the same time, slapped in the face by our own humanness. We struggle to trust. We wobble between our selfish desires to hide out in Christian "exclusiveness" and our call to proclaim the gospel. So, why do we bother?

When I am with people of faith, I become a meaningful part of a larger body. The hospitable acts of receiving, accepting, and encouraging are all a part of the gracious welcome I experience in a Christian fellowship like this. The household of faith always keeps plenty of room on both sides of the door. Keeping company with the faithful makes room for God's embracing love.

Prayer Focus: Pray for God's presence among those with whom you keep company. Give thanks for ways in which their fellowship and hospitality have welcomed you. Offer yourself and your blessing to these people.

September 12 ~ Come to the Table

When he was at the table with them, he took bread, blessed and broke it, and gave it to them. Then their eyes were opened, and they recognized him.
—Luke 24:30-31a (NRSV)

James made a phone call, and three days later he was a guest in the home of his half-brother, Ian. The fact that Ian's father had left his wife and young sons twenty-some years ago was known to James. A job-related move found James just blocks from Ian's home.

Ian and James had never seen each other. Ian answered James's knock and invited him in. Soon they were seated at the table. Food was passed family-style. One of Ian's children noticed that both men aligned the food on their plate in the same manner. The conversation turned to food, and soon they discovered that James shared Ian's dislike for green food. The rolls and butter were passed. Both used their knives to form a butter "twirl."

234

Although it may seem a bit too convenient, this story is true. I was there. I watched as James's mannerisms at the table led to a family's acceptance. I heard a familiar-sounding voice come out of the mouth of a stranger. I listened to the stories as we lingered over dessert and coffee.

The Latin words for company—*com* and *panis*—mean "sharing bread together." At the Lord's Table, we are all company. We may gather as strangers, but soon the familiar actions and stories around the table make room for us to accept and receive. We recognize and welcome one another and the risen Christ as the bread and cup are lifted. The breaking of the bread and the sharing of the cup are true expressions of the larger welcome of God.

Prayer Focus: In your mind's eye, picture a time when you were welcomed to the Lord's Table. Give thanks for the familiar mannerisms and stories that you associate with this sacrament.

September 13 ~ Pushing Away from the Table

"For who is greater, the one who is at the table or the one who serves? Is it not the one at the table? But I am among you as one who serves."
—Luke 22:27 (NRSV)

We regularly meet for lunch. It always takes awhile for everyone to arrive, and no one comes empty-handed. Each of us comes to the table with all the briefcases, keys, and calendars that we need to defend our own good name, status, and life's purpose. By the time our waiter takes our order, there is already so much on the table that there is hardly room for anything else.

We manage to make room for the food when it comes. We move the stuff, but our opinions, prejudice, jealousy, and all our worries still take up plenty of room. It isn't until much later, after the table is cleared and we start to push ourselves back away from the table, that we can really pay attention to one another.

We start to make room to accept and receive as soon as we push ourselves away from the table. If I can leave my stuff right there on the table, then I can serve! Otherwise, all the props that point to me, my efforts, and my qualifications obstruct my vision. My role as "Miss Know-It-All" keeps me from listening. My "shoulds" and "oughts" make it impossible for me to pay attention.

We have nothing to defend once we get our elbows off the table. We can get out of the way. We can hear the call of awe and mystery, and follow. Unhampered by mistrust and the need to prove ourselves, we can be gracious and generous. Once we are away from the table, we are free to serve.

Prayer Focus: Invite God to gently pull you away from the table. Leave your stuff and freely offer yourself as one who will serve.

September 14 ~ Your Life's Purpose

All things are done according to God's plan and decision; and God chose us to be his own people in union with Christ because of his own purpose, based on what he had decided from the very beginning.
—Ephesians 1:11 (GNT)

Dara plays guitar in a couple of bands. Just as soon as his instrument is out of the case, Dara plugs it into an electronic tuner. Each string has its own key. Each is tuned individually. It takes time and a great deal of care. By the time Dara is done tuning, all the strings sound their proper pitch—true and right.

Another full set of six strings waits in Dara's guitar case. The strings are not all the same. An "E" string cannot serve as a "B" string. Each has been specifically manufactured to be strung on a guitar and tuned in a particular way. When the strings are strung and tuned properly, they perform well.

You are like one of these strings. You are marvelously made (Psalm 139:14) and created with everything you need to fulfill your destiny. You have been properly strung. You just need an electronic tuner to plug into God's chosen purpose for your life.

I wish it were that simple to get in tune with the heart of God! I know I am in tune when I have lots of energy. I get in tune when I discover that hours have passed while I've been working on something that is really important to me. Friends affirm my very best work and grab hold of my tuning keys. Even when I don't agree with how I've been strung, God makes room to get past my own deaf ear. God takes the time and care we need to sound true and right.

236

September 15 ~ Gift-Bearers

There are different kinds of spiritual gifts, but they all come from the same Spirit. There are different ways to serve the same Lord, and we can each do different things. Yet the same God works in all of us and helps us in everything we do.
—1 Corinthians 12:4-6 (CEV)

This is a very special gift—it's filled with love inside.
The reason it's so special is it's just for you from me.
You only have to hold this gift and know I think of you.

These lines are part of a longer poem that was carefully attached to a small, wrapped gift box one Christmas morning. It was intended as a gift of love from a child to a parent.

The verse and its gift box point me to the spiritual gifts given by God to each of us. Paul explains that "Christ gave each one of us . . . [a] special gift" (Ephesians 4:7 NCV). This is about working miracles and healing, pastoring and feeding, preaching and teaching—just like Jesus! I am convinced that each of us has a gift such as these, given out of the love that God has for us. These gifts have been planted deep within us. My gift is just for me from God.

As soon as I opened my "gift box" from God, everything began to make sense. I found out that my gift is teaching. Now, everything I do makes room for this gift. I intentionally nurture my teaching abilities. Colleagues graciously receive my work as an instructor. Friends help make sure that I actually spend time teaching. I say *yes* when someone needs my teaching gift and *no* anytime a different gift is what's really needed.

God's generous and loving Spirit gifts each of us. All we have to do is open our own gift box, welcome it, embrace its call, and make room to use the gift.

Prayer Focus: Reach out and receive your gift box from God. Give thanks for Christ's generosity.

September 16 ~ What Some Say

The gifts [Christ] gave were that some would be apostles, some prophets, some evangelists, some pastors and teachers, to equip the saints for the work of ministry, for building up the body of Christ."
—Ephesians 4:11-12 (NRSV)

Dionne's gift is apostleship. I would call her a human chameleon. She can just open a door, walk in, and start carrying on a conversation. She really has a knack for knowing what to say and when to say it. She can just as easily tell a joke as give witness to the Holy Spirit's work in her life. Dionne would be the one I would send if I needed a message to be delivered.

Jeremy's gift is evangelism. As a self-employed businessman, he is able to share a vision that catches clients' attention and energy. He does the same thing with his faith as a member of a Christian rock band. Jeremy's testimony makes room for those listening to catch a glimpse of God's promises and say *yes!*

Lino's gift is pastoring. He happens to be a pastor. Lino is sought out by persons who are facing spiritual struggles and difficult decisions. He offers safe space and unconditional acceptance to all who knock. Lino embodies God's love as he nurtures, cares for, and guides others.

Others embrace gifts that speak. Those gifted as prophets go ahead of us and "forth-tell." Those who serve as our teachers speak to clarify and explain the faith. Still others come up beside us and speak words of encouragement and comfort when we need them most.

Open your own gift box. Make room to listen. Receive these stories. Warmly welcome any clues that the Spirit might be entrusting to your close friends and family. Whether you think yourself to be shy or outgoing, you may be gifted by Christ to make a difference by what you say!

Prayer Focus: *Ask God to free you to hear the voice of the Holy Spirit—in front of you, alongside you, and inside you.*

September 17 ~ What Certain Ones Do

We have different gifts, according to the grace given us. If a man's gift is prophesying, let him use it in proportion to his faith. If it is serving, let him serve; if

238

it is teaching, let him teach; if it is encouraging, let him encourage; if it is contributing to the needs of others, let him give generously; if it is leadership, let him govern diligently; if it is showing mercy, let him do it cheerfully.
—*Romans 12:6-8 (NIV)*

All followers are called to *do* in the name of the risen Christ! I pitch in and help behind the scenes sometimes. I give when the offering plates are passed. I often get stuck leading a group. I might get caught doing something good at Christmas. We all do a lot, and some of the things we do are really important.

Carrie is called to serve behind the scenes doing practical and necessary tasks. She is energized by the chance to get down and dirty. Tim has an entrepreneurial spirit that opens doors. He gives with great delight when there is need. Mike is a leader who shares both power and information. When he stands before a group, everyone is empowered to realize and accomplish their goals. Paula cheerfully welcomes opportunities to stop what she's doing to show compassion and mercy to someone in need. She walks gently with such persons, stands in their shoes, and does practical things to care.

Carrie, Tim, Mike, and Paula are gifted and called to serve, give, lead, and show mercy. They are not acting out of obligation or in response to some "give until it hurts" platitude. They have each been given a spiritual gift that is activated by the pressing needs around them.

Lift the top of your own gift box. Look for clues about these "doing" gifts in the situations that make you want to scream. Pay attention to conditions that keep nagging at you. Make room to wonder if you are called to *do* something about what pulls at your heart. You might be gifted to act boldly!

Prayer Focus: *Pray, "Bother me, God!" Ask God to lead you to know if you might be gifted to "do."*

September 18 ~ Seeing the Signs

To others the Spirit has given great faith or the power to heal the sick or the power to work mighty miracles. Some of us are prophets, and some of us recognize when God's Spirit is present.
—*1 Corinthians 12:9-10a (CEV)*

239

Jesus healed disease, restored sight, and cured the lame. He miraculously turned water into wine and raised a little girl from the dead. As a prophet, Jesus picked up subtle hints and "saw through" the Samaritan woman at the well.

The disciples walked with Jesus. They stood by as Jesus healed. They were in the boat when Jesus calmed the wind and the waves. They came upon Jesus as he was picking up the subtle hints spoken by the Samaritan woman. The disciples, the Pharisees, and others were firsthand witnesses to the God-pointing—but, they couldn't seem to see the signs until the stone was rolled away.

The stone was rolled away! Christ's resurrection revealed the signs and released the gifts. Now, the Holy Spirit points us to the signs of God's continuous presence in our world. Some among us give comfort and make room for the broken to be healed. Others recognize miraculous experiences where God has mysteriously intervened. Some are prophets who can see something deeper, read between the lines, and have a knack for sorting out what's real and what's not.

Unwrap your gift box. Consider the possibility that what you call intuition or coincidence might really be a gift of the Spirit. Make room to test your instincts with an eye toward God instead of the hand of fate. Offer a generous welcome to those "God-pointers" close to you. The power of God to heal, perform miracles, or make sense of things may be waiting to be received.

Prayer Focus: Jesus pointed to God in many ways. Under the cloak of darkness, Nicodemus admitted that none of Jesus' signs could have happened without God. Take a cue from Nicodemus and make room to believe that God is present and working in your life.

September 19 ~ Gifts to Life

The Spirit has given each of us a special way of serving others.
—1 Corinthians 12:7 (CEV)

The relationship between the gifts of the Spirit and how we live out our lives in the world is like a front bicycle wheel. Our God-given gifts are the hub at the center of the wheel. The spokes, which link the hub with the rim, are all the real and obvious ways we use our gifts. The rim, which supports the tube and tire, is all the people and the places where our gifts connect. The tube and tire are the world—so desperately in need of God's love.

The hub of my wheel is teaching. This is a high priority in my life, and I keep it well greased. The spokes are ways that I work—tutoring, teaching in the classroom, preaching, writing, consulting, being a musician, and being an advocate. These are occupations and professions that pay the bills, keep me connected to my center, and make a difference. Along the rim, the spokes are in relationship with federally funded education programs, neighborhood public schools, local churches, and a variety of other public and private councils, boards, and agencies.

The spokes make room for you to give and receive as the rubber hits the road. They are tightened and loosened in relationship to the gift at your hub and the needs of others beyond the rim. The Holy Spirit breezes through the spokes to energize you and free you for optimum performance and best tire wear.

Look clear down into the corner of your gift box. Find the tiny bicycle wheel. Insert your gift into the hub. Let the Spirit set your wheel in motion, and begin to roll along with God's will for your life.

Prayer Focus: *Out of God's love and Christ's sacrifice come gifts. From these gifts comes a joy-filled life. Give thanks!*

September 20 ~ Host and Guest

"Listen! I am standing at the door, knocking; if you hear my voice and open the door, I will come in to you and eat with you, and you with me."
—*Revelation 3:20 (NRSV)*

Our daughter likes to play "Garden View Cafe" at home. She puts on her apron, takes our order, and sets the dining room table. At the given time, my husband and I are escorted to a table for three. Our daughter (the "host") brings in three meals, ducks out one door, throws off her apron, and returns to the table by another door as our daughter (the "guest"). All through dinner she alternates between being the "host" and being a dinner "guest." We try to catch her going through the wrong door or ending up at the dining room table with her apron still on. Our playful hospitality makes room for our "host" to become our "guest" and our "guest" to become our "host."

The Greek word *xenos* means both host and guest. The same holds true in Islamic traditions. The root word of hospitality—*hospes*—claims both the host and guest as one.

Abraham and Sarah hosted three men (Genesis 18). Their hospitality revealed the gift of these guests—the news that Sarah would have a son—new life. At God's command, Elijah went to a widow for food (1 Kings 17). Her provisions were nearly spent. Elijah made room for the widow to release her own fears and become a guest in the presence of this life-bearing prophet. In a post-resurrection appearance, Jesus joined two men on the road to Emmaus (Luke 24:13-35). The men offered to host and feed this "stranger." Their hospitality made Christ known to them as he became host at their table.

Neither the host nor the guest has anything to give unless there is someone to receive. The host and guest need each other. A good host goes to the door and makes room for the door to swing wide open. Once received, the guest is given new life as host, with his or her own gifts to offer.

Prayer Focus: Listen for a knock. Strain to hear the voice that asks you to open the door. Invite God to help you make room to swing the door wide.

September 21 ~ Room to Be Made Known

For the creation waits with eager longing for the revealing of the children of God.
—Romans 8:19 (NRSV)

A good host offers free, friendly, and secure space. How can you make this kind of room for another human being? Offer room for guests to come and go on their own terms. Accept people for who and what they are. Give time for strangers to chew on the events and stories of their lives. Make elbowroom for newcomers to relate without "telling all." Patiently wait for truth. Let guests create themselves without worrying about being "made over" to be like the host. These gentle-hearted actions of hospitality make room for the children of God to be revealed!

Disney's animated film *Beauty and the Beast* speaks volumes about creating hospitable space. Belle, the heroine, is held hostage by a cruel prince who was turned into a beast by a witch. The evil, vengeful spell cast on the

242

castle and the prince can be broken only if the Beast gives up his stubborn pride and begins to truly love another. The supporting characters and story line move Belle from "guest" to hospitable host. Belle makes room for the Beast to be made known. The Beast is transformed! The true nature of the prince is revealed, and the spell is broken.

A compassionate heart can recognize the longings of another human being. An attentive host can make room for a stranger to be revealed as God intends.

Prayer Focus: Lift up the longings of another person to God. Pray about ways you might help this person make room to become all that he or she has been created to be.

September 22 ~ Cherishing Family

When Jesus saw his mother and the disciple whom he loved standing beside her, he said to his mother, "Woman, here is your son." Then he said to the disciple, "Here is your mother." And from that hour the disciple took her into his own home.
—John 19:26-27 (NRSV)

Jill, a single woman and parent of two teenage sons, was diagnosed with terminal cancer. She picked up the phone and called her neighbors, Matthew and Neva. Before Jill could get to the details of her cancer and prognosis, Matthew and Neva were out the backdoor, across the yard, and knocking on Jill's backdoor. They let themselves in and met Jill at her kitchen table. The couple listened and waited through all her tears. Jill explained the diagnosis and told them of her imminent death. Then, she asked Matthew and Neva to assume full parental rights for her sons.

Matthew and Neva made room to ponder. They welcomed the wisdom of close friends and trusted colleagues. The couple went away to visit their families. Matthew and Neva carefully thought about their call as followers of Christ. They contemplated God's gracious love and the gospel command to love. They prayed.

The Holy Spirit moved Matthew and Neva to see with their hearts. Jill died even sooner than expected, and the couple took the two teens into their own home. A few weeks later, in a court of law, they heard the voice of Jesus say, "Matthew and Neva, here are your sons."

243

At our house, family members are our most cherished guests. We open wide the door and pay close attention to our daughter and to our nieces and nephews—all strangers we are getting to know. We welcome family and greet them with open arms. We give and receive love and care. We make room for the struggles and joys that connect our lives.

Prayer Focus: Offer prayers for your family constellation.

September 23 ~ Receiving Friends

Some friends don't help, but a true friend is closer than your own family.
—Proverbs 18:24 (CEV)

There are many friendships in comic strips: Blondie, Dagwood, Tootsie, and Herb; the *Peanuts* gang; mom-friends Wanda and Bunny in *Baby Blues;* and the live-in friends in *Apartment 3-G.* Some days these friends are name-calling, misleading each other, or acting jealous. Other days we catch them opening a door, accepting a heartfelt apology, or making room to play.

The friends in some of my favorite comic strips are just like me. I can give a friend a warm welcome and then turn a cold shoulder. I can be trusted one minute and betray a friend in the next breath. I can give comfort until I start fault-finding. I can make room to forgive a friend as long as she still owes me.

We would never see the story of David and Jonathan (1 and 2 Samuel) in the Sunday morning comics. Their friendship was deep and abiding. Their commitment to each other was enduring and tenacious, even in the face of great risk. When David was in danger, he graciously received help from Jonathan. Later, Jonathan accepted David's generous promises. They related to each other as both host and guest.

David and Jonathan's friendship was not all that special. They were fiercely loyal and protective of each other. But beyond that, all they did was care for each other, according to the law—to love your neighbor as yourself (Leviticus 19:18). David and Jonathan made room for love to be given and received. That made them closer than family.

Prayer Focus: Meet God as you might meet your best friend. Speak openly and intimately as true friends.

244

September 24 ~ Fear Not!

But the angel said to them, "Do not be afraid."
—Luke 2:10 (NRSV)

Fear slams the door on acts of hospitality. There is no room to accept, receive, or believe if there is fear. Fear cannot answer a knock or pay attention to one who is lying by the side of the road.

There is plenty of human fear in the scriptures. Joseph responds to the fears of his brothers. Moses and Joshua say "Do not be afraid" to the Israelites. Boaz said it to Ruth. God said "Do not be afraid" to Abram, Hagar, and Isaac. God sent an angel to deliver "Fear Not!" messages to Zechariah, the virgin Mary, Joseph, shepherds in a field, the women at the tomb, and Paul. Jesus said "Do not be afraid" to the disciples and others so that they could go, do, and believe.

The story of the good Samaritan (Luke 10:29-37) is a story of fear-fed alienation and hatred. Fear moved the priest and the Levite away from the traveler found in need at the side of the road.

John's Gospel adds the threat of oppression and violence to the grief of the disciples (John 20:19-20). This fear didn't scatter the disciples; it trapped them behind a locked door for fear of the Jews.

Fear can keep you a "safe distance" away from me. Fear can confine me to a "safe closeness" apart from you. Do not be afraid!

Prayer Focus: The angel is at your elbow, saying, "Do not be afraid!" Pray the words of the angel back to God. Ask God to show you a heart that is free from fear.

September 25 ~ Solidarity with Strangers

You shall also love the stranger, for you were strangers in the land of Egypt.
—Deuteronomy 10:19 (NRSV)

Julian was at Sanya's place when the phone rang. When Sanya got off the phone, she was shaking. Her mother had been in a terrible accident and had been transported to a metropolitan area medical center's intensive care unit. Sanya's father, Doi, met them there. A shadow of confusion

245

and bewilderment clouded his face. Sanya's parents had resettled in the United States almost twenty years ago, but they had never really learned the language of their new country. In the time it had taken Julian and Sanya to get to the hospital, Doi had been barraged with all sorts of hospital staff and paperwork.

Sanya bridged the language barrier between the hospital staff and her father. She turned to Julian to help make sense of the paperwork and what the doctors were saying about her mother's injuries and treatment. But, there he sat—a stranger to insurance jargon, treatment form lingo, and medical terminology. Julian had lived in this country all his life. This language was his language. But now he was a stranger in need of help.

Julian did not need to be turned into an insurance agent, medical record clerk, or a doctor. He just needed help understanding what seemed foreign to him. At one time or another, we all get caught by the "unknown" and become strangers in our own way. Whatever our own "strangeness" may be, it makes room for us to graciously meet the needs of other strangers.

Prayer Focus: Invite God to give you a stranger's insight. Ask Jesus to point to ways you might reach out to someone as one stranger to another.

September 26 ~ Generosity with the Poor

Since there will never cease to be some in need on the earth, I therefore command you, "Open your hand to the poor and needy neighbor in your land."
—Deuteronomy 15:11 (NRSV)

Jesus promises God's favor and blessing on the poor. Politicians debate the terms of newly proposed economic sanctions. Local school district advisory committees make connections between family economics and academic success. Anti-gambling groups picket casinos as ATM machines are installed on-site. The disciples witness the gift-giving of a poor widow.

Hope, power, policies, and offerings—are we talking about the same poor and needy neighbors here? How can there be need in both scarcity and abundance? How can the poor have nothing yet possess everything? That's the paradox of the poor.

From beginning to end, the Scriptures call us to love our neighbor and keep the paradox. The law of the Torah commands that an open hand be extended to the poor. The Gospels give warm welcome to a widow who gives at great cost. Paul's second letter to the church at Corinth preaches equity, justice, and fair balance between abundance and need.

I want to keep the paradox. I want to pay attention to the needs of others as others point to my need. I want to give to a mother out of my economic abundance and graciously accept parenting advice from that same mother of five. I want to give a hat to a child and receive his song. I want to feed a man and let him tell me about a love that has no strings attached. I want to make room for the poor to turn the world upside down and welcome God's kingdom!

Prayer Focus: Pray that you might bring to life the wise words of one apocryphal writer: "Stretch out your hand to the poor, so that your blessing may be complete" (Sirach 7:32 NRSV).

September 27 ~ Welcoming Those Who Are Lame

"But when you give a banquet, invite the poor, the crippled, the lame, the blind, and you will be blessed."
—Luke 14:13-14 (NIV)

The well-loved children's book series *Clifford, the Big Red Dog* is now an animated show on public television. In a recent episode, dog-friends T-Bone and Cleo talked through the fence to a dog who was visiting in the neighborhood. They invited him to come and meet Clifford on the beach. As the gate was opened, they saw that their new friend had only three legs.

The stranger became strange-er. The missing back leg was all that the two friends could think about. T-Bone and Cleo were ambivalent about playing with this dog. They introduced Clifford and were quick to point out the stranger's three-leggedness. The dogs squirmed when one of their people walked right up to the new dog and began to pet him without seeming to see. They made excuses for not running on the beach. They were afraid that they might catch "leg losing" germs, so they didn't get too close to the stranger and wouldn't play with his ball. Clifford suggested a hillside climb. That climb made room for the three-legged stranger to be accepted.

To be unable to walk is strange to me. Like T-Bone and Cleo, I can get so stuck on the disability or occupied with my own emotions, opinions, and assumptions that there isn't enough room to swing the door open.

When company comes, the table is cleared off and set for the meal. There is plenty of room for something to happen—for guests to tell stories, show their artistry, sing songs, offer gifts, and play. Strangers cast off their "strangeness" and become human. The table is a welcoming place where nothing human can possibly be "strange."

Prayer Focus: Invite God to clear out all the feelings, questions, and ideas that grip you when you are in the presence of someone "different". Ask God to make you ready to receive the precious gifts strangers so eagerly offer.

September 28 ~ Liberating the Oppressed

The spirit of the Lord GOD is upon me, because the LORD has anointed me; he has sent me to bring good news to the oppressed, to bind up the brokenhearted, to proclaim liberty to the captives, and release to the prisoners.
—Isaiah 61:1 (NRSV)

The Spirit's power had made room for Jerrod to get re-acquainted with his home church. God had done for him what he could not do himself. One Sunday Jerrod stood up, grinned, and announced that it was his third anniversary—of sobriety. Applause, cheering, hugs, and prayers of thanksgiving filled the sanctuary all at once. There was much to celebrate!

Jerrod had been held captive by alcohol since the beginning of high school. He was addicted to the exciting lifestyle associated with booze. But, he was also a prisoner of his own choices, held hostage by binge drinking and oppressed by regret. Jerrod made his way to Alcoholics Anonymous (A.A.) a couple of years after college. Before he called and asked me to be his 5th Step partner, folks around the church hadn't seen him for more than ten years.

Jerrod came to me on his own terms. He had his written inventory and needed me to listen without judgment or condemnation. For Jerrod, this meeting was a life and death matter; I needed to pay attention and stay out of his way. I opened the door and made room to fully understand and accept this stranger's story. I received the many details of Jerrod's life "under the influence." His generous humility, fearlessness, and honesty made room for me to connect his story to my own.

The welcome of two open hearts loosened the bonds of alcohol and claimed God's accepting and forgiving love.

Prayer Focus: The Prayer of Saint Francis of Assisi begins, "Lord, make me an instrument." Invite God's Spirit to make you an instrument of grace and freedom to persons who are burdened and bound.

September 29 ~ Enemies at Table

You prepare a table before me in the presence of my enemies.
—Psalm 23:5 (NRSV)

A coworker undermines the work of a colleague. A sibling takes another's toy. A wife confronts a dishonest husband. A student resists a teacher's authority. A husband challenges his wife to tell the truth about her gambling. A customer disputes a bill. A parent bullies a child on the playing field. A patient has qualms about a doctor's diagnosis. A son defies his father.

Confrontation, suspicion, and revenge make us all enemies. Coworkers and customers become rivals. Family members become adversaries. Helpers become attackers. Neighbors become foes. If we were all invited to eat lunch somewhere together, our opposition to one another might keep us from going to the door. Doubt could make us afraid to open the door. Our vindictiveness would make it impossible to swing the door wide enough to enter in.

Whenever we have to defend ourselves, everyone else becomes our enemy. We cannot take our place at the table unless we disarm ourselves. Whether our enemies are our own family members or total strangers, we have to dump all that we think we have to guard. We have to lay aside our pride, put down all our trappings, and empty out all previous experience and foregone conclusions. Then, there is room!

The psalmist describes a setting where God is "host." God has the power to demobilize our attacks, incapacitate our weapons, and reconcile our antagonism. At the table we are welcome and changed from *hostis* (enemy) into *hospes* (guest).

September 30 ~ Finding the Door

The LORD went in front of them in a pillar of cloud by day, to lead them along the way, and in a pillar of fire by night, to give them light, so that they might travel by day and by night. Neither the pillar of cloud by day nor the pillar of fire by night left its place in front of the people.

—Exodus 13:21-22 (NRSV)

There was a robin inside the airport concourse. The immense open space was apparently enough to make the bird believe that she could fly. The walls of clear plate glass brought the blue sky and sunshine in from the outside. The bird instinctively flew toward the sky and smacked right into the glass. After a couple more collisions, she fell to the ground and was carried to an open door.

There really wasn't enough room inside the airport concourse for the robin to fly. The glass was in the way. There were no welcoming windows. The bird was so busy running headlong into the glass that she did not notice there were people trying to help her find a door. The bird took a real beating before she found the room she needed to fly.

Are you banging your head against a wall with no windows or knocking yourself out trying to make a door? God promises to help you find the door! By day, God is present in that great cloud of witnesses who accept you as you are, cherish your giftedness, and pay attention to your needs. God leads you to strangers who need to be warmly received as guests. A pillar of fire welcomes the holy, even in the dark. God's steadfast love never leaves you.

God is leading you right to the door! Make room to open it!

Prayer Focus: *God holds you by the hand and shows you the way. Welcome God's leading!*

October

LIFE QUESTIONS

Elizabeth Hunter

October 1 ~ What Am I Doing?

Jesus answered, "The work of God is this: to believe in the one he has sent."
—John 6:29 (NIV)

*L*ife is full of questions. And through the years I've come to realize that asking the "right" questions is even more important than finding the "right" answers, for the questions we ask have dramatic and eternal effects on our lives. This month we'll seek to deepen our faith by exploring some of these questions. Some are big; some are small; but all are significant.

For example, at twenty-nine, I still don't know what I want to be when I grow up, and I'm okay with that. But seven years ago, I felt harassed by some of life's big questions: *Am I living up to God's expectations? Where does God want me to be? Is the work I do really what God has in mind? Am I making the right choices?*

It didn't get any easier after my boyfriend asked me to marry him. Even in the throes of happiness, we wondered: *Are we ready? What if we make the wrong decision?*

A year later we married and found different questions: *Are we ready for a family? Do we have what it takes to stay married?* Confused, I stressed out trying to fulfill ideas of a successful career and relationship passed on by "helpful" parents and friends.

Then I discovered something: God calls each of us to one basic work—

251

love. The fact that my career and married life may change over my lifetime is okay, because God's notion of success is simply living a life of love. Such success makes God happy. It makes us happy. Without it, all other success is worthless.

Prayer Focus: What gifts has God given me that I'd enjoy using in my family, workplace, church, and community? Do I need God to reveal those gifts or give me confidence to use them?

October 2 ~ Whom Do I Listen To?

Fools think their own way is right, but the wise listen to advice.
—Proverbs 12:15 (NRSV)

Sometimes we hear God's voice from unlikely people. One morning I was rushing to get to a meeting on time. As I hurried from the parking garage, across the pavement, through the revolving doors, and onto the elevator, I looked at my feet to avoid eye contact with anyone who might slow me down.

"Hi," someone said as the elevator doors closed.

"Hi," I answered, punching number seven. As I glanced sideways for half a second, I saw a young man with Down syndrome staring at me and smiling.

"How are you?" he said.

"Fine, and you?" I said, looking down again and "willing" the doors to open. I looked at my watch: less than a minute left.

"I'm fine," he said. Before getting off the elevator on the fourth floor, he touched my arm. Surprised, I looked up. But there was only kindness in his eyes.

"You know, you should look people in the eye when you say hello. It's much nicer," he said. "Have a good day!"

Then the doors shut, and I was alone. I felt ashamed. How could I be too busy for simple kindness when here he was, unafraid and not too busy to care for a stranger?

Now I look at "mundane" conversation in a whole new light.

Prayer Focus: Whom do I listen to? Where in my life could I be more open to hearing God's message from an unlikely source or direction?

October 3 ~ When Does Sex Please God?

Present your bodies as a living sacrifice, holy and acceptable to God, which is your spiritual worship. Do not be conformed to this world, but be transformed by the renewing of your minds, so that you may discern what is the will of God— what is good and acceptable and perfect.
—Romans 12:1-2 (NRSV)

"With my body, I thee worship," said the bride, repeating the words of commitment to the man who would be her husband.

It was one of the few times I'd heard sexual intercourse mentioned within a church service. Yet outside the church, it is a constant topic for media, advertisements, friends, lovers, and our own thoughts—which often ignore spirituality.

Sex concerns more than simple physical pleasure. True love-making doesn't use or take but creates a holy and sacrificial bond of spiritual intimacy and trust. Such love serves and fills another's needs, which works best when two people marry, making a long-lasting commitment to each other.

Without such commitment, it's too easy to use someone for personal satisfaction or to let sexual pleasure mask underlying problems. Sex without commitment may seem like a solution, but it's an empty promise.

To make love within a marital commitment is to be transformed by serving and caring for another. Because we don't push for it, ignoring each other's needs, our pleasure is a blessing.

Prayer Focus: How is God renewing my mind? Do I need patience to trust God's will for me as I share my sexuality in God-pleasing ways?

October 4 ~ Why Pray?

On the day I called, you answered me, you increased my strength of soul.
—Psalm 138:3 (NRSV)

Do you have someone you talk to every day? How does it feel to have someone you check in with on a daily basis?

253

When I have someone like that in my life, talking about life's joys and pains becomes part of my daily routine. It reminds me I'm not alone in life. But in those times when I feel there's no one I can phone or talk to, I try not to forget I can still call on God—a best friend who loves me no matter what. I appreciate our conversations, which renew and refresh me. Because prayer is an act of love for God, I believe God appreciates my prayers, too.

Before I knew how to listen to God's voice, prayer had a cathartic value for me, but it felt one-sided. Now I'm able to hear God in several ways, such as when my heart is quietly convicted if I've hurt someone, when I overhear a snatch of conversation in passing that "coincidentally" speaks directly to me, or when I re-read a Bible passage differently after prayer.

If you have trouble finding time to pray, you might try placing a notebook by your bedside as a prayer journal. Regardless of when or where you do it, prayer is a time to be nurtured and sheltered by God's love, acceptance, and forgiveness. It's a time to gain strength and hope.

Prayer Focus: How might prayer become a bigger part of my life?

October 5 ~ Should I Give to the Homeless?

"'Lord, when did we see you hungry . . . ?' The King will reply, 'I tell you the truth, whatever you did for one of the least of these brothers of mine, you did for me.'"

—Matthew 25:37, 40 (NIV)

While waiting at the stoplight, I see a man holding a sign: "Will Work for Food." At a grocery store exit, a woman asks me, "Can you spare a dollar?" and, extending her hand, reveals an arm with needle marks that "connect the dots" between broken green veins.

Each time I run through the options: *Do I give? Do I pretend not to see this person? Do I say no?* It's something I've struggled with over and over. I know it's not a good idea to give people money they may use to buy drugs or alcohol, but if I have a little money, I'll buy the person a sandwich or beverage. Once I saw a guy try to sell the lunch I'd given him. But most of the time, people seem to appreciate respect and a little help. Just in case, I try to keep a loose dollar handy in my pocket.

254

Whatever I do, I can always pray for the person, smile, and say hello. I also can donate my time or money to a soup kitchen, shelter, or other ministry. Perhaps the question to ask ourselves is not *Should I give to the homeless?* but *How should I give to the homeless?*

Prayer Focus: How do I treat homeless people? What stereotypes might I need to lose? How might I safely help?

October 6 ~ Is God Calling Me to Have Children?

Children's children are a crown to the aged, and parents are the pride of their children.

—Proverbs 17:6 (NIV)

After two friends of ours had a miscarriage, I realized more than ever that even for those who have the commitment and maturity to raise a child, having children isn't something to be taken for granted. Having and raising children are precious abilities, yet they make one vulnerable.

Parents and other caregivers are given a deep, demanding responsibility to raise children in the right way (Proverbs 22:6). We've seen those close to us struggle with both the joys and grief of trying to raise a child. Yet we've seen others settle on having no children of their own while enjoying the privilege of helping raise nieces, nephews, godchildren, or other young people in their communities. Perhaps you can remember some biologically child-free people who helped raise you.

The Bible is full of stories about parents, grandparents, godparents, surrogate parents, and children. Even for those who, like the apostle Paul, have no children, there are many opportunities to care for a young person. "I have no one else like [Timothy]," Paul wrote. " . . . As a son with a father he has served with me in the work of the gospel" (Philippians 2:20*a*, 22*b* NIV). Whether or not we decide to have children ourselves, we can play important roles in the faith, life, and development of young people.

Prayer Focus: Might God be calling me to allow children to play a part in my life? What kind of role might God lead me to take?

October 7 ~ Why Is a Good Marriage So Important?

A capable wife who can find? She is far more precious than jewels.
—Proverbs 31:10 (NRSV)

Who you marry can make a big difference in your life. For her first marriage, a fun-loving, charming friend of mine chose unwisely. She married a man who was passionate about her, but who led her into a life of drugs, wild parties, and atheism. Though she cared about him, she came to realize that they didn't want the same things anymore. She wanted to find a deeper meaning in her life, but he didn't. His negativity was slowly dragging her down. Eventually, they divorced.

After several years of living a single life and seeking a new vocation, she found work that she loved. She also found Christ's acceptance and love. She married another man, who was positive and supportive of her, who believed in the same things she did, who believed in Christ, and who believed in her! It was amazing to see the two of them mutually blossom under their love and support for each other.

If you are looking for someone to share your life with, consider what qualities would best support you as you live a life of faith in God. Even if you're not looking for someone, consider what personal qualities of your own help you live out your faith.

Prayer Focus: How can I and my spouse or significant other best support and encourage each other in life? Do I need God to show me issues I'm overlooking? If I'm single, how can I best nurture in myself qualities that best serve God?

October 8 ~ How Is Economic Justice Relevant to My Life?

A poor man's field may produce abundant food, but injustice sweeps it away.
—Proverbs 13:23 (NIV)

The hard-working farmer should be the first to receive a share of the crops.
—2 Timothy 2:6 (NIV)

About a year ago, the office where I work started buying fairly traded coffee from Equal Exchange, a fair trade coffee grower's cooperative.

Many coffee distributors did not pay poor coffee farmers in Latin America a good price for their product. So when a nonprofit cooperative formed to help the farmers find markets that would pay a fair price, we supported it. Why not? It wasn't that difficult—just a little more expensive, and the product tasted better. Anyway, buying coffee was a justice issue.

So is buying other groceries. Even now poor farmers from small farms in the United States struggle to pay living expenses with commodity prices being far from fair. Many have lost their family farms. According to 1999 USDA figures, even though bread prices went up, wheat farmers only received approximately four cents for every loaf of bread bought—well below the cost of wheat production. With multinational corporations and distributors receiving the lion's share of the profits, many small farmers are losing their hope.

To support small farmers with a better share of a commodity, consider buying produce from farmers markets or asking your grocery store to stock locally grown products. And you can always pray for those who grow our food. Economic justice isn't just for social activists; we really can make a difference—even in simple, everyday ways.

Prayer Focus: Could my food-buying habits be more "just"? How can I help others economically by the choices I make each day?

October 9 ~ What Is Home?

Now the LORD said to Abram, "Go from your country and your kindred and your father's house to the land that I will show you. I will make of you a great nation, and I will bless you."

—Genesis 12:1-2a (NRSV)

When God told Abraham to go to a new land and leave the familiar behind, Abraham did just that. He must have worried about his family's safety, the possibilities of famine in Canaan, and the potential of danger and crime in Egypt. Still, when God opened up a door that held promises of such rich blessings, Abraham had faith and went.

My husband and I decided to live in an ethnically diverse community near the city's edge. We could have picked a "safer" neighborhood where most of the people looked, thought, and acted alike—one not bordered by a tough, slowly revitalizing district. But our new neighbors—people of varied cultures, ages, and family situations—blessed us with their hospitality and acceptance. An African neighbor shares his family's basketball rim. An older Chinese couple offer friendly greetings. A ten-year-old African American neighbor, upon seeing me struggle to dig my car out of two feet of snow, brought a shovel and worked alongside me, pushing away offers of money because she "just wanted to help." What blessings we would have missed if we'd opted to stay with the familiar.

Venture beyond the familiar today and discover the blessings that await you.

Prayer Focus: When God opens a new, unfamiliar opportunity, do I look at it seriously? What new opportunities may God be calling me to explore?

October 10 ~ Is Taking Care of My Body Important for My Spirit?

Or do you not know that your body is a temple of the Holy Spirit within you, which you have from God, and that you are not your own? For you were bought with a price; therefore glorify God in your body.
—1 Corinthians 6:19-20 (NRSV)

I wanted to be in better shape, but at first I didn't like the idea of working out in the morning. I am not a morning person. So I focused on how I'd feel post-workout: glorified.

Exercising helped me have a more positive spirit about the day ahead, as well as a sense of accomplishment. What a great way to start my day! With morning exercise, I've already achieved something—even before I come into contact with potentially demanding and stressful people or work. Maybe it's just me, but on days I exercise things just seem to go better.

Likewise, a hot shower in the morning awakens and refreshes me. Wearing clothes that are comfortable and cheery also raises my spirits, as does surrounding myself with calming colors, refreshing objects, and uncluttered, organized spaces.

The way I figure it, if we respect and care for our bodies like holy temples every morning, it is that much easier for us to welcome God's Spirit to dwell within us and help us throughout the rest of the day.

October 11 ~ How Can I Ever Forgive . . . ?

Clothe yourselves with compassion, kindness, humility, gentleness and patience. Bear with each other and forgive whatever grievances you may have against one another. Forgive as the Lord forgave you.

—Colossians 3:12-13 (NIV)

During a visit to Sierra Leone, a war-torn country on Africa's western coast, I met Muctarr, a twenty-six-year-old playwright who had been brutally maimed by rebel soldiers known for chopping limbs off thousands of civilians. To take away what he most valued, they cut off Muctarr's writing hand. As he begged and wept, they laughed, believing his hope was destroyed.

When Muctarr was released, he found the Nigerian army, who provided him with lifesaving medical care. Eventually, he learned to write almost perfectly with his left hand. A year later, after a shaky peace, the former rebels who had maimed him walked through his village. "I know you," he called loudly, confronting them. "You are the ones who did this to me." One of the terrified men wet his pants as they all pleaded with Muctarr and his family not to take revenge. "I could have killed them, and they knew it," Muctarr said.

The former rebels wept with surprise when Muctarr said he forgave them and told them never to forget what they had done. Just as with Muctarr, forgiveness is a part of our healing process and a way of over coming evil with good.

Prayer Focus: When I speak words of forgiveness, do I mean them, or am I really holding back? Whom is it difficult for me to forgive? Why? How can God help me?

October 12 ~ Why Should I Volunteer?

"Love your neighbor as yourself."

—Matthew 22:39 (NIV)

259

Loving your neighbor as yourself means loving and caring equally for two people: your neighbor and yourself. Our church mentoring program pairs adults with youth members. I mentor Mae, who's fifteen, and spend time with her at least twice a month. We have a lot of fun hanging out, making things, visiting people and places, going to plays or movies, and playing games. I enjoy her creativity, wisdom, and opinions—however different they are from my own. I want her to feel capable of doing anything and to know that her opinions are respected. She knows that I care about what happens to her and that I want the best for her.

Volunteering as a mentor also has helped me to love and care for myself. I know I'm important to Mae, and I feel needed. A hug from Mae, or a genuine question about my life or my opinion, assures me that she cares about me, too. It seems that the more time I spend with her, the more she shares, responds with trust, and asks when we'll get together again.

Loving your neighbor as yourself doesn't require big, grand events; usually love works quietly through small, everyday acts.

Prayer Focus: How could my life expand by loving someone through volunteering? What other ways does God call me to love my neighbor as myself?

October 13 ~ Am I "Keeping It Real"?

God saw everything that he had made, and indeed, it was very good.
—Genesis 1:31a (NRSV)

"Keeping it real" is slang for being true to ourselves and our roots. It means to take care of business in a genuine or natural way. In a sense, there is a reference to "keeping it real" in Genesis 1, when God creates the earth and calls it good. If we read between the lines, we can find a clear call for us to respect the earth's roots in Almighty God and to keep the earth "good."

Keeping the earth naturally beautiful and good implies a variety of life decisions, both small and large. Carpooling can cut back on fuel emissions. Recyling aluminum, plastic, paper, wood, and leaves can reduce waste, landfills, and toxins. Even new systems of organization can make it easier for us to place God's creation above the seeming conveniences of throwing everything away, littering, and consuming energy. Many towns provide trash bags or bins of different colors for various types of recyclables. New electronic products come with energy ratings. Some cars give better fuel efficiency than others.

With a small amount of discipline, we all can easily follow better systems for keeping the earth real.

Prayer Focus: How can I better keep God's creation "real" through my care for the environment?

October 14 ~ Do I Put God First in My Life?

I have learned the secret of being content in any and every situation, whether well fed or hungry, whether living in plenty or in want. I can do everything through him who gives me strength.
—Philippians 4:12-13 (NIV)

Deidre, a woman in our church choir, sings her heart out praising God. This beautiful, positive, talented woman, who has earned several degrees, gives generously of whatever she has. During the passing of the peace, Deidre tells me she has been greatly blessed by God. When you see her, you'd never guess that she's lost all her close family members except her two sons. You wouldn't know that she is divorced or that she has lost several jobs or that she was once evicted from her apartment. Both she and her youngest child struggle with chronic, often debilitating medical problems and hospitalizations. But her attitude is amazingly upbeat. I've wondered time and again how she manages to stay sane, let alone positive. She says that she has gained another family through the church. She calls Jesus the love of her life. And she starts every prayer, "Giving honor to God, who is the head of my life. . . ." Perhaps that's her secret: She faces the right direction. She puts God first in her life.

Prayer Focus: Do I put God first in my life? Do I "face" God at all times, even during difficult circumstances? Do I want God to have a greater place in my life, focusing me in positive directions?

261

October 15 ~ Is Gossip Really That Bad?

A perverse person spreads strife, and a whisperer separates close friends.
—Proverbs 16:28 (NRSV)

The four of us were really mad. "Can you stand her?" "She's got a lot of nerve!" "Did you see how she was acting?" "Who does she think she is, anyway?" "She actually told me that . . ."

Gossip can be juicy. But even true gossip is hurtful. It's a way of avoiding direct honesty with the person being talked about. Such opposition groups a gang of people who are "in the know" against the victim of the gossip. Perhaps you, like me, have experienced being the victim and, at one time or another, also have been the perpetrator.

It's difficult to avoid becoming part of it. There's a fine line between blowing off steam and being unnecessarily critical or cruel. Though gossip can create a sense of togetherness among those participating in the discussion, it often leads to a feeling of superiority, and it always has a sickly aftertaste.

I feel better when I stop gossip as soon as it starts, whether it comes out of my mouth or someone else's. The gossipers are not always happy with me, but it's a cleaner way to live.

Prayer Focus: What have you said lately that you wish you could take back? What have you said that was life-giving?

October 16 ~ Why Can't I Have It My Way?

Everyone should be quick to listen, slow to speak and slow to become angry, for man's anger does not bring about the righteous life that God desires.
—James 1:19-20 (NIV)

Once while waiting in line at a drive-thru, the driver ahead of me grew angry at the order-taker. Cursing loudly, she threw her drink at the drive-thru window, which closed just in time. As she streaked away, trailing burnt rubber and fast-food items, a child in the backseat threw his fries out the window.

We live in an age of rage. We even have special names for it: sports rage, air rage, and road rage. Road rage, for example, can range from using a baseball bat to settle differences, to calling other drivers names, whether they can hear us or not. Such incidents of uncontrolled, violent anger are becoming common responses to everyday problems and stresses. Somehow we believe that we have a right to lash out when people get in our way.

Because we live in community with other people, we are bound to get in one another's way. And because it's human nature to feel some anger or hurt when we are inconvenienced or treated rudely, we must be intentional about avoiding the destructive response of rage. Living in community requires us to sacrifice our desire to always have our own way and, instead, to become peacemakers. Living in community necessitates a focus on God's way, not my way.

Prayer Focus: How often do I speak or act from rage? How can or do I cope with not having it "my way" all the time?

October 17 ~ How Do I Manage Debt?

Do not be one of those who give pledges, who become surety for debts. If you have nothing with which to pay, why should your bed be taken from under you?
—Proverbs 22:26-27 (NRSV)

A financial expert recently told me that twenty-somethings have an average consumer (not educational) debt of over three thousand dollars— more than that of any previous generation starting out.

I remember when my first credit card—with a three thousand dollar limit—arrived in my college mailbox. I thought, *What a good idea for emergencies.* And it was. Problem is, I haven't used credit cards for emergencies only. I've used them to pay tuition, fix my ailing car, and even cover normal living expenses. It didn't take long for me to start carrying a monthly balance.

For me, repaying that debt continues to be a headache, involving credit cards that charge as much as 20 percent interest. Even "refinancing" by transferring a balance to a new lower-rate card would last only so long, and there would be the temptation to use another credit card for other needs. Buying now and paying later may be one of the most dangerous procrastinations I've ever faced.

So I've reduced my credit cards to two, and I rarely use them except for traveling and real emergencies. If I don't have the money now, why chance having my bed taken from under me?

October 18 ~ Am I Looking Heart-ward?

"The LORD does not see as mortals see; they look on the outward appearance, but the LORD looks on the heart."

—*1 Samuel 16:7b (NRSV)*

Eva, a kind but gruff seventy-year-old Polish woman, both terrified and delighted children in our neighborhood when I was growing up. She was known as "the dog lady" because she collected dogs—stray dogs, abused dogs, pretty much all kinds of dogs—averaging seven dogs at a time. Some kids were afraid of her. They threw rocks at her dogs and made fun of her wild, long, white hair, her rough clothing, and the garbage bags she used to line her rubber boots. But my brothers and I loved her.

If we weren't at our house, we were at Eva's—playing with her dogs, helping with her flower garden, or listening to her stories of World War II, when she worked as a telephone operator. Our parents trusted her completely, and she considered us her family. "You're my children, too," she'd say, placing our scrawny dandelion offerings in places of high honor where the dogs couldn't reach them.

I remember how, on one of her birthdays, Eva dyed her white hair bright red, put on lipstick and a gorgeous red sari, and threw a Hawaiian luau for the entire neighborhood. Everyone said what we already knew: how beautiful she was.

Praise God for looking beyond our flawed exteriors into our hearts, which simply want to love and be loved.

Prayer Focus: *When do I look at outward appearances? When do I look heart-ward?*

October 19 ~ Why Do I Procrastinate?

A little sleep, a little slumber, a little folding of the hands to rest, and poverty will come upon you like a robber, and want, like an armed warrior.

—*Proverbs 24:33-34 (NRSV)*

Has waiting until the last minute or resting when there's work to be done ever gotten you in trouble? Do you remember how pulling an all-nighter could leave you sleep-impoverished?

Procrastination can cause "poverty" in our lives in many ways. About six years ago I lost touch with a good friend. She was last to be in touch. I should have been next, but I kept putting off contacting her because I was angry about something I didn't know how to discuss with her. She had hurt me deeply.

When I had showed her my engagement ring, I had expected her to share my joy. Instead, she had looked at it pityingly, saying my husband-to-be should have at least spent one month's salary on it. I had felt shocked and betrayed, as if I'd never really known her. But I never called to discuss it. I just let the wound fester.

When we talked again a year later, it was too late. Our relationship was too damaged. I don't know if we ever could become good friends again, but I deeply regret what happened—especially the fact that I procrastinated in confronting her with my feelings.

Since it only takes a little to fall behind, we must be careful not to put off what is truly important.

Prayer Focus: Is procrastination a factor in any areas of my life? Why? How can I keep poverty from coming upon me in those areas?

October 20 ~ To Love or Not to Love?

"Let anyone among you who is without sin be the first to throw a stone at her."
—*John 8:7b (NRSV)*

Years ago, Mark, a young intern pastor at our church, was struck by a stone as a group of young boys jeered and called him names, hoping to make him react or run. Instead he walked toward them and grabbed Jay, the tall ringleader. "Come with me," Mark said.

Instead of yelling or sending him home, Mark sat and talked to the youth, introducing himself, asking questions, and listening to the answers. He invited Jay to come back and talk some more, to come to church, to hang out with the youth group.

That stone changed Jay's life. Once just a kid struggling on his own to deal with a deeply dysfunctional home life, Jay heard in Mark's invitation an acceptance and love he hungered for. And Jay started coming to youth activities, worship services, fellowship meals, and even children's choir. The church became a surrogate family to Jay, and he became a respected leader—a big brother the rest of us younger kids looked up to.

Thanks to Mark's invitation, Jay grew up surrounded by hope and love; married a wonderful young woman; and became a father, a role model, and a trusted friend who continues to give back to others.

Prayer Focus: How have you been loved and accepted (by others or by God) despite your sin? How do you, in turn, offer grace?

October 21 ~ Do I Really Need Friends?

Every time I think of you, I thank my God.

—Philippians 1:3 (CEV)

Every time I think of my friend Anne, I thank my God! Anne and I have been friends for many years because we both have made a big effort, despite life's changes, to maintain our friendship. We don't drift away from each other because we are intentional about talking on the phone or sending e-mail. At one point last year, after we hadn't talked for a couple of months, Anne left a message on my answering machine: "Hey, we haven't been talking enough, and we need each other!"

She's right: We do need each other. In today's fast-paced world, I sometimes forget how important friends are. It would have been harder for me to forget in biblical times. Then, people had to rely on each other for encouragement, support, and even financial assistance. All those benefits came from family and friends—not counselors, Social Security, or welfare and unemployment systems.

Friendships are also important to our faith. Too often we fail to invest in friendships, which offer gifts of grace and honesty, and help us during spiritual lows. But the good news is that we can always make new friends and maintain those relationships by being a friend.

Prayer Focus: Who am I a friend to? How do we both maintain our friendship? How can I be a better friend?

October 22 ~ What Does It Mean to "Be the Church"?

A friend loves at all times, and kinsfolk are born to share adversity.
—Proverbs 17:17 (NRSV)

"Let's not talk about 'going to church.' Let's talk about 'being the church'!"

Lutheran theologian Marva Dawn once said this to me and several others at a retreat. Her words reminded me of the old children's finger play "Here is the church; here is the steeple." She was saying, "Open the doors. See all the people!"

Being the church is not place-centered but people-centered. When we are being the church, not only are we worshiping with one another, but we are living in companionship through the good and bad times.

When I think of "being the church," I think of Jay and Linda, two friends we worship with on Sundays. They live out their faith by being companions. When a church member broke his hand in several places and couldn't finish a home repair project, Jay showed up at his house in old clothes and did the work for him. According to an elderly member of our church, Jay also cleaned her bathroom. Linda regularly brings small gifts and care baskets to church when someone's going through a tough time. I know because she once gave me one. And together Jay and Linda regularly invite couples to their home, lifting our spirits with prayer, genuine honesty, delicious meals, music and dancing, and the wacky inventions they've made.

Being the church means being there for other people.

Prayer Focus: Who has been the church for you? How are you the church for others?

October 23 ~ Can I Kick This Habit?

Whatever is true, whatever is honorable, whatever is just, whatever is pure . . . if there is anything worthy of praise, think about these things. Keep on doing the things that you have learned and received and heard and seen in me, and the God of peace will be with you.

—Philippians 4:8-9 (NRSV)

You know how some folks have really elegant, well-manicured hands? Not me. I bite my nails. It's such a lovely habit, rich in germ potential and lending my fingers a well-gnawed look. Sarcasm aside, I don't like the habit, but it's hard to kick once you start. And when I do quit, it's easier for me to fall off the wagon than it would be for a non-biter. The first nibble is automatic permission, and it's all downhill from there.

But I keep trying to quit, and I'm making it longer between "relapses." I've learned the triggers: worry, loneliness, fear, and boredom. I've learned good habits—like carrying a small bottle of lotion and nail clippers with me, or doing work with my hands—to take my mind off the need to nibble.

Likewise, continually doing things that are good can carry us through the habits we want to kick. Like traveling a path or a route, traveling a good habit often enough makes it well-worn and natural, leaving us at peace.

Prayer Focus: What habits do I want to subtract or add?

October 24 ~ Without a Significant Other, What's My Significance?

And so we know and rely on the love God has for us.

—1 John 4:16 (NIV)

"I feel like only half a person without him."
"I'll do anything to keep her."
"I'd be nothing without you."
"I have to have a girlfriend to be happy."
"You're still single? Don't worry; you'll find someone eventually."
All these statements were parts of real conversations I've been involved in. A few of them don't even sound that bad. But at the root of each statement is this assumption: Without the love of a significant other to rely on, one's own significance suffers.

But 1 John 4 offers us an alternative vision—the proper vision. To know and rely on God's love is what gives us real significance. Only when God is the object of the above statements are they really true. God's love comes before any other relationships, and God's love is the most important love in our lives. We can rely on divine love, because whether singles or couples, we all are significant to the One who made us.

Prayer Focus: Am I content with myself outside a romantic relationship? If I'm in a relationship, is God involved? Is God at the center?

October 25 ~ Should I Go Back to School?

The wise get all the knowledge they can.
                                                —*Proverbs 10:14a (GNT)*

A team of researchers recently did a study on Alzheimer's disease among a community of Catholic nuns. Study results suggested that an advanced or continued education could lessen one's chances of developing Alzheimer's. And one nun with an extremely large vocabulary and complex writing skills showed no signs whatsoever of Alzheimer's, although she had the disease. So continuing education may make a big difference for our brains as we age.

But continuing education has more obvious and certain benefits, as well. It can help us improve our living and working conditions, whether it's a two-day class on building web pages, coursework toward a bachelor's or higher degree, a challenging book to read, or a stimulating debate with friends. It's not that degrees or certificates make us more important; rather, learning keeps our minds continually growing and can help us place ourselves and our families in a better position. Like physical exercise, exercising and stretching our mental capacity can make us more supple and fit to handle new ideas.

Prayer Focus: Why would I consider going back to school or attending a workshop or class? Why not? What kind of continuing education experiences might best fit my needs or my family's needs at this point in my life?

October 26 ~ Am I Successful Enough?

"[A] child is the greatest in the kingdom of heaven."
                                                —*Matthew 18:4 (NRSV)*

Nkosi, a little boy in South Africa, spoke out about AIDS when most people were afraid to admit they had the disease. Nkosi was one of millions of African children dying of AIDS—children who have not amassed great fortunes, obtained professional degrees, carried out paradigm-shifting research, or invented cures for major diseases. Most will not live to become adults. Yet, according to Jesus' words in Matthew 18, these children are the greatest in the Kingdom.

If children are the greatest, how can we measure ourselves by earthly successes? When our lives become focused on our work and achievements, everything is fine only as long as we are successful. If we believe that our identity consists of our achievements, then, if we fail, we believe that we are failures.

I believe God wants us to see ourselves not as what we do, but as whose we are. We are greater than the sum of our failures and successes. We are great because we are God's. Though we don't need to stop working toward success, it's important for us to place that success behind a childlike faith in God and our God-given abilities. Children are continually learning and growing, and so are we.

Prayer Focus: Who are you? Whose are you? Look at your past, your present, and your dreams for the future. How are you more than what you have done and will do?

October 27 ~ Are the Best Things in Life Really Free?

And he said to them, "Take care! Be on your guard against all kinds of greed; for one's life does not consist in the abundance of possessions."
—Luke 12:15 (NRSV)

The really convincing commercials aren't just on TV anymore. They've also taken over the classical station I sometimes listen to in my car—telling me I need the "best things in life," such as a luxury SUV, a mansion, a piano, a fur coat, or a sound system. I find myself examining other cars, wondering if I'd be better off with a car with no rust, lower mileage, a CD player, and leather seats; but my car is paid for and in good shape!

Often ads suggest that *stuff* will bring us the "best things in life," because we've earned them or because we deserve them. When prices are mentioned, we're assured of a good deal. But stuff is meant only to be useful, not to be definitive of who we are. While possessions might become tem-

270

porary fixes, they can't truly fulfill us or give life meaning. That meaning comes from love—love from God, family, and friends. The best things in life—gifts of love—can't be earned or deserved. Jesus was right to warn us to be on our guard. Because the best things in life really are free.

Prayer Focus: Do I need the stuff I buy? How do I relate to my possessions? Do I want them to fill a need that only God or a loved one can fill?

October 28 ~ Do I See the Truth?

"I am the way, and the truth, and the life."

—*John 14:6 (NRSV)*

Can you remember a time when it was difficult to see or search for truth?

I can. I grew up thinking that my parents were perfect, and that our family, although less affectionate and more critical than some, was somehow better than other families. I grew up constantly afraid of failing their high standards. Even though I regularly went to church and heard of God's grace and mercy, I felt deep down that these truths applied only to other people. I tried to earn or deserve love from others—even God.

Thanks to my friends, I've figured out that I have issues, and that my parents, though good people, didn't and couldn't do everything right. Perhaps part of growing up is being both blessed and "warped" in some way by our parents or caregivers—until, with God's help, we make peace with ourselves and with them.

Even now, that peace comes to me as I am reminded of the truth: Jesus loves each of us unconditionally, in a way we can never earn.

Prayer Focus: In what part of my life is it difficult for me to see truth? Have I unburdened my heart to God so that I can hear God's message of grace and forgiveness?

October 29 ~ Is That a Wrinkle?!

My flesh and my heart may fail, but God is the strength of my heart and my portion forever.

—*Psalm 73:26 (NRSV)*

271

Who says wrinkles are bad? What first attracted me to my husband were his deep smile lines—unusual in someone so young. I absolutely love the lines in people's faces. Whether straight, curvy, zigzag, practical, or decorative—lines are amazing to me. They direct our eyes, convey meaning, and "connect stuff." They show the beauty of life.

While visiting my grandmother before she died, I looked—really looked—at her face. There, like the crazing on delicate porcelain, lines etched her beauty in generous smile-lines, a perpendicular worry-line between her eyebrows, and crow's feet that could make her eyes sparkle with humor. The lines welcomed and embraced me just as surely as the strong, thin lines of her arms.

Written in our faces, our lives, and our loves, such lines connect us to one another and to life, marking us like a loved and adored teddy bear. What if wrinkles are not a curse but a blessing, a sign that we are loved?

Prayer Focus: *How do I feel about aging? How would God have me react to our culture's obsession with youth as perfection?*

October 30 ~ Why Praise?

O sing to the LORD *a new song, for he has done marvelous things.*
—Psalm 98:1 (NRSV)

Spend at least five minutes today reflecting on the marvelous things God has done in your life. A marvel is anything amazing that causes you to be thankful. A marvel can be a baby's first cry, the smell of the ocean, a true friendship, the feel of grass beneath bare feet, a hug of forgiveness, or a message that is right on time. Praising God for marvels could take the form of a prayer, a poem, a drawing, a photo, a dance, or a gift to someone else who needs it. How can we ever praise God enough for such amazing marvels?

As you reflect on marvels in your life, think of a few words that stand out for you. Then, try to create a haiku prayer. A haiku, a traditional three-line Japanese poem, has a line-by-line syllable count of 5-7-5. Here are two examples:

Great and gracious God/You gave us people to love/And good gifts to share.

Because you're perfect/I know I don't have to be/Thanks for saving me.

Try writing your own haiku prayer. You may be amazed at what you come up with.

Prayer Focus: In what ways do I praise God? In what different ways can I use my gifts or skills to offer praise?

October 31 ~ What Does It Mean to Put God First?

You shall have no other gods before me.

—Exodus 20:3 (NRSV)

In all your ways acknowledge [God], and [God] will make your paths straight.

—Proverbs 3:6 (NIV)

As much as I love my husband, God did not mean for me to make my husband the most important thing in my life. The same goes for my family, friends, job, dog, cat, possessions, or even myself. But it can be a constant struggle to make God my top priority. Other people and things in our lives can fulfill us in part, because they are part of God's blessing—but only part. Only God can fulfill us wholly and perfectly, unconditionally and unfailingly, no matter what.

The Bible focuses on helping us put God first. Sometimes the message is simple. In Exodus, the first commandment tells us to place nothing and no one before God. At other times, the message is confusing. Jesus says, "Whoever comes to me and does not hate father and mother, wife and children, brothers and sisters, yes, and even life itself, cannot be my disciple" (Luke 14:26 NRSV). It may seem that Jesus is asking us to hate people we love, but that isn't the case. Jesus also tells us to love others as ourselves. So, in this verse he doesn't mean that we should hate others, but that we should love others less than God.

As much as we love and respect others, we must acknowledge God's desires above theirs. Of all the life questions we have, what putting God first means for the way we live may be the most important of all.

Prayer Focus: How willing am I to put God first? What does that mean for my life now?

273

November
GROWING TOWARD FULL HUMANITY

Esther Cho and Richard Evans

November 1 ~ Dangerous Faith

But he began to curse, and swore an oath, "I do not know this man you are talk-ing about." At that moment the cock crowed for the second time. Then Peter remembered that Jesus had said to him, "Before the cock crows twice, you will deny me three times." And he broke down and wept.
—Mark 14:71-72 (NRSV)

I come from three generations of clergy, originally from North Korea. During the Korean War, families were divided and stranded on opposite sides of the 38th parallel. In the North, Christianity was outlawed. Churches were destroyed, and Christians were imprisoned, persecuted, or killed.

For decades, there had been no exchange of family information. Recently, my uncle was able to visit North Korea, and he arranged a pub-lic meeting with some relatives—a couple and their five-year-old son.

They spoke formally and briefly. When their time was over, the five-year-old boy was sent to bow his formal good-byes to "grandfather." As the boy leaned over on my uncle's chair, he whispered quietly in his ear, singing in Korean, "Jesus loves me this I know . . ." For this act, they could have been beaten, imprisoned, even executed. After generations, in a song

275

memorized in secrecy, the little boy reassured my uncle that the faith had been preserved and carried through the years. Dangerous faith.

Really believing in something is dangerous. Belief that is more than an intellectual consent to an idea, or a tacit agreement to something that sounds right, is a dangerous thing. It can get you in trouble. Sometimes killed. Crucified on a cross. At first, Peter ran from a dangerous faith. But, ultimately, he was transformed through his struggle. The same Peter lived out the rest of his life as a changed man, helped shape the history of the world, and faced his death with a newfound courage.

Faith is a dangerous thing. You might really see yourself. You might be moved to grow, to be transformed. You might be moved to take a chance, to take a risk, and to really live. What stands to be gained is authentic life—authentic faith.

What does it mean to be a human being, to live life authentically, to grow toward full humanity as we see it in Jesus Christ? This month we invite you to explore your faith and what it means to live life with your name on it.

Prayer Focus: Imagine a life in which we really live all that we say we believe. Imagine a life in which our decisions about where we spend our time and money, and where we invest our whole selves, really come out of our deepest beliefs. In taking your faith seriously, what risks are you willing to live?

November 2 ~ Faith of a Mustard Seed

"For truly I tell you, if you have faith the size of a mustard seed, you will say to this mountain, 'Move from here to there,' and it will move; and nothing will be impossible for you."

—Matthew 17:20 (NRSV)

Jesus tells us parables to help us see life in a new way. But instead of confronting us head-on, which would cause us to see what is coming and get our resistance up, he tells a parable. A parable sneaks up on us and enters into our lives with a surprise. Jesus never uses parables to illustrate common wisdom and morality. He uses them to challenge our usual way of seeing things. Take, for example, the parable of the mustard seed.

The disciples have just returned from trying to be disciples. They have tried to help someone, and they have failed. They have fallen on their faces. They don't know why, but they have a hunch. Their assumption is that faith is a quantitative thing—something you can store up, so that the more you have, the more you can do. Jesus confounds that idea—turns it upside-down, as he does with everything else. He says that if you have faith the size of a mustard seed, the smallest seed there is, then you can move mountains—which means faith opens up possibilities for life beyond what you have imagined. You don't need a lot of faith, because faith is not a thing. It is not something quantitative. It is qualitative. Faith is a relationship with God.

So what? So we can see ourselves and life in amazing, new, hopeful ways!

Prayer Focus: Faith requires us to loosen our grip or control over life, to open our eyes and hearts so we may see life in new ways. Consider those things in your life that you are struggling to control. Pray for the faith to let go of each one as you lift it up to God, who hears our prayers and can open up possibilities for life beyond what we have imagined.

November 3 ~ Throw Deep

Surely, this commandment that I am commanding you today is not too hard for you, nor is it too far away. . . . See, I have set before you today life and prosperity, death and adversity. . . . Choose life so that you and your descendants may live, loving the LORD your God, obeying him, and holding fast to him; for that means life to you.

—Deuteronomy 30:11, 15, 19b-20a (NRSV)

Ken Stabler once was a quarterback for the Raiders. During training camp one year, a newspaper reporter, who recently had visited Jack London's memorial, read some of London's prose to Stabler:

I would rather be ashes than dust! I would rather that my spark should burn out in a brilliant blaze than it should be stifled by dry rot. . . . The proper function of [a person] is to live, not to exist. I shall not waste my days in trying to prolong them. I shall use my time.

Then the reporter asked Stabler, "What does that mean to you?" Stabler said, "Throw deep" (James S. Hewett, ed., *Illustrations Unlimited,* Wheaton,

Ill.: Tyndale, 1988, pp. 100-101). In the Deuteronomy 33 account of Moses' farewell address, the people had been wandering around for years, trying to find their way—trying to find hope when there didn't seem to be any. They were about to cross the Jordan, to take the next step toward full life in the promised land. And they were feeling a little wobbly. In so many words, Moses said, "This is not so esoteric that you can't get it. You can do this!" His appeal to them was that they would have the faith and hope to discover again what it truly means to be a human being in relationship with God.

This was the worst of times for them. They were facing the actual threat and promise of life. So Moses addressed their faith, courage, and hope. Moses wanted them to see life in a new way—to see that the future was open. He said, "I have set before you today life and . . . death. . . . Choose life. . . ." In other words, "Throw deep!"

Prayer Focus: Imagine what it would mean for you to "throw deep" in your life. Is there something limiting you from experiencing life in all its fullness? Is there something that feels like a wall closing you in, keeping you from living the kind of life you want to live and from becoming the kind of person you really hope to be? Remember, God promises that the future is open—and possible!

November 4 ~ Words of Life

He said to me, "Mortal, can these bones live?" I answered, "O Lord GOD, you know." Then he said to me, "Prophesy to these bones, and say to them: O dry bones, hear the word of the LORD. . . . I will cause breath to enter you, and you shall live. I will lay sinews on you, and will cause flesh to come upon you, and cover you with skin, and put breath in you, and you shall live."
—Ezekiel 37:3-6 (NRSV)

Great-grandmother was born in the 1880s in Korea, when Protestant missionaries began proselytizing. Grandmother's eldest daughter gained literacy in the Christian missionary schools. When she became sick, she wrote to her mother of her newly found faith. Noble women were not allowed outside the inner pavilion of their households, and Grandmother was unable to be at her daughter's home as she lay dying. But, this letter of confession, she did receive. Through the words of this letter, she heard the gospel of Jesus Christ, which spoke of the one loving God, Creator of the universe, who promised liberation from death and sin and all earthly bondage—who promised a new creation.

Hearing these words, she found herself enraged at her bondage and empowered to take control. The "spirit-sites" erected all around the house and grounds, she resolved to tend no longer, as society required, with constant rituals, food offerings, and upkeep. In an unprecedented moment of impertinent courage and unthinkable initiative, empowered by the Spirit of the Word of God, she picked up a broom; she swept the spirits, their offerings, their altars, and their very threat of terror and destruction into the courtyard in a heap; and she lit them, consuming them in a great conflagration!

Then, against all those who would forbid her, she stepped for the first time outside of the gates of the courtyard, which had enclosed her all her life, and headed for the missionary church! Four generations of Methodist ministers have come out of my family, from the surprising courage of one old woman brought to life through words of life. The vision of dry bones in Ezekiel speaks of the living words of God—*words that can achieve* the impossible. The Word of God offers not only the possibility but also the promise of life from the dead.

Prayer Focus: What holds you in bondage? The past? Do you regret what cannot be changed? The future? Are you a slave to plans, needs, anxieties, uncertainties, or fears? The present? Are you bound by anger, pain, disillusionment, abuse, illness, addiction, depression, guilt, self-pity, or stress? What are the "deaths" that keep you from being really alive? Remember that God continually offers us new life, even from death.

November 5 ~ Plant and Dream

Thus says the LORD of hosts, the God of Israel, to all the exiles whom I have sent into exile from Jerusalem to Babylon: Build houses and live in them; plant gardens and eat what they produce. . . . Multiply there, and do not decrease. But seek the welfare of the city. . . . I will fulfill to you my promise and bring you back to this place. For surely I know the plans I have for you, says the LORD, plans for your welfare and not for harm, to give you a future with hope.
—Jeremiah 29:4-7a; 10-11 (NRSV)

279

On the last night of our mission trip to Cambodia, where we helped to construct a community center for vocational training, we celebrated with an open banquet and communion service. Over three hundred people from the village came to share a feast—and soft drinks, something most of them couldn't afford. Kids were given sandwiches. They hardly knew what to do with them; they had never seen sandwiches before. Most had never been to a worship service, but they knew there was something different there. In the midst of poverty, tragedy, and barriers of language and culture, we shared joy, hope, and life!

As we spoke these words for communion, we felt that we were one: "We bring bread from a world where some have enough to eat, and many are hungry. We bring juice from a world where some have leisure, and many struggle to survive." And in that setting, we remembered these words from God to any who suffer from pain, significant losses, or hopelessness; to any who struggle to live: "Plant gardens. . . . Have sons and daughters. . . . Seek the welfare of the city. . . . I know the plans I have for you . . . plans for your welfare and not for harm, to give you a future with hope."

Wherever you are, live life in fullness. Never live so boxed in or closed off that the future is not open to God's call. Never live so comfortably yourself that you forget the vision of a full life for all.

Prayer Focus: The Spanish Christian philosopher Miguel de Unamuno said that if you want to know what a person's real faith is, you have to find out what the person really hopes for—the person's dream. So I ask you: What is your dream? Why? Share these most cherished dreams of your heart in your prayer.

November 6 ~ Dealing with Life's Disappointments

We are afflicted in every way, but not crushed; perplexed, but not driven to despair; persecuted, but not forsaken; struck down, but not destroyed. . . . So we do not lose heart. Even though our outer nature is wasting away, our inner nature is being renewed day by day. For this slight momentary affliction is preparing us for an eternal weight of glory beyond all measure, because we look not at what can be seen but at what cannot be seen; for what can be seen is temporary, but what cannot be seen is eternal.

—2 Corinthians 4:8-9, 16-18 (NRSV)

In the opening scene from *Annie Hall*, Woody Allen's alter ego, Alvy Singer, expresses his philosophy of life when he relates the story of two elderly women who were at a Catskills mountain resort. One of them said, "Boy, the food at this place is really terrible." The other one replied, "I know, and such small portions." Alvy says, "That's essentially how I feel about life. Full of loneliness and misery and suffering and unhappiness, and it's all over much too quickly."

Disappointments—life is full of them. None of us gets to live all of life on the basis of our first choices. When facing disappointments, we may wish for an earlier time, a time when everything seemed to be in place. We may get stuck in thinking "if only." But we can't become mature adults unless we give up the illusion that life is always fair, that we should get what we want, that we *deserve* what we want.

Paul could have had a "good life" as a Roman citizen. Instead, he followed Jesus and was shipwrecked, imprisoned, beaten, betrayed, deserted, and disappointed. He expected Jesus' imminent return, but it didn't happen. And in spite of all that, he could write, "We are afflicted in every way, but not crushed. . . . 'I believed, and so I spoke'" (2 Corinthians 4:8a, 13b NRSV).

When life doesn't go the way we hoped, when we discover again how infinitely complex and mysterious and crazy life can be, we may need to be reminded to trust that there are new possibilities for life that we sometimes don't see, or refuse to see, or are afraid to see. Sharing life in the community of faith helps make hope and meaning come alive. As Saint Augustine said, "I believe. Help my unbelief."

Prayer Focus: *Reread today's scripture. Are there times when you feel like "losing heart"? Hear and pray that you might believe.*

November 7 ~ I Will Be There for You

I am one who has seen affliction under the rod of God's wrath; he has driven and brought me into darkness without any light. . . . Though I call and cry for help, he shuts out my prayer. . . . But this I call to mind, and therefore I have hope: The steadfast love of the LORD never ceases, his mercies never come to an end; they are new every morning. . . . For the Lord will not reject forever. Although he causes grief, he will have compassion according to the abundance of his steadfast love; for he does not willingly afflict or grieve anyone.

—Lamentations 3:1-2, 8, 21-23, 31-33 (NRSV)

She came into my office, sat down sideways, and looked at the floor. She was in her early thirties—a mom with two children. Her psychologist had referred her to me, because the psychologist was on vacation, and because "she has some theological questions she wants to ask you."

I tried to open the conversation, but she would not respond. Finally, still looking down, she said, "I'm angry with God, but I don't think God would understand." I had been reading some of the angry psalms, ones that end in praise but begin in lament. I read them to her. She listened, looked up, faced me, and began to tell her story. She had been the victim of incest by her father, brothers, and neighborhood men—all arranged by her father, who used an obscure passage in Leviticus to justify his behavior. At the end of the story she cried. She said, "First I prayed for them to die. Then I prayed for me to die. I believe in God—but I'm not sure God believes in me."

What could I say? In Exodus, God defines God's self to Moses: "I AM WHO I AM," which Gerhard von Rad translates from the Hebrew, "I will be there (for you)" (Gerhard von Rad, *Old Testament Theology*, Vol. I [New York: Harper and Row, 1962], p. 180). No matter what happens, no matter where you go, "I will be there for you." But how was God there for her?

Although her primary experience was of God's absence, she never gave up her search. Through the stormy darkness of her life, she kept hoping, reaching for God. And God reached back. Although she had been through a wilderness from which she will never entirely recover, she later asked to be baptized, along with her children. It was a witness of courage, hope, and new life.

Prayer Focus: What have been some of the darkest, most painful moments of your life? As you search through these dark hours, look for the presence of God. God walks with us, before us, and ahead of us all the time. Let us learn from the dark hours behind us; let us be hopeful wherever we are walking now; let us not fear the road that lies ahead, knowing that we are not alone.

November 8 ~ Earth Has No Sorrow That Heaven Cannot Heal

Thus says the LORD: A voice is heard in Ramah, lamentation and bitter weeping. Rachel is weeping for her children; she refuses to be comforted for her children, because they are no more.

—Jeremiah 31:15 (NRSV)

"Blessed are those who mourn, for they will be comforted."

—Matthew 5:4 (NRSV)

On April 20, 1999, two students entered Columbine High School with the intent to destroy everything and everyone in it. When they were finished, fourteen students, including themselves, and one teacher were dead. Two of the dead students were related to our church in Highlands Ranch, Colorado—as were other students, teachers, and rescue and medical personnel who were involved in the incident. The following is part of the church service from the Sunday following the tragedy:

There are times when we must be together, as a community of faith, in this sanctuary, in this holy place, in this synagogue. "Synagogue" means "place of coming together." We come together affirming that all people are a part of the family of God. We come together affirming love and not hate. We come together affirming the presence of the God who says, "I will always be there for you."

We may find words for what we are thinking and feeling. There may just be "sighs too deep for words" (Romans 8:26). Still, we have to say something, to begin the struggle to make meaning, to find words and to share them. As we share our personal stories, they become part of our collective story. And by telling them, we both hold on to them and let go of them. We begin to heal. But right now we grieve. We struggle with our losses, or with a new sense of vulnerability. We have been reminded how valuable life is. We may have a new or renewed appreciation that we need one another at the deepest level. That is how God made us.

After the shock and numbness wear off, we begin to ask questions—for some, questions about God. Some people see life's unfairness and decide, "There is no God; the world is nothing but chaos." Some people say, "Life is not fair." That's right. It isn't. At the service Wednesday night, a high school girl said, "Students shouldn't have to know words like 'shrapnel.' Students shouldn't be killing each other. I want to throw up." We all wanted to throw up.

We may look for someone or something to blame. The truth is, we are probably all implicated in some way. We look for explanations. We ask, "Why?" Our minds cannot tolerate a vacuum. We want an answer. There is probably no satisfying "answer" that will make sense of it all. The word "answer" can also mean "response" as well as "explanation."

So the question is not, "Why did this happen?" but, "How will we respond?"

As we mourn, we are comforted. The word "comforted" implies strengthening, as well as consolation. There is a Hebrew word for "hope," which means "to twist or entwine." Not today, but maybe soon for some of us—or not for a long time for others of us—this experience will entwine with many others, and life will again be strong and hopeful. "Earth has no sorrow that heaven cannot heal."

Prayer Focus: "Come, ye disconsolate, where'er ye languish, come to the mercy seat, fervently kneel. Here bring your wounded hearts, here tell your anguish; earth has no sorrow that heaven cannot heal" (Thomas Moore, "Come, Ye Disconsolate," 1816). For what sorrow do you seek healing?

November 9 ~ And Me?

[Peter] saw the heaven opened and something like a large sheet coming down, being lowered to the ground by its four corners. In it were all kinds of four-footed creatures and reptiles and birds of the air. Then he heard a voice saying, "Get up, Peter; kill and eat." But Peter said, "By no means, Lord; for I have never eaten anything that is profane or unclean." The voice said to him again, a second time, "What God has made clean, you must not call profane." . . . On Peter's arrival Cornelius met him. . . . And [Peter] said to them, "You yourselves know that it is unlawful for a Jew to associate with or to visit a Gentile; but God has shown me that I should not call anyone profane or unclean."
—*Acts 10:11-15; 25*a, *28 (NRSV)*

Several years ago, my son, David, and I were watching the television show *FBI: The Untold Stories* together. David is Korean, and at that time one of his best friends was an African American named Alex.

The show that evening was about the FBI's pursuit and capture of some people from a neo-Nazi hate group called The Order, who several years ago assassinated a radio talk show host for his pugnacious attitude toward white supremacists.

At the end of the show, as the FBI agents were leading these guys away, David asked, "Are those bad guys?"

"Yes."

"Why?"

"Because they don't understand, David, that all people belong to the family of God," I said. "And if you don't believe like they do, if you aren't 'Christian' like they are, if you don't look like they do, if you aren't white like they are, they might kill you."

"Even Alex?"

"Yes."

"And me?"

"And me?" is not just one little boy's question. Who among us could not be excluded—for whatever reason—from someone else's notion of the family of God? Who among us could not ask, "And me?"

After Peter had a vision, which we read about in Acts 10, he said, "You yourselves know that it is unlawful [that is, taboo] to associate with or to visit a Gentile [that is, anyone who is different]; but God has shown me that I should not call anyone profane or unclean." But, in spite of what Peter had said, in the second chapter of Galatians, we see that he refused to eat at the same table with the people he had said were a part of the family of God.

It's easy to identify with Peter. A lot of us like to divide the world into us and them. But we all are more alike than we are different. There is no us and them—just us. Regardless of our differences, we human beings are all laced together. In church language, we are all brothers and sisters in the family of God.

Prayer Focus: Have you ever felt excluded and alone? Is there someone who might need an invitation to feel included? In prayer, consider ways you might work to be more inclusive in your life, and think of those around you who might welcome an invitation.

November 10 ~ At the Well

A Samaritan woman came to draw water, and Jesus said to her, "Give me a drink." (His disciples had gone to the city to buy food.) The Samaritan woman said to him, "How is it that you, a Jew, ask a drink of me, a woman of Samaria?" (Jews do not share things in common with Samaritans.) Jesus answered her, "If you knew the gift of God, and who it is that is saying to you, 'Give me a drink,' you would have asked him, and he would have given you living water."

—John 4:7-10 (NRSV)

The United States is now the most religiously diverse place on Earth, with more Muslims than Presbyterians, and people of every conceivable cultural background living together in its cities. Our challenge is to learn to share life amidst diversity with honesty, courageously stepping into intimate relatedness, daring to trust, and allowing for real dialogue. The scene of the woman at the well gives a glimpse of what it is to share life, giving and receiving of our innermost selves, in spite of real differences.

Jesus and his friends stop to rest in Samaria—not a choice location for Jews to linger. Most self-respecting Jews would rush through this part of the country without stopping. (Samaritans had a deep-rooted quarrel with Jews.) Yet, Jesus sits alone at a well.

A Samaritan woman comes near to draw water. Feeling uneasy, she lowers her bucket without lifting her eyes. He walks slowly toward her as she tugs hastily to retrieve the water, not wanting to be seen with a Jewish man. He comes closer, looks her in the eye, and speaks to her. Quietly, he asks her for a drink of water. Now, face-to-face, the woman answers him with honesty and courage: "How is it that you, a Jew, ask a drink of me, a woman of Samaria?" Jesus responds genuinely to her challenge: "If you knew the gift of God, and who it is that is saying to you, 'Give me a drink,' you would have asked him, and he would have given you living water."

This is a most remarkable scene. We see two courageous people sharing their humanity with each other, although each seems to be radically different from the other. Jesus' gospel of the kingdom of God breaks down and jumps over very real and deeply entrenched barriers, which divide humanity, with a transcending message of inclusive life and love.

Prayer Focus: Are there people you are intimidated to approach because of your differences? Remember that life comes to us in surprising and amazing ways. Pray for courage to share, to trust, to give and receive, and to be open to being changed through our relationships with those around us.

November 11 ~ Celebrate Diversity

There is no longer Jew or Greek, there is no longer slave or free, there is no longer male and female; for all of you are one in Christ Jesus. And, if you belong to Christ, then you are Abraham's offspring, heirs according to the promise.
—Galatians 3:28-29 (NRSV)

There is a church in my neighborhood with a big sign out in front that never fails to incite my outrage. In bold letters, it reads, "We celebrate truth, not diversity!" What I find offensive is the idea of a "celebration" of exclusion, which is the message it inevitably sends. It is a way of saying, "Our way or no way; there is only one right way to think and to be, and if you are different, there is no room for you here."

We all have had the painful experience of being excluded, as well as the ugly experience of excluding somebody else. The belittling of those who are "out" by those who are "in" happens all the time, even with children. Against the backdrop of this hopelessly ugly aspect of human nature came a man who lived his life in such a way as to make us hope beyond all hope and believe in the radical dream of a world that claims all people as children of the one God—without exception or rank. This man was Jesus, and the dream is the continuing Christian hope for the kingdom of God.

No wonder Jesus was crucified and Christianity became suspect. It threatened established order—rules about who is "in" and who is "out." Paul writes, "*All of you* are one in Christ Jesus" (emphasis added). This is a message of great liberation to the underdog, but it is a powerful blow to those who are already part of the "in crowd."

If we take this message seriously, self-interest is inseparable from common interest. Nationalism is inseparable from humanism. My profit is inseparable from another's loss. And the well-being of our country and the needs of my life are not privileged values. If taken seriously, these Christian professions of faith present subversive and threatening challenges to the status quo of our world, to my life, and to yours. And yet, this is precisely how we are called to live—to risk justice for the sake of all God's people.

Prayer Focus: Can you envision a world without "outsiders"? Such a world is part of the vision of the kingdom of God. In prayer, consider the words, "Thy Kingdom come, Thy will be done" (Matthew 6:10 KJV) in the context of your own life.

November 12 ~ Not a Single Letter

Mordecai told them to reply to Esther, "Do not think that in the king's palace you will escape any more than all the other Jews. For if you keep silence at such a

287

time as this, relief and deliverance will rise for the Jews from another quarter, but you and your father's family will perish. Who knows? Perhaps you have come to royal dignity for just such a time as this." Then Esther said in reply to Mordecai, "Go, gather all the Jews to be found in Susa, and hold a fast on my behalf. . . . After that I will go to the king, though it is against the law; and if I perish, I perish."

—Esther 4:13-16 (NRSV)

There is a piece of Jewish wisdom that says, "A human life is like a single letter of the alphabet. It can be meaningless. Or it can be a part of a great meaning" (quoted by Anne Lamott in *Traveling Mercies*). So much of contemporary culture stresses the individual. As an oil company commercial puts it, "Don't you wish the world revolved around you?" Well, no, actually. When we spend so much energy trying to define exactly what "letter" we are, we often end up empty, unfulfilled, anxious, depressed, or angry. Who we are as "letters," as individuals, is important. But even more important are the words, sentences, and meanings we spell out together. Like letters of the alphabet, we are intended to be a part of something larger than ourselves.

A word used for *perfection* in the Bible doesn't have to do with being "perfect" or flawless. It's more like being on the right road and making progress. The root of the word suggests never quite getting to the end. It means that we are not primarily ends in ourselves but part of the road to life, part of the meaning for the whole; we are most meaningful in our relatedness to the rest.

As a single "letter," Esther was an enviable person, to be sure. She had become the beautiful and privileged Queen of Persia. Yet it was the weaving of her life with that of her community that left the mark of her great courage and beauty for all of history. By participating in the "writing" of something larger, Esther came to life with great meaning for all.

"A human life is like a single letter of the alphabet. It can be meaningless. Or it can be a part of a great meaning." In what meaningful words, sentences, and volumes does your letter come to life?

Prayer Focus: You are called to be more than what you have become. You are a part of a great meaning—a part of God's continuing creation in the world. What do you have to offer? Ask God to use your "letter"; and consider in what meaningful words, sentences, and volumes your letter might come to life.

November 13 ~ Together at Table

When you come together, it is not really to eat the Lord's supper. For when the time comes to eat, each of you goes ahead with your own supper, and one goes hungry and another becomes drunk. . . . So then, my brothers and sisters, when you come together to eat, wait for one another. If you are hungry, eat at home, so that when you come together, it will not be for your condemnation.
—1 Corinthians 11:20-21, 33-34 (NRSV)

When I was growing up, our church was in a rough part of town and was burglarized regularly. So, when people came banging on the door, demanding assistance, almost everyone was fearful and alarmed—but never Dad, the pastor. He would open the door, listen to their story, and, when asked for money for food, invite them to share his lunch. For those who would take him up on the offer, he would cook up two helpings of spicy Korean Ramen noodles with a healthy helping of kimchee (spicy Korean pickled cabbage), and he would share the simple—and very spicy—meal with them. Maybe it was the kimchee, but not many would come back.

One day Mark came knocking at the church door. He had whiskey on his breath, and he told the regular kind of story. So Dad offered him lunch. He accepted, sharing the meal with Dad. They spent the day working side by side, weeding around the parking lot. Dad put Mark up for the night. One night turned into two, and two nights into a week. Mark did not want to leave. He has lived in that church for many years now as the building superintendent.

During those years, Mark got his life back together. And to this day he says, "Pastor Cho, he's like my father," all because of an invitation to a meal shared together—not a meal *donated to* the poor; not a meal *served to* one in need; but a meal *shared*, nourishing the soul as well as the body through the sharing of each other's humanity. Jesus shared his table with all who would come to him. Everyone was welcome. Yet we read in 1 Corinthians of the earliest Christians already having forgotten the meaning of coming together to the table for shared life. May we not forget the life that is promised in the act of sharing—the sharing of our things and our selves, the sharing of our humanity.

Prayer Focus: *What are the things that "fill" you in life? What are the things that truly sustain and nourish your life? How can you share the most essential things in your life?*

289

November 14 ~ Life in Clay Jars

For it is the God who said, "Let light shine out of darkness," who has shone in our hearts to give the light of the knowledge of the glory of God in the face of Jesus Christ. But we have this treasure in clay jars, so that it may be made clear that this extraordinary power belongs to God and does not come from us. We are afflicted in every way, but not crushed; perplexed, but not driven to despair; persecuted, but not forsaken; struck down, but not destroyed; always carrying in the body the death of Jesus, so that the life of Jesus may also be made visible in our bodies.

—2 Corinthians 4:6-10 (NRSV)

A woman took too many pills. There was too much emotional pain. Lying on her gurney in the Emergency Room, she asked me, "What's your sermon about this Sunday?"

"Brokenness."

"Some of us are more broken than others."

"Yes, but none of us escapes. It is part of life. It's my Humpty-Dumpty Sermon."

"What do you mean?"

You know the rhyme:

Humpty-Dumpty sat on a wall.
Humpty-Dumpty had a great fall.
All the King's horses and all the King's men
Couldn't put Humpty back together again.

The experience is familiar. Humpty-Dumpty speaks some basic truths. First, brokenness is a universal human experience. We all know what it is to have a dream, a goal, health, family, a relationship—something—broken. Second, it's hard to get everything back together again. But Humpty-Dumpty doesn't get the last word.

The apostle Paul wrote of brokenness. He was beaten, whipped, and challenged. His friends didn't defend him. Some thought he was untrustworthy and inconsistent. He felt overworked and underloved. "I've got conflicts on the outside and fears on the inside," he basically said.

This treasure—life—comes in clay jars, he wrote. They can be broken. But knowing the God who said, "Let light shine out of darkness," means we may be struck down, but not destroyed. Paul never expected his faith to protect him from the vagaries of life. He never expected an easy "be good and life will be good" ideal.

We have this treasure in clay jars. They are imperfect vessels. They are vulnerable and can be broken. But regardless of our brokenness or imperfections, there are always new possibilities for life. God is present in our vulnerability and our brokenness—in clay jars like you and me.

Prayer Focus: What brokenness do you bring? What darkness in your life needs light? What pain are you running or hiding from? Pray not that you will never be broken, not that your life will always be protected from all that is dark or painful or unknown, but that God will be present in all these places. Pray that though you may be broken, you also may be remolded through the promise of life.

November 15 ~ "Why Can't I Be Me?"

A man . . . asked him, "Good Teacher, what must I do to inherit eternal life?" Jesus said to him, " . . . You know the commandments: 'You shall not murder; You shall not commit adultery; You shall not steal. . . .'" He said to him, "Teacher, I have kept all these since my youth." Jesus, looking at him, loved him and said, "You lack one thing; go, sell what you own, and give the money to the poor, and you will have treasure in heaven; then come, follow me." When he heard this, he was shocked and went away grieving, for he had many possessions.

—Mark 10:17-22 (NRSV)

In the movie *Forrest Gump,* Jenny asks Forrest, "What are you going to be when you grow up?" Forrest says, "Why can't I be me?"

Good question. We seem to spend so much of our lives avoiding ourselves—avoiding life—by avoiding whatever is puzzling, humiliating, embarrassing, limiting, or challenging.

Despite all his limitations, Forrest was the one character most able to engage life in all its fullness. He was open, courageous, and trusting; and he had a certain wisdom. In the end, he asked his dying mother, "What's my destiny, Mama?" She said, "Forrest, you're gonna have to figure that out for yourself. . . . You have to do your best with what God gave you."

Part of growing up as a person and maturing in faith is moving beyond our narcissism and taking responsibility for our lives. Growing toward life in all its fullness means struggling with the puzzling, challenging, and difficult questions about our faith and who we are. There are a lot of people who will take the struggle out of that for you. They will spell out everything for you and fill in the blanks. But not Jesus.

A man defined by his wealth (known as "The Rich Man") came to Jesus searching for authentic life. He had kept all the commandments, but he felt the hollowness of the fill-in-the-blank answers to eternal life. Jesus saw his striving, loved him, and challenged him to risk his very identity, telling him to sell what he owned, give the money to the poor, and "follow me." Jesus brought the man face-to-face with himself and invited him to struggle with becoming. The man understood, felt unequal to the task, grieved, and walked away with lowered head.

He didn't see that Jesus' invitation to authentic life is possible for anyone willing to risk continually growing, regardless of his or her limitations. Even Forrest.

Prayer Focus: *What are some risks you face in continuing to grow? In what ways are you avoiding life, trying not to be "you"?*

November 16 ~ Abundant Life

So again Jesus said to them, "Very truly, I tell you, I am the gate for the sheep. All who came before me are thieves and bandits; but the sheep did not listen to them. I am the gate. Whoever enters by me will be saved, and will come in and go out and will find pasture. The thief comes only to steal and kill and destroy. I came that they may have life, and have it abundantly."
—John 10:7-10 (NRSV)

We spend much of our time worrying about being successful, caring for our friends, arguing with our opponents, marveling at our children, playing games, sweating finances, regretting mistakes, loving, eating, sleeping, working, crying, and laughing.

Yet we also have the capacity to stop and ask, *What does it all mean?* Part of what it means to be human is to wonder what it means to be human. We are, as John Gardner once put it, "stubborn seekers of meaning." And since life can be frustrating, painful, and even cruel, some responses to the question about the meaning of life are pessimistic: "[Life] is a tale told by an idiot, full of sound and fury, signifying nothing" (Shakespeare's *Macbeth*); "Vanity of vanities, . . . all is vanity" (Ecclesiastes 12:8 NRSV). What, then, does it mean to "have [life] abundantly"?

In today's scripture, the thief is that which only pretends to offer life— that which is, in reality, a wolf in sheep's clothing. So many conventional expectations of "the good life" can fall into this category.

It's tempting to view Jesus as the gate to "the abundant life," meaning "the life I want." But the abundant life that Jesus offers can be found only through entering his gate: living life by the surprising, challenging, courageous, risky, frequently unconventional and upside-down example of his life and words. At the end of the day, the test is, *Was I a more loving, generous, humble, compassionate, grace-full person or not?* That is "the good life."

Prayer Focus: The people who get into heaven are not the ones with "right beliefs" or the current idea of what morality is. But, as Jesus says, "I was hungry . . . naked . . . sick . . . in prison . . . and you cared" (Matthew 25:35-56, author's paraphrase). Whom have you cared for? Who around you may be in need of something you can offer?

November 17 ~ Bananas for All the Children

In that region there were shepherds living in the fields, keeping watch over their flock by night. Then an angel of the Lord stood before them, and the glory of the Lord shone around them, and they were terrified. But the angel said to them, "Do not be afraid; for see—I am bringing you good news of great joy for all the people: to you is born this day in the city of David a Savior, who is the Messiah, the Lord."
—Luke 2:8-11 (NRSV)

How many bananas do you think you eat in a year? In Korea in the 1970s, bananas were very valuable. Regular people never got a single banana—ever. For a few years, some churches in Seoul somehow got their hands on bananas (probably overstocked low-grade ones from an American military base) and handed them out to children on Christmas Eve. This is how my sister and I got our first taste of a banana.

I couldn't believe it. I remember thinking, *Wow! A whole banana for me? This is too much. Why would they waste such a valuable gift on just a kid?* I felt a little guilty.

293

But any child who walked through the doors of the churches—orphan children, dirty children, shoeless children, desperate children who went from church to church collecting bananas—got one. No questions asked! This enormous delicacy was given not to "more important" people but to kids, who were thought to have no place in the scheme of things. It was a gift that had to be eaten right then if it was to be any good—not treasured and stored away for a rainy day but extravagantly enjoyed today.

To me, the banana was an unbelievably huge gift, freely given, to someone who didn't feel worthy. Sounds like life—like the incarnation. Think about it: The message of the birth of the Messiah, who brought life to all people, came first to shepherds—not kings or priests or "more important" people. The message of Christmas is that *all* people in the human family are worth a banana—not because of what we can do or what we have, but because of who we are: children of God. Bananas for all the children!

Prayer Focus: When have you experienced the gift of grace—something that you in no way deserved? What are some wonderful gifts in your life? What are you grateful for? Pray with a grateful heart.

November 18 ~ I Discover Myself with You

And the rib that the LORD God had taken from the man he made into a woman and brought her to the man. Then the man said, "This at last is bone of my bones and flesh of my flesh; this one shall be called Woman, for out of Man this one was taken. Therefore a man leaves his father and his mother and clings to his wife, and they become one flesh.

—Genesis 2:22-24 (NRSV)

If someone asked you what you needed for a full life, what would you say? What would you tell yourself? In the first story in Genesis, the Lord God makes a man and a woman and introduces them to each other. What does the man say? The translation of the original text at this point is "bone of my bones. Flesh of my flesh." What does that mean? What Adam really says is, "What a stroke of luck! With you I find myself; I discover who I am."

You might say that the story answers the question, *Why are boys and girls attracted to each other?* But it also makes a crucial theological point not limited to boys and girls. God loves us and gives us what we need, and what we need is not usually what we think we need. From a biblical perspective, what we need is relationships. God's gift to us is our capacity and need to share life.

But it's a risky thing to share life deeply, to care about one another. Care is often "wrong"—says the wrong thing, does the wrong thing, has the wrong timing, makes mistakes. But on this planet Earth, we all share life. The first story in Genesis says that we are made by God, at the most fundamental level, for relationship with one another.

Prayer Focus: What are some important relationships in your life? Pray that God will be in the midst of those relationships, that those relationships will continue to grow and mature with God, and that, through those relationships, you might continue to discover yourselves and find authentic life.

November 19 ~ Looking for a Place

As they were going along the road, they came to some water; and the eunuch said, "Look, here is water! What is to prevent me from being baptized?" He commanded the chariot to stop, and both of them, Philip and the eunuch, went down into the water, and Philip baptized him.

—Acts 8:36-38 (NRSV)

All of us have questions about things that seem to matter a lot at the time, but may be forgotten tomorrow. And we tend to lose track of the questions that really matter—questions about meaning and value and purpose and place. We all need a place. Place can be an ugly word. "I don't mind them as long as they stay in their place." Place can be a beautiful word. "There's always a place for you here." "You will always have a place in my heart." Ugly or beautiful, place is an important word.

I conducted a funeral for a man who had been very successful, but his identity was so tied up in his work that when he lost his work, he lost his place—his compass. He couldn't find the way back. He was found murdered in a Denver alley.

Philip overheard the Ethiopian eunuch, who was excluded from the temple, reading from Isaiah, and Philip asked if he understood what he was reading. Then Philip told him about Jesus. As they passed by a pond, the eunuch asked to be baptized. So Philip baptized him, and the eunuch went on his way rejoicing. He had a place in God's family.

There is a rabbinic expression for the Creator which means "The Place." Whoever you are, wherever you are in your life, there is a place for you in God's family. Place isn't about geography. It's about life.

Prayer Focus: Are you looking for "home"—a space where you are truly alive, a place where you really belong? This "home" is a reflection of who God is—a place where life is found. God is always so near. There is always a place for you.

November 20 ~ The Truth Will Set You Free

"Therefore I tell you, do not worry about your life. . . . Look at the birds of the air; they neither sow nor reap nor gather into barns, and yet your heavenly Father feeds them. Are you not of more value than they? And can any of you by worrying add a single hour to your span of life? . . . So do not worry about tomorrow, for tomorrow will bring worries of its own. Today's trouble is enough for today."

—Matthew 6:25-27, 34 (NRSV)

What is this word of which Jesus speaks? What does it mean to remain in this word? What truth will we know? And what freedom comes from knowing that truth?

Three years after marrying my younger brother, and eighteen months after having a baby, my sister-in-law lay in a hospital bed, dying of leukemia. About an hour before she died, I was standing on one side of her bed, and her mother was on the other side. Jean looked up and said, "Mama, I don't want to die." Her mom said, "Jeannie, you're not going to die." In a voice both weak and strong, Jean challenged, "Oh, Mama, don't lie to me."

If only before we die, we do want someone to tell us the truth. But what is the truth? And what freedom comes from knowing that truth?

If Jesus' word is the truth, then it must speak to the reality of our lives from the reality of his life. What do we see in Jesus' life? We see one who had disagreements with his parents, who invited children to be with him, who fed 5,000 people dinner, who needed time by himself, who got angry at prejudice and injustice, who forgave those who offended him, who was scared to die, who was able to trust God's providence, and who could com-

296

mit himself to that. If the truth of our lives and the truth of Jesus' life are the same, then we are his disciples when we remain in it—that is, when we remain in life. What kind of truth is that?

It is not the "2 + 2 = 4" kind of truth. It is truth as an undistorted way of living life. That kind of truth can make us miserable—if we wish that life were different than it is. What freedom does that truth bring? *The freedom to see life as it is and to live it.* That does not mean we do not try to change some things. It does mean we have the freedom to enjoy the beauty of moments that do not last; to endure the agony of moments that intrude; to have another chance to redeem individual selfishness, interpersonal prejudice, and international strife; to affirm the satisfactions of caring; to be human; to be part of God's family. Is that really freedom? Yes. And that's the truth.

Prayer Focus: Each of us can create distortions that interfere with our ability to see life as it is—and with our ability to live it. What is the reality of your life? What kind of truth and freedom do you seek?

November 21 ~ Fried Eggs

The cup of blessing that we bless, is it not a sharing in the blood of Christ? The bread that we break, is it not a sharing in the body of Christ? Because there is one bread, we who are many are one body, for we all partake of the one bread.
—1 Corinthians 10:16-17 (NRSV)

When my sister was in the second grade, she was invited to her first slumber party. They were serving spaghetti rings for dinner. Our family had recently immigrated from Korea, and we were not accustomed to much of American cuisine. Alice timidly remarked that she had tried spaghetti rings once and didn't know why people ate it. In response, Mrs. Brown, asked, "Well, then, what *do* you eat at home, dear?" My shy sister, pressured for a quick answer, mumbled, "Fried eggs." Puzzled, Mrs. Brown served Alice two fried eggs at each meal.

The act was intended to accommodate someone who was "different" from the rest, but, sadly, the result was embarrassment and exclusion. If we are to be open to all of God's family, it is not enough to say "everyone is welcome" if that means everyone is welcome to join "us," as we are.

Without going out of our way to learn about each other and work toward having genuine dialogue, we cannot say that we are truly open and participating together in Christian community.

Paul writes about the one bread and body of Christ to address the issue of exclusion. The effects of practicing kashruth ("keeping kosher") made social intercourse between the practicing Jew and the outside world possible only on the terms of the one who observed kashruth. The primary idea of Christian community, however, is that of participating in something of which others are genuinely a part.

A truly inclusive community of faith is a place where all come to the table in a meaningful way—each from a place of strength and unique identity, each with sincere affirmation for all. We must work toward a day when we each will embrace the challenge and promise of fellowshiping with each other, open to being transformed and to transforming others by sharing life together.

Prayer Focus: *Regardless of our differences, we human beings have more things in common with one another than we have things that divide us. Pray for God's people everywhere, who are part of your own family.*

November 22 ~ Find Your Gift and Give It Away

Now there are varieties of gifts, but the same Spirit; and there are varieties of services, but the same Lord; and there are varieties of activities, but it is the same God who activates all of them in everyone. To each is given the manifestation of the Spirit for the common good. . . . All these are activated by one and the same Spirit, who allots to each one individually just as the Spirit chooses.
—1 Corinthians 12:4-7, 11 (NRSV)

In the movie *Mr. Holland's Opus*, Richard Dreyfuss wants to be a composer but reluctantly takes a job teaching high school music in order to pay the bills. At the end of the story, current and former students gather to honor him for the gift of his teaching. He looks at the students, to whom he has given so much, and confesses: "I got dragged into this gig . . . and now it's the only thing I want to do." Teaching, after all, was his gift.

In the Scriptures, it is clear that there are all kinds of gifts of the Spirit— gifts that give life. You have a gift. Where is God calling you? Where do you want to go? What is it that animates, energizes, gives spirit and life to you? Who knows where it might take you or what might be possible. We each need an opus, a work, a project, something we are passionate about, a gift to give back to life.

There is a difference between performing activities or services, and being brought to life through the giving of our gifts. It's like the difference between being clinically alive yet in a coma—just breathing in and breathing out—and experiencing real life, authentic life, the fullness of life brought beyond mere existence. Life is too precious just to "play life." One of life's paradoxes is that you get to keep only what you give away. Find your gift, and give it away.

Prayer Focus: God extends us an invitation to authentic life through the giving away of the deepest, most passionate part of ourselves. When have you been most alive? What are you most passionate about? How can you share that part of your life with others?

November 23 ~ What Should I Do?

The two angels came to Sodom in the evening. . . . But before they lay down, the men of the city, the men of Sodom, both young and old, all the people to the last man, surrounded the house; and they called to Lot, "Where are the men who came to you tonight? Bring them out to us, so that we may know them." Lot went out of the door to the men, shut the door after him, and said, "I beg you, my brothers, do not act so wickedly. Look, I have two daughters who have not known a man; let me bring them out to you, and do to them as you please; only do nothing to these men, for they have come under the shelter of my roof."

—Genesis 19:1a, 4-8 (NRSV)

What should I do? Some decisions seem to be clear. Sometimes, however, the choices life brings us are more ambiguous. The Bible helps us make decisions by telling us the truth about human life on earth. It contains stories of war, deception, betrayal, and loss; stories of love, faithfulness, triumph, and dreams.

Lot offered his virgin daughters to strangers pounding on the door. Joshua fought the battle of Jericho, but what about the Canaanite bodies

299

strewn across his victory trail? Moses and David were murderers. Jacob was a swindler. Judith used sex to seduce a king and then kill him. Peter denied knowing Jesus.

The Bible is not a simple book on ethics. It is a book about real people. And in each story, God is there—a burning bush; a whirlwind; a still, small voice; a baby. The Bible is true, because in it we experience God's truth about life, God's relationship with the human family, and God's hope for us. But the Bible doesn't hand out decisions like sticks of gum. We can't just pick a story and know what to do. As we struggle with who God is and make the stories a part of who we are, we find who God is calling us to be—and to become.

Prayer Focus: Are you wondering what you should do? Do you need God's presence and guidance in the midst of all the noise, uncertainty, and ambiguity in your world? Open your mind and heart to God's word and presence in your life. Ask God to surprise you through other people, times of prayer, encounters with scripture, and even struggles.

November 24 ~ What's in a Miracle?

When he looked up and saw a large crowd coming toward him, Jesus said to Philip, "Where are we to buy bread for these people to eat?" . . . One of his disciples . . . said to him, "There is a boy here who has five barley loaves and two fish. But what are they among so many people?" . . . Jesus took the loaves, and when he had given thanks, he distributed them to those who were seated; so also the fish, as much as they wanted.

—John 6:5, 8-9, 11 (NRSV)

When I was three years old, I was diagnosed with hemophilia. Normally, hemophilia is a genetic disorder that is incurable. But when I was growing up in South Korea, a number of unexplained cases of hemophilia were reported. I was one of these.

My parents were told that there was no cure, no hope. But one day we found out about a drug from abroad that was being tested on third-world patients. I participated, along with many other children. The drug was a failure; all but one of the participants eventually died—either of hemophilia or of complications. But I was that one who survived. Miraculously,

300

my white blood cell and platelet count climbed and stabilized, and it remains so today—without explanation.

Even then, I remember wondering, *Why me and not the other children?* I will never know the "why's" or "how's," but I have learned that life is a gift. The real miracle in my life was not that I lived, but that I experienced God's shaping, transforming message: life belongs only to God. Life is not to be lived selfishly but to be given away.

Miracles are a part of life today just as they were in biblical times. The miracle story in my own life helped define my identity, just as the story of the miraculous feeding helped define the identity of the early Christians. It was a moment of Jesus' self-revelation.

A miracle is God's extraordinary message in the midst of the ordinary world and our ordinary lives. Simply put, a miracle is God's work in the world. God works amidst practical, ordinary reality with real and ordinary human beings; and through God's work, God communicates to us.

Yes, miracles are everywhere, for God is always at work.

Prayer Focus: A miracle is recognizing God's hand in the life that we live, and hearing God's call to each of us. Where is God's hand in your life? To what are you being called? Pray that you might see and participate in the miracles in your life.

November 25 ~ Habits of the Heart

You yourselves are our letter [of recommendation], written on our hearts, to be known and read by all; and you show that you are a letter of Christ, prepared by us, written not with ink but with the Spirit of the living God, not on tablets of stone but on tablets of human hearts.

—2 Corinthians 3:2-3 (NRSV)

We have a basketball goal at our house that can be lowered to about six feet high. The neighborhood children like to play on that goal. One day Jared rang the doorbell and asked if he could play. I said, "Sure, but first you have to answer a question. What's the first book in the Bible?"

"Uh—I don't know."

"What's any book in the New Testament?"

"Umm—I don't know. We don't go to church."

301

"What's any one of the Ten Commandments?"

His face brightened and he said, "You have a right to speak with an attorney."

I thought, *Jared comes from a very nice family, but what is his "core" going to be?*

What shapes our core, our vision of life? Robert Lifton says that without a center, one is just a kind of protean person—one who can take any shape, any form.

If we ourselves are letters of recommendation, "written not with ink but with the Spirit of the living God, not on tablets of stone but on tablets of human hearts" (2 Corinthians 3:3 NRSV), what kind of self is that? If it is written on the heart, what kind of heart is that? What habits of the heart reflect Christ?

One habit of the heart is to live believing that life is worth living. God has given to you and me some of the mystery and miracle we call life, and it is precious. "I have set before you life and death," the Old Testament declared. "Choose life" (Deuteronomy 30:19 NRSV).

Another habit of the heart is to know that the precious life with my name on it—or your name on it—deserves to be lived with integrity. What does that mean? As Melvin Wheatley, Jr., once put it, "I will say what I mean. I will do what I say. I will mean what I do."

A third habit of the heart is to hope. Hope means that the future is open, that there are always new possibilities. "I know the plans I have for you, says the Lord, plans for your welfare and not for harm, to give you a future with hope" (Jeremiah 29:11 NRSV).

Christ centers life, gives us a core, and then sends us back into life—no longer protean, shapeless globs but persons who are alert to the preciousness of life, to integrity with ourselves and others, to hope—to the habits of our hearts.

Prayer Focus: Who is it that centers your life? What are the habits of your heart that shape your core?

November 26 ~ Love Spoken Here

One of the scribes . . . asked him, "Which commandment is the first of all?" Jesus answered, "The first is, 'Hear, O Israel: the Lord our God, the Lord is one; you shall love the Lord your God with all your heart, and with all your soul, and with all your mind, and with all your strength.' The second is this, 'You shall love your neighbor as yourself.' There is no other commandment greater than these."

—Mark 12:28-31 (NRSV)

One night last winter a man came through the front door of our church. His jeans were dirty, and his hair was messy. He was wearing several pairs of socks, but no shoes. He said he needed directions. Under his shirt, he was holding on to something. While we were talking, that item crashed to the floor. He began crying, almost hysterically. He said it was an ostrich egg that Shirley MacLaine had given to him in Aspen. What would it mean for us to love this neighbor?

One day a Pharisee asked Jesus, "Teacher, which is the greatest commandment in the Law?" He wanted to catch Jesus in a trap. We usually think there were only ten commandments, but there were actually hundreds of laws to observe. How would Jesus summarize them? What would he say is most important?

Jesus, whose concern was always truth, didn't fall for the trick. He said that the most important commandment is to love God with all your heart, soul, mind, and strength; and the second is to love your neighbor as yourself.

It's nice to have something so clear: Love God and neighbor. Yet it's not as simple as it seems, for our love is a fragile love. We're more likely to love if we believe it won't ask something of us we don't have. We're more likely to love if we're pretty sure we won't get hurt or look too silly. And we're more likely to love if we think we'll get something in return.

But that's not the love Jesus calls us to. He calls us to a selfless love—a love willing to give freely and to take risks; a love willing to reach out to a lost, disheveled, confused stranger on a winter's night.

Prayer Focus: Love is challenging, painful, fragile, ambiguous, and powerful. It is our greatest task. Talk with God about your challenging, painful, fragile, ambiguous, powerful experiences with love. Invite God to be with you in this greatest of tasks.

November 27 ~ Possibility

We know that the whole creation has been groaning in labor pains until now;

303

and not only the creation, but we ourselves, who have the first fruits of the Spirit, groan inwardly while we wait for adoption, the redemption of our bodies.
—Romans 8:22-23 (NRSV)

When I was a child, I wanted to be a Supreme Court justice. My best friend wanted to be the manager at Baskin Robbins. For children, the whole world is one vast possibility. I'm not sure when it happens, but as we grow up, reality—and a certain sense of fixedness—sets in. Possibility becomes increasingly narrow until, finally, we end up merely accepting life.

Still, no matter what our age, deep inside us sleeps a quiet voice that awakens once in a great while to speak beautiful, faintly familiar words—words of great hope, of breathless expectation, of possibility! And the voice asks, *What is the meaning of my life? Is there something more?* The answer is "yes!"

Our lives are waiting to be born anew, says the apostle Paul, "groaning in labor pains." Yet daring to dream of possibility means daring to risk, to embrace uncertainty. Sometimes the promise is hard to spot, and like many things in life, it's often unclear. And we must simply live with the ambivalence.

Paul uses the image of pregnancy to describe the Christian's state of being. Being a Christian is about becoming new. New life has already formed, but the baby isn't here yet. It's about already being changed, yet waiting with expectation—and living fully all the while. It's about being thankful amidst fear and the unknown.

Many of us are terrified that this "birth" may happen in our lives, that we may be the ones who will have to change, grow, be born. Yet being open to possibility means having hope, faith, and vision; becoming more than we are; moving toward life in all its fullness, as God intended for all creation. It is only in risking life that we discover the promise of possibility in our lives.

Prayer Focus: God's new creation is waiting to be born—here, in this real life, in you! There is great possibility in your life. Be open to all that could be.

November 28 ~ Release from Bondage

Just then there was in their synagogue a man with an unclean spirit, and he cried out, "What have you to do with us, Jesus of Nazareth? Have you come to destroy us? I know who you are, the Holy One of God." But Jesus rebuked him, saying, "Be silent, and come out of him!" And the unclean spirit, convulsing him and crying with a loud voice, came out of him.

—Mark 1:23-26 (NRSV)

The beginning of the book of Mark includes stories about Jesus performing healings and exorcisms—casting out demons. In the Greek, *demon* means something that has power to take over your life. These stories are at the beginning of Mark to say that Jesus has come to defeat the powers that control our lives and keep us from the fullness of life God intends for us. So to call Jesus *Messiah*, according to Mark, means that he is the one who can release you from bondage—from whatever holds you back from authentic life.

According to prophetic images, the coming Messiah was pictured to be at a banquet with members of his kingdom. To see Jesus as the Messiah, then, would mean that all those with whom he shared a meal were now understood to be members of this Kingdom. Yet he ate with all kinds of people in all kinds of bondage—with all kinds of "sinners." The message is this: Everyone belongs, because we don't get there by our own efforts; we get there by grace.

Jesus, once again, turned things upside down. His approach to people was not to condemn them or exclude them; it was exactly the opposite—to include and forgive them, to release them from whatever bondage, whatever "sin," whatever power or demon had taken over their lives.

The Word of God has the power to silence the demons that take over our lives. Once they have been cast out, we are invited—without condemnation, ridicule, or punishment—to a whole different kind of life beyond what we ever may have expected.

Prayer Focus: What demons need to be silenced in you so that you might be set free? Ask God to speak these words of power and transformation in your life.

November 29 ~ Sabbath Rest

God saw everything that he had made, and indeed, it was very good. . . . And on the seventh day God finished the work that he had done. . . . So God blessed the seventh day and hallowed it, because on it God rested from all the work that he had done in creation.

—Genesis 1:31, 2:2-3 (NRSV)

Take a moment to read the creation story in Genesis 1–2:3. Really "hear" the story, as if for the first time.

What did you feel as you read these words? The words speak deeply of love, wonder, goodness, blessing, gift—the essence of what life is meant to be for all of God's creation at every moment. If we were to read this text in Hebrew, we would notice a recurring emphasis on the seventh day. The message to us from the story of creation is an imperative: "Shh—Silence! Be still and aware of God's presence within and all around!"

We often live with the illusion that, somehow, we are in control of our lives; and if we can just manage to do all that needs to be done, we will remain in control. But the truth is, we are never in control. All it takes is a telephone call in the middle of the night, a lab result, or a letter in the mailbox to turn life in a moment. Life and death: The most important realities remain out of control.

An invitation to Sabbath rest isn't about taking a nap. By abstaining from all the "doing," which so often defines our lives and our identities, we begin to understand that each of us is created with intrinsic value; that each of our lives, and each moment of life, is meaningful in and of itself. As children of God, we are called to remember that life is precious, valuable, and meaningful—regardless of how much can be accomplished, produced, or amassed in a lifetime. "God saw everything that he had made, and indeed, it was very good." No need to prove our worth. No need to justify our time.

Take time to rest. Take time to be. Take time to live.

Prayer Focus: *Accept the invitation to Sabbath rest. Look at your life from a completely different angle. Reevaluate your everyday priorities. Reconsider what work means, what you are working toward, and how you value yourself and others.*

November 30 ~ Let's Go Home, Toto!

By faith Abraham obeyed when he was called to set out for a place that he was to receive as an inheritance; and he set out, not knowing where he was going. . . . If they had been thinking of the land that they had left behind, they would have had opportunity to return. But as it is, they desire a better country, that is, a heavenly one. Therefore God is not ashamed to be called their God; indeed, he has prepared a city for them.

—Hebrews 11:8, 15-16 (NRSV)

306

Do you remember in *The Wizard of Oz* when Dorothy says, "Let's go home, Toto"? A sense of "home" is so important for life. But so much of what we try to make "home" is not really home at all. What each of us is looking for isn't as much a place as it is a promise—the promise that what we are doing makes sense, that it has meaning and value. What we are looking for is our real home, our real destination—the same one God offered Abraham.

The story of Abraham and Sarah is the story of faith. God said that Abraham would be the father of a new nation—its children like the stars of the sky and the sands of the sea. But how was that going to be? He and Sarah were nearly one hundred years old. The story says that they were rich—in things, at least—but Sarah couldn't get pregnant; and more important, they had no real home. There was no permanence in their lives. They were always in between, always on the way.

Like Abraham and Sarah, we keep on the move, don't we? We are always between places and on the way—questing after security or permanence or success or love or whatever. In the New Testament, the Greek word for faith is used to describe a relationship characterized by trust, openness, mutuality, and confidence. The home God offers is not a place but a relationship. In faith, Abraham and Sarah responded. How about you?

The journey toward "home" involves risk, brokenness, and hope. We keep on the way, growing toward full humanity, believing that no matter what happens, God says, "I will be there with you."

Let's go home, Toto!

Prayer Focus: Is there a place in your life in which you need to step out on faith? Lift this up in prayer with the knowledge that God does, indeed, hear our prayers.

December

THE OVERCOMERS

James A. Harnish

December 1 ~ Survivors or Overcomers?

And he said unto me, "It is done. I am Alpha and Omega, the beginning and the end. . . . He that overcometh shall inherit all things."
—*Revelation 21:6-7 (KJV)*

Read Revelation 1:1-3.

*I*f you're like me—and 40 million other folks—you probably watched the finale of the first *Survivor* series. To tell the truth, I thought the series took soulless self-interest as an operating assumption. When survival means eliminating everyone else by any means available, it's hard not to end up with the newspaper headline that declared, "Nasty guys finish first." Rather than celebration, the series ended with a grim sense of joyless resignation.

When *Survivor* hit the networks, I was reading the story of the frontier journey of Lewis and Clark and the Corps of Discovery. Talk about survival! Every time they agreed that things couldn't get worse, things did! They did not merely survive; they overcame insurmountable obstacles, and the entire nation celebrated what the Corps had accomplished together.

I write these meditations from a deep conviction that God intends more for our lives than self-absorbed survival. The central theme of the book of

Revelation is that in the power of the risen Christ, we can overcome all the powers of evil, suffering, fear, and death. And at the end, the whole creation will reverberate with joy.

Survivors or overcomers? As we make this journey through the last book in the Bible, we get to choose.

Prayer Focus: Ask God, who overcame the power of death in the risen Christ, to enable you to be among those who overcome.

December 2 ~ A Servant, Brother, and Witness

The revelation of Jesus Christ . . . to his servant John, who testified to the word of God and to the testimony of Jesus Christ, even to all that he saw. . . . I, John, your brother who share with you in Jesus the persecution and the kingdom and the patient endurance, was on the island called Patmos because of the word of God and the testimony of Jesus.

—*Revelation 1:1-2, 9 (NRSV)*

Read Revelation 1:9-11.

John introduces himself to his readers as a servant and brother who testified to all he saw. So, who am I?

I'm a fifty-four-year-old guy whose deepest desire is to live as a servant of Jesus Christ. I've been married to Marsha for thirty-two years. We have two Gen-X daughters and one son-in-law. Like John, I'm a pastor, serving a congregation that is chock-full of young adults who are also becoming servants of Christ. Some of these meditations began as on-line conversations with them in response to a weekly e-mail message to my congregation.

I'm your brother in the way that John described himself as a brother of the Christians in Asia Minor (present-day Turkey). I've shared the hopes and fears, joy and sadness, strengths and weaknesses of an amazing assortment of fellow servants in the congregations I've served. I'm a fellow traveler on the road of human experience.

I'm writing to testify to the way I've seen the overcoming power of the risen Christ at work in my life and the lives of others. I pray that as we share these meditations together, we will become more obedient servants, more supportive of our sisters and brothers, and more daring in our witness to the risen Christ.

Prayer Focus: Pray that God, who called us to be servants, will strengthen our relationships with each other so that we may bear witness to what God is doing in our world.

December 3 ~ Blessed or Confused?

Blessed is the one who reads aloud the words of the prophecy, and blessed are those who hear and who keep what is written in it.
—*Revelation 1:3a (NRSV)*

Read Revelation 1:3, 22:18-19.

Let's tell the truth. John said that anyone who reads the Revelation is "blessed," but most of us are simply confused—not that there's anything new about the confusion. Church leaders in the second century rejected Revelation along with the teachings of Montanus, who predicted that the New Jerusalem would descend in what is now Turkey. In the fourth century, when Eusebius categorized the writings alleged to be scripture as "accepted," "rejected," or "disputed," he listed Revelation as a "disputed" book, though it was included in the canon (the list of authoritative or normative sacred writings). Right down to this day, Christians have more differences of opinion on the interpretation of this book than any other in the Bible.

While some interpret Revelation as a very specific "preview of coming attractions" for the end of the world with direct reference to contemporary nations, most biblical scholars believe that we should begin with the context of its first readers, allowing its truth to speak to us through their experience. Because of this diversity of opinion, contemporary scholar M. Eugene Boring calls Revelation "a happy hunting ground for all sorts of bizarre and dangerous interpretations" (*Interpretation: Revelation* [Louisville: Westminster John Knox Press, 1989], p. 4). And yet, it continues to amaze us and give us hope!

Why write meditations on Revelation for young adults? My answer is an e-mail message that asked, "How can I keep my faith intact and not lose it?

311

I really need this info right now!" Like the seven young churches to which John sent this book, the young adults I know are looking for a way to keep their faith intact in times of radical change, shifting values, and cultural conflict. Like John's first readers, we need power to overcome!

John promised that those who read Revelation *aloud* would be blessed, and guess what? It works! Try reading it aloud, as if you were reading a story to children, and see how it blesses you.

(Note: For further study of Revelation, I recommend M. Eugene Boring's volume *Revelation* in the *Interpretation* series, published by John Knox Press.)

Prayer Focus: *Ask God to break through your confusion or discomfort about the book of Revelation, so that through its witness, you might be blessed.*

December 4 ~ Just Imagine!

Look! He is coming with the clouds; every eye will see him.
—Revelation 1:7 (NRSV)

Read Revelation 1:7, 22:8-9.

The images in Revelation overwhelm our senses. They invite us to see, not with the eyes in our heads, but with the imagination in our hearts.

Do you remember the opening sequence in the original *Star Wars* movie? It was subtitled "A New Hope."

Where does it happen? "In a land far, far away."

What's the situation? C3PO says, "We're doomed."

Who's in power? Darth Vader and the dark power.

What does Princess Leia do? She hides a coded message in R2D2.

What does R2D2 do? He is sent with a message for oppressed people.

What will each character do? Everyone chooses one side or the other.

How will the story end? We know that good will ultimately triumph.

You'd be blind not to see the message of *Star Wars*, just as you'd be foolish to draw literal comparisons to current nations or events. But when you see with your imagination, you find yourself engaged in the struggle between good and evil that is present in all places in every age.

Star Wars creator, George Lucas, said that the movie "works on all the senses. . . . kind of [a] dreamlike experience" (*Time*, April 26, 1999, p. 94). John's vision of the overcoming power of the risen Christ came to the persecuted first-century Christians in Asia Minor through the Spirit-soaked imagination of John in much the same way *Star Wars* came to this generation. It works on all the senses. Look with the eyes of your imagination, and you can experience that power, too!

Prayer Focus: Ask God, who brought new hope to oppressed people through John, to help you see and be strengthened in that same hope today.

December 5 ~ God in Three Tenses

Grace to you and peace from him who is and who was and who is to come. . . . I am the Alpha and the Omega," says the Lord God, who is and who was and who is to come, the Almighty.

—Revelation 1:4, 8 (NRSV)

Read Revelation 1:4-8, 7:9-12, 11:15-17.

Have you ever been asked, "Are you saved?" What did you say?

On the assumption that God's salvation is rooted in God's identity, I understand my experience of salvation in three tenses.

I was saved. The Almighty God acted in Jesus Christ, who "freed us from our sins by his blood" (Revelation 1:5 NRSV). I was saved on that Friday afternoon when Jesus hung on a cross and said, "It is finished."

I am being saved. As I respond to God's saving grace, the Spirit of God works within me to overcome those things that get in the way of his saving purpose in and through my life. It's happening now!

I will be saved. By the power of the Spirit, I am pressing on toward the new life in Christ that will ultimately be fulfilled on the other side of death (Philippians 3:12-16).

When I was serving a rural congregation, I asked a farmer how he was doing. The old boy said, "Preacher, I'm not the man I used to be, and I'm not yet the man I'm going to be, but by God's grace I'm more the man I'd like to be than I've ever been before." I'd say he knew the God who is, who was, and who is to come!

313

December 6 ~ No Fear!

When I saw him, I fell at his feet as though dead. But he placed his right hand on me, saying, "Do not be afraid; I am the first and the last, and the living one. I was dead, and see, I am alive forever and ever; and I have the keys of Death and of Hades."

—Revelation 1:17-18 (NRSV)

Read Revelation 1:12-20, 14:1-7, 15:1-4.

Have you noticed all the angels that are showing up these days? They're everywhere! You'll find them on everything from calendars and greeting cards to refrigerator door magnets. I saw a specialty shop named "Nothing but Angels." Most of them are cheerful little cherubs with chubby cheeks and smiling faces that incite a warm, cozy feeling the moment you see them. In fact, many of them could use a Slim Fast liquid diet and several hours in the gym!

There's not a single angel in the Bible who would make it in our contemporary angel market. With disturbing consistency, everyone who runs into a biblical angel is scared to death, and there's not a single cherub in the entire book of Revelation. In the same way, John's first vision of the risen Christ scares the living daylights out of him. The first thing Christ says is, "Do not be afraid."

Let's face it. We all have good reasons to be afraid. You can find out about more than five hundred human fears at www.phobialist.com. What things cause you to be afraid? Go ahead; name them. Now, I ask you, when you confront those fears, whom would you rather have on your side? A chubby cherub that makes you feel warm and cuddly, or one who has been to death and back and is strong enough to scare you with his overcoming power?

In this world, it's good to know who's on your side!

Prayer Focus: *Ask the risen Christ to overwhelm you with his power, so that in him you might overcome your fears.*

December 7 ~ Learning to Listen

I was in the spirit on the Lord's day, and I heard behind me a loud voice like a trumpet. . . . Then I turned to see whose voice it was that spoke to me. . . . And his voice was like the sound of many waters.

—Revelation 1:10, 12a, 15c (NRSV)

Read Revelation 1:10, 17-19, 19:6-10.

I received an e-mail from a bright, well-educated young man. He asked, "How can we listen to God? How do we distinguish God's voice from the myriad of other things we listen to (such as our own thoughts)?"

I heard essentially the same question on NBC's hit series *The West Wing*. President Bartlet was disappointed when NASA lost contact with a space probe on Mars. As the show ended, he stepped out of the Oval Office into the Rose Garden, gazed up into the night sky, and said softly, "Speak to us."

Deep within each of us is a longing to hear a living word that comes not so much from within us as to us from God. John said that he was in the Spirit on the Lord's day—Sunday, the day of resurrection—when he heard a voice that he recognized as the voice of the risen Christ. It took him by surprise while he was practicing the regular spiritual discipline of worship.

Here's a spiritual principle that's been proved by faithful people across the centuries: People who hear the voice of Christ have learned to listen through the spiritual disciplines of worship, Bible study, and prayer. Who knows? If we listen, we may even hear that same voice speaking in the deepest places of our souls.

Prayer Focus: Ask the risen Christ, who spoke to John, to speak to you as you listen in the spiritual discipline of worship.

December 8 ~ Overcoming Confused Priorities with Love

"I have this against you, that you have abandoned the love you had at first. Remember then from what you have fallen; repent, and do the works you did at first. . . . To everyone who conquers, I will give permission to eat from the tree of life that is in the paradise of God."

—Revelation 2:4-7 (NRSV)

Read Revelation 2:1-7, 3:19.

Though no one knows who said it first, we've all heard the line by now: The main thing is keeping the main thing the main thing. John invites us to listen to the words of the risen Christ to seven young churches in Asia Minor. He told the folks in Ephesus to keep first things first.

A young woman's e-mail described a spiritual "Aha!" in her life. "I'm so fulfilled and joyful in being clay and knowing God is the potter. Sure takes the pressure off while giving a sense of direction. . . . This is what I was made to be like!"

We were made to be like Jesus and to experience a life that fulfills the loving purpose of God. God's love was the "main thing" for John Wesley, the eighteenth-century founder of the Methodist movement. He said, "First. The love of God. . . . Such a love is this, as engrosses the whole heart, as takes up all the affections, as fills the entire capacity of the soul, and employs the utmost extent of all its faculties" (*The Works of John Wesley*, Vol. 5, p. 21).

But how easily we forget our first love and allow other things to take its place! In Revelation, John offers three steps to help us keep the main thing the main thing.

1. Remember. Be like the runaway son who remembered who he was (Luke 15:17).

2. Repent. Turn in the direction of God's love revealed in Jesus.

3. Do the works of loving reconciliation that will re-ignite the fire of love. Find tangible ways to express the love you seek by serving someone in need, writing a letter to a friend, offering forgiveness to someone who has hurt you, or letting someone know how deeply you value him or her.

Rediscovering the love of God is like eating from the tree of life in paradise. It's finding the joy for which you were created.

Prayer Focus: Ask God, who created you in love, to help you maintain the priority of love.

December 9 ~ Overcoming Suffering with Faith

"Do not fear what you are about to suffer. . . . Be faithful until death, and I will give you the crown of life. . . . Whoever conquers will not be harmed by the second death."

—Revelation 2:10-11 (NRSV)

316

Read Revelation 2:8-11.

Rachel Scott died at Columbine High. I've heard Christian people claim that her death was an act of God that was intended to spark a spiritual revolution. But I don't buy it. I'm confident that God can use her witness to ignite a flame of faith in people's lives, but that's a long way from saying that God caused it—at least not the God who loved us all the way to the cross (see Romans 8:31-39).

Where is God when we suffer? That was no academic question for John, who was in political exile on the island of Patmos (off the coast of Asia Minor), or for the Christians in Smyrna (north of Ephesus), who could see persecution coming. The Revelation emerged out of the real suffering of real people who had to wrestle with God's faithfulness in their persecution.

John was like Martin Luther King, Jr. writing his "Letter from the Birmingham City Jail" with the sound of police dogs in the street and the names of arrested people on his heart. He was like Nelson Mandela, imprisoned on Robbin Island. He heard Christ promise that people who are faithful will receive the crown. In the suffering, death, and resurrection of Jesus we can find power to overcome suffering with hope.

Does God cause suffering? I doubt it, although the struggle with evil in Revelation makes it clear that in giving freedom to this Creation, the God who will ultimately overcome suffering, allows it. Can God use suffering to ignite hope and faith within us? You can count on it! Will God ultimately overcome all suffering? You bet!

Prayer Focus: Ask the God who meets us at the cross to meet you in your place of suffering with strength and hope.

December 10 ~ Overcoming Temptation with Strength

"I know where you are living, where Satan's throne is. Yet you are holding fast to my name, and you did not deny your faith in me even in the days of Antipas my witness, my faithful one, who was killed among you, where Satan lives. . . . To everyone who conquers I will give some of the hidden manna, and I will give a white stone, and on the white stone is written a new name that no one knows except the one who receives it."

—Revelation 2:13-17 (NRSV)

317

Read Revelation 2:12-17.

Reality television took a lusty turn on *Temptation Island*. Four unmarried couples tried to resist the allure of a tropical island inhabited by swinging singles. With a straight face, one TV executive said, "It's not about sex." Sure. And Washington isn't about politics!

Here's the truth: I'm capable of getting as much sensual pleasure out of watching a bunch of yuppies with toned and tanned bodies lust after each other as the next guy. It's called voyeurism, and there's plenty of it going around. But in one sense, the TV executive got it right. It's not just about sex. It's about temptation that feeds on the animal instincts that evolution never quite sifted out of our human psyche. It's about using other people for our own satisfaction; about confusing love with lust; about trading moral integrity for personal pleasure; and about doing it for corporate profits.

What's a Christian to do? The Bible says the only way to deal with temptation is to resist it (James 1:12-15). We all live on "Temptation Island." We are all tempted to something less than the life God has called us to. We all need the inner strength of the Spirit and the external support of fellow Christians to overcome temptation and maintain our identity in a world "where Satan lives."

Prayer Focus: Name the temptation in your life and ask God, whose Son overcame temptation in the wilderness, to give you the power to overcome.

December 11 ~ Overcome Confusion with Conviction

"Only hold fast to what you have until I come. To everyone who conquers and continues to do my works to the end, I will give authority over the nations; to rule them with an iron rod, as when clay pots are shattered—even as I also received authority from my Father. To the one who conquers I will also give the morning star."

—Revelation 2:25-28 (NRSV)

Read Revelation 2:18-29.

"Will it be coffee, tea, or He?"

318

Charles Krauthammer asked that question in *Time* magazine. In the article he recalled a time when he was checking into the hospital, and the admissions secretary asked, "What is your religious preference?" He says that he was tempted to answer, "'I think Buddhism is the coolest of all, but I happen to be Jewish'" (*Time*, June 15, 1998, p. 92). He reflected on a time when religion shaped identity and expressed his concern for a culture in which belief has become nothing more than a "preference."

Krauthammer is onto something important there. There was a time when creeds really mattered. Sometimes, sadly, they mattered enough to lead to Crusades and Inquisitions. But when belief is defined as a "preference," conviction is traded for convenience.

Conviction was casual in Thyatira. That's why the word came like "a flame of fire" to challenge easy tolerance of pagan practice and to ignite fresh loyalty to Christ. Later, convictions became critical. Under the emperor Domitian, every Roman citizen was required to swear that "Caesar is Lord." It was utterly irreconcilable with the Christian claim that "Jesus is Lord." Their creed became a life or death deal.

Let's never return to the Inquisition! And let's give thanks for a healthy tolerance that provides mutual respect for freedom of thought and personal conviction. But genuine Christianity is still a life or death deal—not in the sense of martyrdom (though that does still happen), but in the way belief in the Lordship of Christ shapes our thoughts, actions, relationships, political choices, and economic responsibilities. It is more than a preference; it's a conviction that determines our identity—or should.

Prayer Focus: Pray that God, who searches our minds and hearts, will give you clarity about the central convictions of your faith in Christ.

December 12 ~ Overcoming Lethargy with Life

"Wake up, and strengthen what remains and is on the point of death. . . . If you do not wake up, I will come like a thief, and you will not know at what hour I will come to you. . . . If you conquer, you will be clothed like them in white robes, and I will not blot your name out of the book of life; I will confess your name before my Father and before his angels."

—Revelation 3:2-5 (NRSV)

319

Read Revelation 3:1-6.

Eugene Peterson says that "Revelation pulls us out of our complacent daze and puts us on our feet" (*Reversed Thunder* [San Francisco: HarperSanFrancisco, 1988], p. 25). Its vibrant images are a wake-up call for our lethargic souls.

I met with a group of twenty-something guys who were reading C. S. Lewis. His words had connected with a practical reality in their lives:

> The real problem of the Christian life comes . . . the very moment you wake up each morning. All your wishes and hopes for the day rush at you like wild animals. And the first job each morning consists simply in shoving them all back; in listening to that other voice . . . letting that other larger, stronger, quieter life come flowing in. *(Mere Christianity)*

Each of the guys in the group knows how it feels to wake up with "wild animals" rushing into his mind. My problem is e-mail. If I read my e-mail before I pray, I will never get around to praying! But when I shove those things back and take time to listen for that "other voice," I experience the presence of the one who can pull me out of my daze and keep my feet moving in the right direction.

As the Nike company (from the Greek word meaning "conquer" or "overcome") has taught us, the challenge is to "Just do it!"

Prayer Focus: *Push everything aside so you can spend some time in prayer, listening for a fresh word from the risen Christ.*

December 13 ~ Overcoming Indifference with Life

"These are the words of the holy one, the true one, . . . who opens and no one will shut, who shuts and no one opens: . . . I have set before you an open door, which no one is able to shut. . . . If you conquer, I will make you a pillar in the temple of my God; you will never go out of it."

—Revelation 3:7, 8, 12 (NRSV)

Read Revelation 3:7-13.

Have you walked through any open doors lately?

One of my all-time favorite movies is *Dead Poets Society*. Robin Williams played the iconoclastic teacher who taught his students to say, *Carpe diem,* meaning "seize the day." His passion opened new doors for their thinking, living, and being. It changed the way they lived.

Living with the book of Revelation can open new doors in our souls. Let's not get hung up on end-of-the-world books and movies. For heaven's sake (literally, for Heaven's sake!), let's not try to rigidly identify every character in John's vision with twentieth-century nations and leaders. The long hall of church history is cluttered with the sad ruins of faithful people who were absolutely sure that the end would come in their time, but they were, and are, always disappointed.

If we allow John's word pictures to do their work, they can touch a deep place in our lives. We may discover that we are being lifted out of the mundane corridors of our human existence into a higher place—with a stronger faith and a more vibrant awareness of the overcoming power of the risen Christ. We may feel his Spirit energizing us to claim each moment as a fresh opportunity to bear witness to our faith.

The risen Christ challenged the folks in Philadelphia (Asia Minor, not Pennsylvania!) to see an open door. Acknowledging their human weakness, he promised them strength to overcome their fear and to claim their identity as witnesses to the living God. Just as he opened new doors of opportunity for them, he opens new doors for us and calls us to follow the way that leads to new life.

Prayer Focus: How often are you tempted to settle for the ordinary or mundane when all of God's power is available for you? Ask God, who opens new doors, to energize you to seize the opportunities of this moment in your life.

December 14 ~ Overcoming Cynicism with Passion

"I know your works; you are neither cold nor hot. I wish that you were either cold or hot. So, because you are lukewarm, and neither cold nor hot, I am about to spit you out of my mouth. . . . Listen! I am standing at the door, knocking; if you hear my voice and open the door, I will come in to you and eat with you, and you with me. To the one who conquers I will give a place with me on my throne, just as I myself conquered and sat down with my Father on his throne."
—Revelation 3:15-16, 20-21 (NRSV)

321

Read Revelation 3:14-22.

Jedediah Purdy is a Gen-Xer. He was a twenty-four-year-old Yale law student when his book, *For Common Things*, was published. One review called it a "passionate attack on the dangers of modern passionlessness. . . . A precocious diatribe against the sort of media-savvy detachment that passes for intelligence and maturity in the age of Letterman" (*Time*, September 20, 1999, p. 74).

In a sense, Purdy's critique is a contemporary version of the hard words of the risen Christ to Laodicea. Neither hot nor cold, they had become complacent, comfortable, content with a lukewarm religious experience, which demanded little and never came into conflict with the culture around them. Bland indifference, passionless apathy, shallow religious practice without compassion was enough to make Jesus sick!

There's plenty of cynicism going around these days, and it isn't just on Letterman, whose spontaneity and humor make me want to say, "Hey, Jedediah, lighten up!" But I don't find that cynicism among the young adults with whom I share the life of faith. They are alive, passionate, and energetic about life. They know how to laugh and cry. They care about each other and about the world around them. They have discovered that the best way to overcome lukewarm religion is to allow the risen Christ to take up residence in their human experience. If it could happen in Laodicea, it can happen here for us!

Prayer Focus: Listen for a knock at the door of your heart and invite the risen Christ to come into your life in a fresh, new way today.

December 15 ~ Who Is Worthy?

Then I looked, and I heard the voice of many angels surrounding the throne and the living creatures and the elders; they numbered myriads of myriads and thousands of thousands, singing with full voice, "Worthy is the Lamb that was slaughtered."

—Revelation 5:11-12 (NRSV)

Read Revelation 4:1–5:14.

A number of years ago on *Saturday Night Live*, Wayne and Garth often fell on their knees shouting, "We're not worthy!" They got that right! But who is?

In the messages to the seven churches, Christ spoke in this world. Now, he lifts John into an experience of sensory overload in which one thing is crystal clear: There is a throne at the center of the universe, and it is not empty. Contrary to the way things often appear, the universe is not in chaos. There is "one seated on the throne" who is worthy of glory, honor, and power.

"Worthy art thou" was the acclamation used to greet the Roman emperor. Domitian demanded that he be addressed as "Lord and God." John recycles those terms to point to the one who supersedes every earthly power.

But here's the surprise! At God's right hand is a slaughtered Lamb. The one who is worthy to open the scroll is also the one who died on the cross. The ultimate power in this world is not the military, political, and economic superpower in Rome, but the self-giving, nonviolent love of Jesus who gave himself for us (Revelation 1:5-7).

Who, do we believe, is on the throne? What's the nature of the power at the center of existence? Who is worthy of our devotion, loyalty, and praise?

Prayer Focus: In your imagination, picture the throne at the center of your life. Who or what is reigning there?

December 16 ~ How Long?

I saw under the altar the souls of those who had been slaughtered for the word of God and for the testimony they had given; they cried out with a loud voice, "Sovereign Lord, holy and true, how long will it be before you judge and avenge our blood?"

—Revelation 6:9-10 (NRSV)

Read Revelation 6:1–7:17.

The echo of the martyrs' voices under the altar forces us to ask some pretty heavy questions. In the call and response of the African American

323

preaching tradition, Martin Luther King, Jr. would ask, "How long?" The reply would come back from the congregation, "Not long!" It rocked with the rhythm of hope, born out of generations of suffering. He would tell his followers that the arch of history may be long, but it bends toward justice. They'd sing "We shall overcome someday" and go back into the struggle again.

The saints beneath the altar ask the question that lurks beneath every experience of suffering or injustice: *How long, O Lord? How long until you set things right? How long until your vision of justice, mercy, and peace is fulfilled? How long until our world will be saved?*

John doesn't answer with a span of time. Instead he lifts our eyes to a triumphant vision of those who have already overcome, singing praise to the God who saw them through the struggle. Our tear-filled eyes catch a vision of that day when God will wipe away all tears and the Lamb at the center of the throne will lead us to the water of life.

The visions of Revelation will never accomplish their work in our lives until we see them through the eyes of those who suffer injustice and feel the hope that we shall indeed overcome someday.

Prayer Focus: Where is the "How long?" in your life? Do you really believe that you will overcome someday? Ask the Spirit of the risen Christ to strengthen you in the hope that Revelation proclaims.

December 17 ~ How Does God's Kingdom Come?

And there were loud voices in heaven, saying, "The kingdom of the world has become the kingdom of our Lord and of his Messiah, and he will reign forever and ever."

—Revelation 11:15 (NRSV)

Read Revelation 8:1–11:19.

Almost every child who grew up sitting on a church pew learned to pray, "Thy kingdom come, thy will be done on earth as it is in heaven." In Revelation, the heavenly voices declare it as an already accomplished fact: "The kingdom of this world has become the kingdom of our Lord."

But how does the Kingdom come? How does God's will get done around here? Eugene Boring writes, "The path to the kingdom goes through, not around, the woes of history" (*Interpretation: Revelation*, p. 134). Frankly, John's surrealistic images are hard to take. If we analyze them too closely, they become almost impossible to comprehend. But if we hear the trumpets, smell the incense and sulfur, feel the fire, imagine locusts and scorpions, we might begin to feel the turmoil of a world that insists on going its own way and refuses to repent (Revelation 9:20-21).

The plagues in Revelation parallel the plagues in Exodus, when the purpose was to challenge Pharaoh to repent and to liberate the children of Israel. Similarly, the images in Revelation are a means of liberation. They are a trumpet call for the whole creation to turn in the way that leads to life. But when the intransigent world refuses, God calls to his faithful witness, "Come up here."

God's kingdom comes through the very real turmoil of an unrepentant world, but for those with eyes to see, it is already here! We saw it in the leadership of Martin Luther King, Jr., as he called this nation to live up to its creed. We saw it in the witness of Desmond Tutu and the Christians of South Africa who led the way in the ending of apartheid. We can see it in the lives of men and women who break free from self-destructive addictions and turn in the direction of a healthy life. We can feel it in the inner strength that the Spirit gives when we face pain or injustice. In sometimes obvious and often subtle ways, we can see the Kingdom coming and God's will being done on earth, in us, even as it is already fulfilled in heaven.

Prayer Focus: Where do you see God's kingdom coming and God's will being done in your world? How can you be part of it?

December 18 ~ Praying with the Saints

Another angel with a golden censer came and stood at the altar; he was given a great quantity of incense to offer with the prayers of all the saints on the golden altar that is before the throne. And the smoke of the incense, with the prayers of the saints, rose before God from the hand of the angel.
—Revelation 8:3-4 (NRSV)

Read Revelation 8:1-5, 5:6-8.

I don't have much experience with incense. Although I know it's a hot item these days, I'm not into burning incense at home and, being a Methodist, I have no experience with lighting or swinging a liturgical incense pot (more accurately known as a "censer") around the altar. But not long ago I participated in a graduation service in an Episcopal church. As we processed into the chancel, the smell of the incense filled the air—just the way John described the incense in Revelation, rising with the prayers of the saints before the altar. It's a sensory expression of the deepest hopes and longing of faithful people reaching out to God.

New Testament scholar Walter Wink says that people "who pray do so not because they believe certain intellectual propositions about the value of prayer, but simply because the struggle to be human in the face of suprahuman powers requires it." He describes prayer as "the interior battlefield where the decisive victory must first be won, before any engagement in the outer world." He calls intercessory prayer "spiritual defiance of what is, in the name of what God has promised" (*Sojourners*, October 10, 1990, p. 10).

My most profound experiences in prayer have not been those times when I reflected on a theoretical concept about how the Almighty God connects with us through prayer. Rather, they have been in those experiences of inner struggle when I knew that a decisive victory needed to be won in my own soul before I could face the needs and concerns of the world around me. It happened in places where I wrestled with those things in my life that were keeping me from being the whole, loving, joyful human being God intended for me to be.

The saints pray in Revelation because they know that it is the only way to overcome the powers of evil and death. Their praying goes beyond pious platitudes or rational thought. It moves into the deep, sensory places that can be reached only by the scent of incense and the Spirit of God. Their praying can teach us to follow the Spirit of God into the deep recesses of our souls until we begin to feel that our prayers, like incense, are lifting us into the presence of God.

Prayer Focus: Pray that the Spirit of God will take you into some deep place of hopeful prayer.

December 19 ~ Power in the Blood

Then I heard a loud voice in heaven, proclaiming, " . . . But they have conquered him by the blood of the Lamb and by the word of their testimony, for they did not cling to life even in the face of death."

—Revelation 12:10-11 (NRSV)

Read Revelation 12:10-12, 5:9-10.

Author Kathleen Norris says that the only folks who seem to appreciate the old gospel hymns about the blood of Jesus are children like her nine-year-old nephew who find in them "a welcome opportunity to be 'totally grossed out' in church." But Norris also says it's our loss. "Christians have grown adept at finding ways to disincarnate the religion," she writes, "resisting the scandalous notion that what is holy can have much to do with the muck and smell of a stable, the painful agony of death on a cross. The Incarnation remains a scandal to anyone who wants religion to be a purely spiritual matter, an etherized, bloodless bliss" (*Amazing Grace* [New York: Riverhead Books, 1998], pp. 113-14).

Norris is probably correct. Across my early years in ministry, we carefully avoided the biblical images of blood. If the hymnal had included the old gospel song "Nothing but the Blood of Jesus," we never would have sung it in worship. But along came AIDS, and reality caught up with us. When was the last time a nurse took your blood or a dentist worked on your teeth without latex gloves? We know there is, in fact, power in the blood, and it's nothing short of the power of life and death.

The biblical images of blood are rooted in the belief that blood carried life. In the sacrificial traditions of the Old Testament, a person's guilt, sin, or "uncleanness" was transferred to the sacrificial lamb so that the repentant person was made clean by the shedding of the blood. So, how do those biblical images speak to you? When have you felt that you were "unclean"? What did it take for you to feel clean again? Maybe the old hymn got it right. "What can wash away my sin? Nothing but the blood of Jesus."

Prayer Focus: What is the sin that needs to be washed away in your life? In a spirit of prayer, reflect on the image of the sacrificial blood of Jesus, and feel its power to cleanse your soul.

December 20 ~ Will We Endure?

Here is a call for the endurance of the saints, those who keep the commandments of God and hold fast to the faith of Jesus.

—Revelation 14:12 (NRSV)

327

Read Revelation 12:1–14:20.

Erik Weihenmayer is a big-time overcomer. He's the thirty-two-year-old blind man who climbed Mt. Everest. Talk about endurance! A team member said his spirit just wouldn't quit.

People who are blind depend on consistent patterns in their environment, but absolutely nothing about Mt. Everest is consistent. Risk and danger are constant companions. The mountain destroys those who are unaware of its dangers or unprepared for its challenges.

A world where evil is real is a world filled with danger. Like a dragon, the power of evil seeks to devour those who resist its sinister influence. The early Christians identified that power with Nero (the numerical equivalent of 666) and those who were marked with his name. But in baptism, now as then, Christian disciples are marked with God's name. With the first readers of the Revelation, we are called to "follow the Lamb wherever he goes" (Revelation 14:4 NRSV), just as Erik Weihenmayer followed a bell attached to the climber before him. The first-century Christians endured Rome's oppressive power with the self-giving love of the Lamb, even when following the Lamb meant following him in death.

The only way I know to develop that kind of spiritual strength is through the spiritual disciplines of Bible study, prayer, worship, and fellowship with other Christians. With those tools, we, like the first-century Christians, can discover the strength to follow the Lamb wherever he goes. In the sixteenth century, Martin Luther taught the Reformers to sing:

And though this world, with devils filled, should threaten to undo us,
We will not fear, for God has willed his truth to triumph through us.

Prayer Focus: Are you developing the spiritual strength that will enable you to endure the unpredictable power of evil? What spiritual disciplines do you need to practice to equip yourself to endure?

December 21 ~ Where Is God's Justice?

"Lord, who will not fear and glorify your name? For you alone are holy. All nations will come and worship before you, for your judgments have been revealed."
—*Revelation 15:4 (NRSV)*

328

Read Revelation 15:1–16:21.

Kelly Wiglesworth was runner-up on the first *Survivor*. In an aside to the camera she asked, "How do you stay true to yourself and maintain integrity and still play this game?" She answered her own question: "You can't" (*New York Times,* August 25, 2000, p. B25).

The question confronts us in a multitude of very practical ways: Can we maintain our integrity and play this game? Can we be faithful to Christ and continue to live the modern life like "any old pagan" in our culture? Of course we can and, unfortunately, we often do. But John is convinced that things can't function that way forever. Ultimately, we can't have life both ways. In the end, the opposing powers of good and evil will collide. But the outcome is clear. The one who sits on the throne, the one who is worthy because he went to the cross, the one who is just and true will ultimately overcome injustice and corruption. Like the writer of Exodus recounting the plagues that brought liberation for the children of Israel, John paints a spectacular picture of the final work of God's justice in a corrupt and blasphemous world.

I stood in awe in the Jefferson Memorial in Washington, D.C., and read again his words: "I tremble for my nation when I reflect that God is just; that his justice cannot sleep forever." God's wrath is not the anger of a peeved deity. It is the inevitable working out of God's justice and truth. Since we can't have it both ways, we must choose. Even now we can sing with the hosts of heaven, "O Lord God, the Almighty, your judgments are true and just!" (Revelation 16:7).

Prayer Focus: Ask God to give you wisdom to know the way of justice and to walk in it.

December 22 ~ What Makes a Nation Great?

"These are united in yielding their power and authority to the beast; they will make war on the Lamb, and the Lamb will conquer [overcome] them, for he is Lord of lords and King of kings, and those with him are called and chosen and faithful."
—Revelation 17:13-14 (NRSV)

Read Revelation 17:1–18:24.

Have you been to our nation's capital?

329

I finished writing these meditations in Arlington, Virginia. From the balcony of the condominium where I was staying, I could look due east across the Patomac to see the Lincoln and Washington Memorials in perfect alignment with the Capitol. The Jefferson Memorial and the Kennedy Center stood to the right and left. These buildings and monuments are visual reminders of the highest ideals and greatest moments of our history. The place makes me reek with patriotism!

But I must admit that the capital of the world's reigning "superpower" was a disturbing place for me to reflect on John's overlapping images of Rome and Babylon, and to hear the melancholy lament, "Fallen is Babylon the great!" (Revelation 18:2 NRSV). It's no small thing to include "under God" in the Pledge of Allegiance. Great empires rise and fall, and every empire stands under the mercy and justice of God. Our history is marked by times when we have fulfilled the vision of "liberty and justice for all," and times when we have failed miserably.

John wrote in the heyday of Rome's greatness, but he could see the fault lines of arrogance and corruption that would bring Rome down. His vision stands as a daring challenge to those who "are called and chosen and faithful," by the one who is Lord of lords and King of kings, to live faithfully in our nation today.

Prayer Focus: Ask God, who rules over all nations, to show you the way to be faithful to Christ in your life as a citizen.

December 23 ~ Why Go to Church?

Then I fell down at his feet to worship him, but he said to me, "You must not do that! I am a fellow servant with you and your comrades who hold the testimony of Jesus. Worship God!"

—Revelation 19:10 (NRSV)

For this reason they are before the throne of God, and worship him day and night within his temple.

—Revelation 7:15 (NRSV)

Read Revelation 19:1-10; 7:9-17.

The question came by e-mail, but it was as old as the hills: "What difference does worship make? Do I really need to go to church to be a Christian?"

The folks who study culture say that young adults today are "spiritual" but not "religious." They want to experience God, but they're not interested in organized religion (an oxymoron if ever I heard one!) or formal worship services. To tell the truth, when I compare the bland, boring, lifeless worship I see in some churches to the high-intensity worship I see in Revelation, I think they may be correct!

The word *worship* appears in Revelation more than in any other book in the New Testament. Most of the time it describes heavenly worship, which is consistently marked by these three things. Worship in heaven is

Christ-centered: worship that celebrates what God has done and is doing in Christ

Continuous: worship that shapes existence by an ongoing practice of praise

Communal: worship that always includes multitudes of diverse people uniting their voices in song

Out of my background as a college actor and dramatist, I am a regular viewer of *Inside the Actors Studio* on the Bravo cable channel. The actors and directors who are interviewed on the program are all asked what they hope to hear God say when they get to the gate of heaven. As I remember it, actor Ben Affleck replied, "Your friends are in the back room. They've been expecting you."

Vital, active worship with the body of Christ on earth is one of the ways we practice for life in heaven. Worship on earth that is in tune with the worship in heaven reminds, challenges, and enables us to become Christ-centered people who live with a continuous spirit of praise and who share their lives in the community of friendship and faith.

Prayer Focus: When have you experienced worship on earth that resonated with the qualities of worship in heaven? As you reflect on John's visions of heavenly worship, allow them to shape your expectations for worship on earth.

December 24 ~ The Ultimate Overcomer!

Then I saw heaven opened, and there was a white horse! Its rider is called Faithful and True. . . . He is clothed in a robe dipped in blood, and his name

331

is called The Word of God. . . . On his robe and on his thigh he has a name inscribed, "King of kings and Lord of lords."

—Revelation 19:11, 13, 16 (NRSV)

Read Revelation 19:11-16.

A twenty-something guy with no recent church experience showed up in worship. When asked what brought him, he said someone gave him the "Left Behind" books. He didn't buy their vision of the future, but they got him thinking about Jesus. And that's precisely what Saint John intended!

I believe that if we hear the Revelation through the experience of John's first readers, we will not interpret it as a timeline of future events but as a kaleidoscopic collage of spectacular images to describe the ultimate victory of the risen Christ. That victory will come as the grand conclusion to human history, but Jesus made it clear that we are not to spend our time in futile attempts to set the calendar for the end of time (see Acts 1:6-8). Looking at the images in Revelation is a lot like looking at the ceiling of the Sistine Chapel. Our eyes may focus chronologically on one figure at a time, but it is the painting as a whole that overwhelms our senses.

In the vision in Revelation 19, the central figure is the rider on the white horse whose name is King of kings and Lord of lords. Because he is still the Lamb (Revelation 5:6), the blood on his robe must be his own. It is the sign of the sacrificial, nonviolent love that cleanses the white-robed saints who follow. The one who went to the cross has overcome all the powers of darkness, injustice, evil, and death that nailed him there.

M. Eugene Boring writes, "At the End we meet not something but Someone. . . . At the End of all things we meet not a stranger or newcomer but One we know" (*Interpretation: Revelation*, p. 197). If the one we meet at the end is the Lamb who died for us, then there's nothing to fear—in this world or the world to come.

Prayer Focus: Allow your imagination to carry you into the vision of the overcoming Christ. How does this image make you feel?

December 25 ~ A Feast of Judgment or Joy?

And the angel said to me, "Write this: Blessed are those who are invited to the marriage supper of the Lamb."

—Revelation 19:9 (NRSV)

Read Revelation 19:6-8, 17-21.

When George Lucas was asked what lessons people were taking from *Star Wars*, he replied, "This is a world where evil has run amuck. But you have control over your destiny, you have many paths to walk down, and you can choose which destiny is going to be yours" (*Time*, April 26, 1999, p. 93).

John's horrendous images point to a basic reality: Our choices matter. The end we reach is determined by the means we choose. The nightmarish "slaughter-meal of the vanquished," as M. Eugene Boring calls it, is the polar opposite of the wedding feast of the Lamb (*Interpretation: Revelation*, p. 200). The contrasting meals convey the vivid contrast between the final destination of a world that rejects God's way of salvation, and the joyful reunion of God's family.

If I wasn't the happiest father of the bride who ever danced with his daughter, I don't know who was! Both families were bubbling over with joyful gratitude for the love that had brought their children together. I wouldn't trade the memory of that wedding for anything short of the wedding feast in heaven. But I get a hint of that heavenly feast of joy every time we celebrate Holy Communion. Horatius Bonar describes it as "giving sweet foretaste of the festal joy, the Lamb's great bridal feast of bliss and love" (*The United Methodist Hymnal*, p. 623). Like Bonar, when I celebrate communion with something like the visionary faith of John in Revelation, it brings into my life that same joyful anticipation of the uniting of Christ with his bride, the church, in heaven.

Our task on earth is to live in faithful anticipation of the ultimate bridal feast in heaven.

Prayer Focus: *Are the means by which you are living consistent with the end you hope to reach? If not, what changes need to be made in your life?*

December 26 ~ The Power of Evil Versus the Power of God

Blessed and holy are those who share in the first resurrection. Over these the second death has no power, but they will be priests of God and of Christ, and they will reign with him a thousand years.

—Revelation 20:6 (NRSV)

Read Revelation 20:1-10.

According to George Lucas, Darth Maul, the sinister villain in *Star Wars: Episode 1*, is the image of evil. He said, "If you're trying to build an icon of evil, you have to go down into the subconscious of the human race over a period of time and pull out the images that equate to the emotion you are trying to project. . . . He's the evil within us" (*Time*, April 26, 1999, p. 90).

John went down into ancient biblical and cultural traditions for his image of evil and his picture of the way God ultimately overcomes it. Although these visions are open to a variety of interpretations, most biblical scholars would encourage us to refrain from identifying the binding of Satan, the thousand-year reign, and the fiery defeat of Gog and Magog (systemic and cultural antagonists of God's will) with specific chronological events in identifiable times and places. These interpreters would see these passages as dramatic pictures of the ultimate fulfillment of God's salvation that was initially demonstrated at the cross. Their emotive power gave persecuted Christians fresh confidence to remain faithful to Christ, even in the face of martyrdom. The fire that consumes evil envisions God's answer to the prayer, "Deliver us from evil."

The liturgy for baptism in my faith tradition calls us to "renounce the spiritual forces of wickedness, reject the evil powers of this world," and to "accept the freedom and power God gives [us] to resist evil, injustice, and oppression" (*The United Methodist Hymnal*). John's pictures call us to do just that!

Prayer Focus: Can you name specific ways in which you have experienced the "power of evil" within your life? How do you experience the power of evil in the world? Pray that God will strengthen you to reject the power of evil and to live in the power of God.

December 27 ~ Trembling Before the Throne

Then I saw a great white throne and the one who sat on it; the earth and the heaven fled from his presence, and no place was found for them. And I saw the dead, great and small, standing before the throne, and books were opened. Also another book was opened, the book of life.

—Revelation 20:11-12 (NRSV)

334

Read Revelation 20:11-12.

We Floridians took a lot of heat over the 2000 presidential election debacle. After all the political and legal wrangling, the final decision rested with the United States Supreme Court. The Court was the end of the line, the final judgment in a very ambiguous time.

Reflecting on the authority of the court, one editorial writer said, "Some things are best left unseen. In the television age, the way to avoid trivialization is to remain veiled. . . . The very opaqueness of its workings have helped the court maintain its unmatched authority and supremacy. People tremble before it. Quite an achievement in an age in which people tremble before very little" (*Time*, December 18, 2000, p. 104).

We tremble before the "great white throne" not because of its opaqueness, but because of its clarity; not because we cannot see through it, but because the one who sits on the throne sees through all our attempts to hide or mask who we really are. Nothing is veiled; everything is seen.

My guess is that we all know of things in those books that would be best left unseen. But there is another book. The Lamb's book of life contains nothing but the names of those who have overcome by the sacrificial gift of the Lamb's suffering on the cross. The powers of death will be destroyed, but the names in the book of life will last forever.

Prayer Focus: Allow your imagination to look into John's symbolism of the book of judgment and the book of life. How do these symbols help you understand your life and your faith in Christ? When the books are opened, what will they say about you?

December 28 ~ No More Death!

Then Death and Hades were thrown into the lake of fire.
—Revelation 20:14 (NRSV)

Read Revelation 20:12-15.

We might as well talk about death because there's sure a lot of it going around these days. By the time we reach adulthood, we've already seen a lot of death. We know its power. We've felt its pain.

335

I have a friend who was a student at Notre Dame when Father Robert Griffin was the campus chaplain. Looking toward his own death from cancer, "Griff" said, "Death is a bully whose nose should be tweaked, and I hope to be one of the tweakers."

That's so good, I wish I'd said it! He went on: "I grow weary of fearing death, for myself and for my friends. . . . I want to be present at death's judgment; I want to hear God say that death must die. I want to be present at resurrections that defeat death's victories. I want to see the fallen sparrows renewed in their flight. I want to greet death, when he comes irresistibly, with insolence and swagger, as though I were a baggy-pants clown to whom the final snickers belong" (*Notre Dame Magazine*, Winter 1999–2000).

There was absolutely no question in John's mind that death will not get the final word in this creation. With Paul, he lived in the confidence that "[Christ] must reign until he has put all his enemies under his feet. The last enemy to be destroyed is death" (1 Corinthians 15:25-26 NRSV). John could see death's judgment, and by faith in the risen Christ, we will overcome it, too!

Prayer Focus: Are you afraid of death? Can you identify with Father Griffin's attitude toward death? Ask God to help you face your fear of death with confidence in the risen Christ.

December 29 ~ Seeing a God-Made World

Then I saw a new heaven and a new earth. . . . And I saw the holy city, the new Jerusalem, coming down out of heaven from God, prepared as a bride adorned for her husband. . . . Then he said to me, "It is done! I am the Alpha and the Omega, the beginning and the end. To the thirsty I will give water as a gift from the spring of the water of life. Those who conquer will inherit these things, and I will be their God and they will be my children.

—Revelation 21:1-2, 6-7 (NRSV)

Read Revelation 21:1-26.

Helen Keller, born deaf and blind, said, "I can see, and that is why I can be happy, in what you call the dark, but which to me is golden. I can see a God-made world, not a manmade world" (*New York Public Library Book of*

Twentieth-Century American Quotations [New York: Warner Books, 1992], p. 356).

John, exiled on Patmos, could see a God-made world. He could see a world where God was at home with his people; a world where all tears were wiped away; a world where death and crying and pain would be no more; a world where there is no darkness because God is the light in which everyone lives.

The final vision of the Revelation is the first vision of the new creation. In a world of darkness, the vision of that city shines like gold. It is the final consummation of God's saving purpose toward which the whole biblical story has been moving.

But this vision was not given merely to encourage us to expect "pie in the sky by and by." John recorded his vision of the next world to strengthen faithful people in this one. By describing the ultimate fulfillment of God's kingdom in heaven, he described what it might look like for us to live in the partial fulfillment of that Kingdom on earth. This Kingdom-shaped vision of the future is the master plan by which faithful followers of Jesus shape their lives. It defines the values by which they attempt to influence the world in which they live. By looking to the future, we receive guidance and strength to overcome the darkness in our world today.

Prayer Focus: How does your vision of the future influence your life today? What will it mean for you to shape the life you live today around your vision of the kingdom of God coming on earth? Ask the Spirit of God to give you a vision of the future that will empower you for faithful living in the present.

December 30 ~ From Here to Kingdom Come

And he said to me, "Do not seal up the words of the prophecy of this book, for the time is near. Let the evildoer still do evil, and the filthy still be filthy, and the righteous still do right, and the holy still be holy."
—Revelation 22:10-11 (NRSV)

Read Revelation 22:10-11.

When I met Morris Hintzman, we were both young adults in seminary. He has given most of his career to leading Metropolitan Ministries of Tampa, which has grown from a modest outreach program for a few

337

downtown churches into one of the most effective ministries with home-less families in our nation. Not long ago I heard Morris say, "From here to heaven, I want to do everything I can to make sure that every homeless family in our city has the opportunity to move toward a stable, productive life." The way he said it left no doubt that he meant it. It is the motivating passion at the core of his being.

After studying near-death experiences, Carol Zaleski said, "The proper function of our conceptions of the afterlife is to provide not knowledge but orientation" (Quoted in *Context,* July 15, 1997, p. 7). The proper function of John's multisensory images of heaven is not to give us the meas-urements of the pearly gates, but to give a sense of direction to our lives—to challenge us to keep on doing that which is right and keep on being faithful to Christ. When it comes down to it, overcomers are simply ordi-nary people who have found an extraordinary orientation for their living. Their driving passion is to be faithful witnesses for Jesus Christ.

What would you commit yourself to be or do "from here to heaven"? What deep inner passion sets the direction for your life? Bob Dylan used to sing, "You're gonna have to serve somebody." Who or what are you going to serve from here to heaven?

Prayer Focus: What's the basic orientation of your life? Who will you serve from here to eternity? Ask God to plant within you a clear direction for your life.

December 31 ~ Come, Lord Jesus!

"See, I am coming soon. . . . I am the Alpha and the Omega, the first and the last, the beginning and the end." . . . The one who testifies to these things says, "Surely I am coming soon." Amen. Come, Lord Jesus!
—Revelation 22:12-13, 20 (NRSV)

Read Revelation 22:12-21.

In his spiritual autobiography, C. S. Lewis said that before Jesus came into his life, "what mattered most of all was my deep-seated hatred of authority. . . . No word in my vocabulary expressed deeper hatred than the word *Interference.* But Christianity placed at the center what then seemed to me a transcendental Interferer. . . . There was no region even in the

338

innermost depth of one's soul (nay, there least of all) which one could surround with a barbed wire fence and guard with a notice No Admittance" (*Surprised by Joy* [New York: Harcourt, Brace and Company, 1955], p. 172).

The Revelation ends where it began. First and last, beginning and end, Jesus comes as the "Divine Interferer." When God's salvation is complete, there will be no corner of Creation that will be hidden from the love that died to save us. The final prayer of the Bible is that the one who has overcome evil and death, will come to us.

A young woman's e-mail to me bore witness to the coming of that saving presence in her experience: "The meaning of salvation gives me goose bumps. It means that in my darkest hour, in my most sinful moment, at the time when it is hard for me to love myself, there is One who found me worthy to risk all that he had to give me hope. My salvation was where Christ met me, slipped into my heart and made me see things with a new perspective. This World can give us its best, but there is something far greater waiting. It allows me to see the gates of heaven shimmering right here on Earth."

I began these meditations with the prayer that by living with John's vision of the risen Christ, we would become more obedient servants, more supportive sisters and brothers, and more daring witnesses to the risen Christ. I hope this prayer has been answered for you. I know it has happened for me! May the overcoming presence of Christ continue to be at work within us until the promise is fulfilled that "we shall overcome someday!"

Prayer Focus: How have you experienced the overcoming presence of the risen Christ? How has God's salvation come to you in this life? Give praise to God for the work of his overcoming power in your life.